Building World Order

Building World Order

How the Christian Faith Fosters Global Peace, Prosperity, and Justice

Mark R. Amstutz

ROWMAN & LITTLEFIELD
Lanham • Boulder • New York • London

Published by Rowman & Littlefield
An imprint of The Rowman & Littlefield Publishing Group, Inc.
4501 Forbes Boulevard, Suite 200, Lanham, Maryland 20706
www.rowman.com

86-90 Paul Street, London EC2A 4NE

Copyright © 2025 by The Rowman & Littlefield Publishing Group, Inc.

All rights reserved. No part of this book may be reproduced in any form or by any electronic or mechanical means, including information storage and retrieval systems, without written permission from the publisher, except by a reviewer who may quote passages in a review.

British Library Cataloguing in Publication Information Available

Library of Congress Cataloging-in-Publication Data Available

ISBN: 979-8-8818-0562-3 (cloth : alk. paper)
ISBN: 979-8-8818-0564-7 (ebook)

∞™ The paper used in this publication meets the minimum requirements of American National Standard for Information Sciences—Permanence of Paper for Printed Library Materials, ANSI/NISO Z39.48-1992.

For
Ariana Schmidt
and
former students who have served, or are serving,
the public interest in government and nongovernmental organizations

Contents

Introduction	xi
Conflict, Poverty, Inequality, Instability	xiii
Promoting Peace and Prosperity in the World	xv
The Role of Citizens	xvi
The Plan	xvii
Notes	xx
1 Advancing Peace and Prosperity in the World	1
The Basic Building Blocks of Global Society	3
The Emergence of Nations	3
The Rise of State Sovereignty	5
The Responsibilities of States	6
The Development of the International Community	8
The Emergence of Global Society	8
The Rise of International Organizations	10
Sources of Disorder and Injustice	12
Domestic Sources	12
International Sources	14
Environmental Sources	15
Governmental Responses to Disorder and Injustice	15
The Responsibility to Protect	17
Confronting Global Challenges	17
Notes	19
2 A Christian Approach to Global Politics	23
Basic Principles of Christianity	24
God's Sovereignty	24

	Human Dignity	25
	The Universality of God's Love	25
	The Pervasiveness of Human Sin	25
	Caring for the Poor and Vulnerable	26
	The Need for Justice	26
	Protestant Teachings	27
	The Dual Nature of Citizenship	28
	The Legitimacy of Government	29
	The Priority of Individual Responsibility	29
	Stewardship	29
	The Need to Manage Government Power	30
	The Primacy of Spiritual Life	30
	Catholic Teachings	31
	The Christian Faith and Politics	33
	The Bible and Politics	35
	Political Engagement Principles	37
	Notes	40
3	Strengthening Nation-States	43
	The Nature and Role of Nation-States	44
	The Nature of Nation-States	44
	The Role of Nation-States	46
	Shortcomings of Nation-States	47
	Is the Nation-State in Trouble?	48
	Is Nationalism Important?	50
	Christianity and the Nation-State	53
	The Challenge of Christian Nationalism	55
	Strengthening Nation-States	57
	State Building	57
	Nation Building	59
	Notes	61
4	Strengthening Global Society	65
	The Emergence of International Organization	66
	Alternative Conceptions of Global Society	67
	Communitarianism	68
	Cosmopolitanism	69
	Justice and the International Community	70
	Christianity and the International Community	71
	Christians and Global Problems	74
	Strengthening Global Interdependence	76

	Obstacles to Solidarity	76
	Strengthening Integration	78
	The Problem of World Order	81
	Notes	82
5	The Christian Faith and Migration	85
	The Importance of International Migration	86
	International Law and Migration	88
	Alternative Conceptions of Migration	89
	Caring for Refugees	90
	The Challenge of Irregular Migration	93
	The Christian Faith and Migration	95
	How to View the World	96
	Church Documents	96
	Applying Faith to Migration	98
	Notes	101
6	The Christian Faith and Development	105
	The Basic Condition of Life: Privation	106
	The Nature of Economic Growth	108
	The Problem of Inequality	108
	The Nature of Development	109
	Cold War Development	110
	The Impact of Globalization	112
	Development in the New Millennium	114
	The Christian Faith and Development	117
	Christianity and Economic Growth	117
	Christian Principles and Community Development	120
	Notes	121
7	The Christian Faith and Climate Change	125
	The Nature of the Problem	126
	Domestic (Chiefly US) Responses to Climate Change	129
	International Responses to Climate Change	131
	The Christian Faith and Climate Change	132
	Church Declarations	132
	Christian Ethics and Climate Change	136
	Notes	139
8	The Christian Faith and Global Health	143
	Global Health and Pandemics	144
	HIV/AIDS	146
	COVID-19	147
	Ebola	149

	The Christian Faith and Global Health	150
	The Church and HIV/AIDS	151
	The Church and COVID-19	153
	Humanitarian Aid	155
	Notes	157
9	The Importance of Public Service	161
	Serving the Public Interest through Government	163
	Serving the Public Interest through Nongovernmental Organizations	165
	The Vital Role of Individuals	167
	Five Case Studies	170
	Notes	176
Bibliography		177
Index		185
About the Author		195

Introduction

On August 2, 1990, Iraq carried out a massive surprise invasion of its tiny neighbor Kuwait. Iraq's much larger and qualitatively superior military forces smashed through Kuwait's defensive positions, and within days of the invasion, Saddam Hussein, Iraq's dictator, announced the formal annexation of the country. How should Christians have responded to this act of aggression? Many believers viewed the military action as having little to do with the gospel, others responded by encouraging the international community to find a peaceful settlement, and still others believed that the United States and other democratic nations should use force to undo the illegal annexation. After the UN Security Council passed a resolution calling on Iraqi forces to leave Kuwait, Christian groups debated whether military force was necessary.

Some, favoring a pacifist disposition, supported negotiations backed by economic sanctions. Others, using a just war perspective, argued for the use of military force as a last resort. The National Council of Churches, the association of Mainline Protestant denominations, after carrying out a "peace pilgrimage" to the Middle East, declared that resorting to force to settle the conflict was "morally indefensible." They claimed that forcibly liberating Kuwait would result in hundreds of thousands of casualties. On January 15, the day before the air campaign was to begin, Protestant leaders visited the White House and again urged President Bush not to resort to war. As we now know, a day later the United States initiated the bombing campaign against Iraqi military installations. After destroying the country's air force and important military installations, allied ground forces carried out a four-day campaign that destroyed much of Hussein's army and liberated Kuwait.

Iraq's aggression against Kuwait presented clear legal and moral issues. Most contemporary concerns, however, are more ambiguous. Problems such as climate change and migration, for example, are morally complex and present greater challenges in developing collaborative action. Given the complexity involved in addressing global problems, how can concerned citizens, and Christians more specifically, contribute to the development of prudent public policies that are consistent with Christian values? What contribution can Christian churches make to the development of a more humane world and the alleviation of human suffering?

I have written this book because I believe that Christians have an obligation as citizens of their own country to help address global concerns but also because I believe that Christian morality can contribute to actions that can reduce violence and suffering and foster a more peaceful world. Since any effort by concerned citizens to help advance a just and prosperous world will require knowledge of the structure of global society, it is essential that they have a basic understanding of international political affairs. Additionally, if Christian values are to help structure political analysis and action, citizens must also possess knowledge of biblical political ethics—that is, principles derived from Scripture that are relevant to political and social life. Given the probabilistic nature of policy making, the integration of political knowledge and biblical morality, along with political advocacy, should be guided by competence, tolerance, and humility.

Although Christian believers are the primary agents for illuminating and applying Christian morality to global affairs, non-Christian citizens can also play a role in integrating Christian values with the issues and challenges confronting the international community. The world's common good is not found exclusively in the Christian religion. Because God loves the entire world, he shares his love and concern with all human beings—a truth Christian theologians call "common grace." Consequently, Christians and non-Christians can share many ideals and values, such as peace, justice, human dignity, and compassion for the vulnerable. But in applying a Christian worldview to the temporal affairs, believers have a special responsibility to discern, articulate, and apply Christian morality to political issues in nations and the world itself.

This book describes essential elements of contemporary global affairs and sets forth a Christian perspective for assessing major political and economic challenges currently facing nations and the international community. Although the Christian religion is chiefly about God's relationship to human beings, the Christian faith involves values and perspectives that can contribute to global peace and prosperity. Such a task requires not only an understanding of biblical faith but also a knowledge of international politics. Because I am a Christian, a US citizen, and a scholar of international relations, I write with the hope that all American citizens, and especially those who are Christian, will be inspired to become more aware of, and involved in, public affairs, both at the national and international levels. Only through wise, prudential political action can citizens foster a better world based on human rights, prosperity, and peace.

CONFLICT, POVERTY, INEQUALITY, INSTABILITY

Despite significant social and economic improvements throughout the world, many states continue to face intractable challenges because of disease, malnutrition, civil wars, political oppression, mass migration, and degrading poverty. At the same time, a growing number of states are unstable and weak, and their institutions are incapable of maintaining domestic order or protecting human rights. Other states are fragile because of increased domestic polarization and the absence of public policies that meet basic human needs. As a result, despite significant economic development, as well as advances in science and technology, the world is beset with many problems that impair human flourishing. The following are examples of human suffering within nation-states in 2024:

- *Sudan:* Since a military coup toppled the government in October 2021, the country has been run by a council of generals. In April 2023, a bitter conflict arose between Sudan's army and a paramilitary opposition force. The fighting has left nearly half of the country's population in dire need of aid.
- *Afghanistan:* After the US military toppled the Taliban government in 2002, the US government sought, through military and economic assistance, to create a more humane Afghan society. Despite massive aid over nearly two decades, nation building was unsuccessful. As a result, President Joe Biden ordered the removal of all remaining military forces in mid-2021, leading to the immediate collapse of the Afghan government and the return of Taliban rule. As of 2024, the country remains isolated internationally, with widespread human suffering.
- *Haiti:* As of mid-2024, Haiti remains a failed state. The presidency has been vacant following the 2021 assassination of its president, while its legislature is vacant because the lawmakers' terms expired in early 2023. By 2024, its acting prime minister had been forced out and was replaced by an interim governing council tasked with holding elections in 2025. Since criminal gangs have taken over much of Port-au-Prince, the country's capital, the country was awaiting the arrival of a UN-approved foreign police force (from Kenya) to help restore order.
- *Venezuela:* Nicolás Maduro, Venezuela's strongman, has sought to build a socialist society but, in the process, has destroyed the economic institutions of society, precipitating untold suffering on its people. While oil exports provide revenue to sustain the governing elite, most people face extreme

poverty and political oppression. The conditions are so extreme that more than seven million of its citizens have fled the country, most to neighboring countries.
- *Yemen:* An eight-year civil war between government forces and Houthi rebels has resulted in more than four million people being displaced from their homes and nearly a quarter of a million deaths. Since most food must be imported, the conflict has resulted in severe hunger, resulting in several hundred thousand deaths.

In addition to such state-based concerns, the international community itself continues to face significant regional and international problems. Examples of such issues include the following:

- *Hamas-Israel War:* In October 2023, hundreds of Hamas terrorists crossed Israel's security fence surrounding Gaza and attacked numerous Jewish settlements nearby. The attack resulted in the massacre of more than twelve hundred Israeli citizens and some 240 hostages. Israel's military forces responded by intervening in Gaza to destroy the Hamas fighters responsible for the atrocities and to free hundreds of hostages. As of mid-2024, the Israeli-Hamas war is ongoing, having resulted in more than thirty-five thousand deaths and widespread physical destruction in Gaza.
- *Climate change:* Since there is a broad consensus that the burning of fossil fuels contributes to greenhouse emissions, the international community has sought to develop a framework for reducing gas emissions. In 2015, 190 countries signed the Paris Agreement that called on nations to establish emissions ceilings. Since these ceilings are voluntary, the quest to address climate change remains a major challenge in international affairs.
- *Democracy:* According to Freedom House, an influential nongovernmental organization that measures the level of freedom in countries, global freedom in 2023 declined for the seventeenth consecutive year. Although the number of democratic states increased in the last half century (from forty-four countries in 1973 to eighty-four countries in 2022), in recent years democratic regimes have faced stiff opposition as domestic political conflicts and the allure of authoritarian rule have forced a retrenchment in political and civil rights and freedom of expression and assembly.[1]
- *Poverty:* Despite significant economic growth in most countries in recent decades, extreme poverty continues to afflict roughly seven hundred million people, mostly in Asian and African countries. One of the major aims of the United Nation's Sustainable Development Program is the elimination of extreme poverty in the world.
- *Refugees:* According to the UN High Commissioner for Refugees, the international organization responsible for refugees and internally displaced

persons, more than one hundred million people were forcibly displaced from their home in 2022. Of these, more than twenty-nine million persons were refugees—persons who have found safety outside of their homeland.[2]

In view of these and other challenges, how can the world be made more prosperous and peaceful? What role can Christians, and concerned citizens in general, play in strengthening domestic and global justice?

PROMOTING PEACE AND PROSPERITY IN THE WORLD

Because the task of creating and sustaining humane communities is one entrusted to humans, all persons, regardless of social status or nationality, are members of a political community and are therefore partly responsible for conditions in their own homeland. Additionally, since people are members of the universal society of humankind, they also bear responsibilities toward persons in foreign lands. While people's primary obligations are to those nearby—family members, fellow parishioners, neighbors, citizens of their nation—they also bear responsibilities to all persons in global society.

The task of caring for our world involves numerous levels of engagement—private, local, national, and global. At the private level, citizens express their love and care to family and friends. At the local level, citizens express love and care by serving on local boards, participating in neighborhood gatherings, and providing financial support to neighbors. In addition, local aid can be distributed indirectly through churches, nongovernmental organizations, and civic clubs. At the national level, citizens contribute to their nation by obeying its laws, serving in the armed forces, paying taxes, and advancing national concerns through nongovernmental organizations. Finally, individuals, as members of the international community, can foster the global common good through government or through direct service. When a government provides foreign aid or humanitarian assistance, it does so indirectly, on behalf of the citizens of the donor country. By contrast, direct action occurs when people provide care to peoples in need, bypassing governments altogether. The two types of service are complementary and contribute to the global common good.

A central theme of this book is that citizens can contribute to the peace and prosperity of their nation and the international community itself. Not everyone has the time and inclination to be concerned with public affairs, but every person can show love and concern to a neighbor. Although this book is primarily concerned with national and international political action, I conclude this book by highlighting the importance of individual action in serving the common good. Every person can give something—time, money, ideas—to advance a community's welfare.

The international community is more divided and chaotic than at any time since the end of Cold War. The rules-based system (frequently defined as the liberal international order) that prevailed during the Cold War has weakened in the postwar era. Major undemocratic states, especially Russia and China, are challenging Western democratic norms. While economic modernization has contributed to improved living conditions and increased longevity, especially in the developing nations in Asia and Africa, much suffering persists in the world. Civil wars and interstate conflicts have resulted in over 108 million people, or 1 percent of the world's population, being displaced.[3] Autocratic governments continue to abuse human rights, while religious persecution persists in many countries. And the recent COVID-19 pandemic, which caused the death of millions of persons, demonstrated anew the importance of cooperation in controlling and curbing disease.

THE ROLE OF CITIZENS

The world's eight billion people live in states. While some people may be unaware of their membership in one of the world's countries, most people are aware of their nationality. While the terms "nationality" and "citizenship" are frequently used interchangeably, technically they have distinct meanings. Nationality, the most basic concept, simply refers to people's status as members of a nation. The Universal Declaration of Human Rights declares (Article 15) that all people have "a right to a nationality." By contrast, citizenship, which is not mentioned in the Universal Declaration, refers to the formal or legal relationship of a person to a particular sovereign state. People can live in nation-states as non-citizens, but only citizens have the legal ties to the sovereign state that give them special rights, such as voting, and impose specific obligations, such as military service. Citizenship is thus the formal acknowledgment of full membership in a nation-state. Because I am especially concerned with the role of Christians in national and global affairs, I emphasize citizenship rather than nationality.[4]

A key theme of the book is that a knowledgeable citizenry is essential in sustaining a responsible, benevolent government and in sustaining a humane international community. Given the complexity of many domestic and global issues, citizens rarely have the time and background to develop a competent understanding of the world's major problems. This does not mean that people should remain uninvolved in the affairs of the nation and the world. Rather, an informed citizenry can help inspire action that contributes to a humane public order. At the same time, a concerned and knowledgeable citizenry can foster greater accountability for actions or inactions taken by leaders of national and international organizations.

Given the problems besetting nations and global society, the current challenge in international affairs is twofold: first, how to sustain benevolent, constitutional states and help rehabilitate those that are weak and failing; and second, how to foster a more prosperous, peaceful, and just global order. In short, the challenge is how to strengthen existing nation-states and how to renew global order through interstate cooperation.

This book does not provide policy prescriptions. Indeed, the book assumes that there are no simple solutions to the world's difficult and often intractable challenges. Rather, the aim is to provide a framework for assessing some of the world's major issues and problems. My hope is that with increased conceptual and theoretical knowledge, along with greater knowledge of the role of institutions, especially the nation-state, citizens will be able to develop a more informed political engagement about domestic and international issues confronting our contemporary world.

It is also important to stress that this book is not a theoretical study of theological or political ethics. Rather, it is a study in applied political morality. Its purpose is to describe and assess how a Christian perspective can contribute to an improved world order. Attempting to make the world a little better is a daunting task since such an undertaking requires both political and moral knowledge. Theorizing about a more peaceful, harmonious, and productive world is an important and demanding task—one best undertaken by philosophers and ethicists. My task as a scholar of international relations is different. It is to describe and assess global issues to improve the human condition.

The task of building and sustaining a peaceful and prosperous world may seem like an elusive goal. But every person can contribute something to a better world. And if persons are to pursue such work, they need both political and moral knowledge as well as the commitment to the common good.

THE PLAN

Two perspectives inform the book's analysis. First, I write as a Christian, who seeks to apply biblical principles to the challenges of temporal life. Second, I write as a scholar of international relations who is concerned with the promotion and sustenance of political and economic justice within nation-states and the world. I argue that Christians, and concerned citizens in general, can contribute to a more humane world by integrating Christian values with domestic and international politics.

Christians have historically interpreted the relationship of the Kingdom of God and the Kingdom of Man in a variety of ways.[5] In this book, I rely on a

Reformed (Calvinist) theological perspective, which H. Richard Niebuhr has called the "Christ transforming culture" approach. While acknowledging the duality of spiritual and temporal realms, this theological perspective calls on believers to serve as God's agents in reforming and transforming temporal political and social affairs.

International relations scholars have approached world politics from a variety of perspectives, such as liberalism, idealism, realism, and constructivism. In this study, I analyze international relations as a principled realist—a scholar who approaches global issues by integrating political morality with the reality of power politics. Moral ideals are important in setting forth goals and purposes, but in politics what ultimately matters are outcomes, not intentions. The moral task of politics is to improve human welfare, protect human rights, and maintain public order.

Finally, given the broad scope of our inquiry, it is important to say a word about the nature of world order. To begin with, I use the terms world order and global order interchangeably. Further, I use the term as a description of the overall condition of international stability among nation-states.[6] Global order is important since it enables political communities to maximize their people's economic, social, and political wellbeing.

Since the major political communities in the world have changed over time, and since their influence has grown or declined in response to their economic, political, and economic power, the characteristics of world order have similarly shifted over time. These changes range from an imperial structure to a more collaborative order, where leading states pursue interstate order through formal and tacit agreements based on power. Political observers of international relations frequently refer to the world as an international community. They do so not because the world is an established political community; rather, they do so because the political communities of the world need to be a part of a global society that facilitates human flourishing. World order emerges because stability in interstate relations is a precondition for the peace and prosperity of its constituent members.

Since the mid-seventeenth century, the world's primary political communities have been sovereign states. The political order that emerged from the Peace of Westphalia (1648) was based on principles, including nonintervention in the domestic affairs of other states, the inviolability of territorial borders, state sovereignty, and the development of international law to structure international relations. The United Nations is essentially the expression of the Westphalian order, which calls on states to respect the autonomy of other states, avoid aggression, and settle disputes peacefully. According to Henry Kissinger, the Westphalian system is essentially a procedural order that provides rules on interstate relations but neglects the values that are to guide the behavior of states.[7] Thus, while the UN system seeks to advance international peace, it avoids such issues as democracy, rule of law, human rights, or religious liberty. How societies are constituted is up to each state. This is one of the major shortcomings of the Westphalian order and provides an opportunity for Christians to illuminate values and perspectives of the Christian faith that can foster global peace and prosperity.

The book's organization is as follows. First, I describe the domestic and international institutions that are essential in advancing peace and prosperity in the world and highlight some of sources of global disorder and injustice. In chapter 2, I set forth basic principles of the Christian faith that are relevant to political and social life. In chapter 3, I highlight the essential role of the nation-state in the world and explore initiatives that might strengthen states. I also address the contested notion of nationalism. Chapter 4 examines the nature of global society and explores initiatives for strengthening the international community. Chapters 5 to 8 examine how a Christian perspective might contribute to the framing and analysis of four global issues: migration, development, climate change, and health. Chapter 9 highlights the importance of public service. If advancing the national and global common good is important, then citizens, and in particular Christians, should be involved in public affairs by addressing shared needs at the local, national, and international levels. Public service, whether in governmental or nongovernmental organizations, remains an important task.

This book represents the culmination of more than four decades of teaching and scholarship on international relations and more particularly the ethics of global affairs. Because I am a Christian, and because I believe that Christians have a responsibility to care for the world, I have sought throughout my academic career to integrate the Christian faith with the field of international politics. This book reflects my personal quest to address important global concerns from a Christian perspective.

My understanding of the world and the Christian faith has been influenced by countless international relations scholars, ethicists, and theologians. Those that have been especially important include thinkers such as Samuel Huntington, Abraham Kuyper, Hans Morgenthau, Reinhold Niebuhr, Michael Novak, and Michael Walzer. And since teaching and scholarship is a collaborative effort, I am especially grateful to my former students and faculty colleagues at Wheaton College who, through conversations, discussions, comments, and challenges, contributed to my analysis of international political ethics.

Finally, I am especially grateful to readers who offered comments on draft chapters. Albert Gombis and James Skillen each read a chapter and provided helpful suggestions for strengthening the analysis. Ariana Schmidt, a former student, read the entire manuscript and provided invaluable comments and suggestions that strengthened the clarity and focus of the book. Ariana has worked in refugee affairs and is completing a PhD degree in international affairs. She hopes to continue working in global humanitarian affairs, thereby modeling public service called for in chapter 9. Because serving the common good is vital, I dedicate this book to her and other former students who have served, and continue to serve, the public interest in government and nongovernmental organizations.

NOTES

1. Freedom House, "Freedom in the World 2023," https://freedomhouse.org/sites/default/files/2023-03/FIW_World_2023_DigtalPDF.pdf (August 6, 2024).

2. UN High Commissioner for Refugees, "Global Trends 2022," www.unhcr.org/global-trends-report-2022 (August 6, 2024).

3. UN High Commissioner for Refugees, "Global Trends 2023," www.unhcr.org/global-trends (August 6, 2024).

4. Citizenship, like nationality, is acquired in one of three ways: birth, family ties, and naturalization. According to the first tradition (*just soli*), citizenship is acquired where one is born. This is the tradition in the United States and is articulated in the Fourteenth Amendment, which declares that all persons born or naturalized in the United States are US citizens. The second tradition, *jus sanguinis*, assigns citizenship based on the nationality of one or both parents. This tradition is common in Europe and means that a child born in a foreign country to French parents is a French citizen. Finally, naturalization is the legal process by which a non-citizen acquires citizenship. In the United States, for example, an immigrant can apply for citizenship after living in the country for five years as a legal permanent resident. The application involves several requirements, including some knowledge of the US government and basic English proficiency.

5. In *Christ and Culture*, H. Richard Niebuhr sketched five classic theological approaches: Christ Against Culture, Christ and Culture in Paradox, Christ Transforming Culture, Christ of Culture, and Christ Above Culture. See H. Richard Niebuhr, *Christ and Culture* (New York: Harper & Row, 1975).

6. Scholars have defined the concept in at least three ways: first, as a description of political rules and institutions governing the world; second, as a prescription for a desired system of international order; and third, as an overall condition of international stability. The first approach highlights the rules, principles, and institutions of the international community. The second emphasizes the preferred framework for conducting diplomacy among states. The third highlights the necessity for interstate order if states are to succeed in caring for their own people. This study relies on this third definition of world order.

7. Henry Kissinger, *World Order* (New York: Penguin Press, 2014), 363–64.

Chapter 1

Advancing Peace and Prosperity in the World

I was first confronted by the challenge of global poverty as a college junior. I was one of thirty students participating in a four-day Washington, DC, seminar in the fall of 1963. The program introduced students to key issues in national and international affairs through presentations from government and political officials in their respective offices. When we visited the Department of State, we were briefed by a mid-level diplomat who had just returned from serving in the US embassy in Peru. He described how the US government was encouraging literacy and health care among the indigenous people in the highlands of the country. He concluded his presentation by calling on students to consider a public service vocation to advance human dignity in poor, less-developed countries. The presentation was a decisive moment for me, for it demonstrated how a government official could influence social and economic life in developing nations. Accordingly, it led me to focus my vocational interests on international affairs and, more particularly, on caring for people in poor countries. Although I did not become a diplomat, throughout my academic career I continued to view my calling as equipping students to pursue public service vocations. My challenge to them was, "develop your gifts and abilities and then give them away for a cause other than your immediate self-interest."

Since first hearing about the human needs in Peru in 1963, the world has made dramatic improvement in living conditions, especially among the low-income countries. The gains in increased longevity, decreased illiteracy, and poverty reduction have been especially noteworthy in most low- and middle-income countries. The following are some important social and economic achievements in the past half-century:

1. Despite wars and domestic conflicts, the world has been relatively stable, permitting significant economic growth.
2. More than a billion persons are no longer in abject poverty, while the standard of living for most of the world's people has improved.
3. Infant mortality has declined worldwide.
4. World health has improved and longevity in most countries has increased.
5. The spread of HIV and COVID-19 viruses has been curtailed.
6. Despite the continued threat from weapons of mass destruction, their use has been contained.
7. The spread of modern communications technology has given all people, but especially those in poor countries, greater access to information resulting in more freedom, better health, and greater mobility.

At the same time, the world continues to face major threats and problems, such as the following:

1. The persistence of international war. Currently major military conflicts exist between Russia and Ukraine and between Israel and Hamas in Gaza.
2. The persistence of ethnopolitical conflicts within states, thereby fostering domestic disorder and regional instability. Currently, such conflicts persist in numerous countries, including Libya, Sudan, Syria, and Yemen.
3. An increase of civil wars leading to more internally displaced people and refugees.
4. The growing influence of nondemocratic regimes, thereby threatening the existing rules-based global order.
5. The rise of militant groups—such as Hamas in Gaza, Hezbollah in Lebanon, and Islamic State in Iraq—that carry out indiscriminate violence and destabilize states.
6. Significant economic inequality within and among nation-states—a condition that contributes to political polarization and instability.
7. The growth in irregular migrants from failing states, contributing to domestic social and economic challenges.
8. The rise of protectionist trade policies that threaten the liberal trading system established by the West.

In this chapter, I examine the challenge of promoting and sustaining a stable international community. Global order is essential if member-states are to advance economic prosperity and secure human rights. While the nation-state remains the foundational political community of the world, states can prosper only if they cooperate and collaborate on shared concerns with other states. Such collaboration demands a stable international system. Just as political order is fundamental to the peace and prosperity of nation-states, so, too, world order is essential to the peace and prosperity of the international community. National self-sufficiency (autarky) is not a viable strategy. If states want peace and prosperity, they need to do so in the context of the international society of nation-states.

The chapter has four sections. First, I describe the emergence of nations and states and then explore the rise of an international society of member-states. In the third part, I examine sources of disorder and injustice in the world. Finally, I examine the challenge of confronting global issues and problems.

THE BASIC BUILDING BLOCKS OF GLOBAL SOCIETY

The structure of the international community is based on the nation-state. Fundamentally, the nation-state is a composite of three elements: state, nation, and sovereignty.

Although the terms nation and state are used interchangeably, it is important to differentiate them. A state is a legal and political concept referring to the people and territory controlled by a government. Basically, a state entails land, people, and government. A nation, by contrast, refers to social and cultural conglomerations of people. When people share a common language, culture, economic system, and history, they develop common bonds, values, and attitudes, which collectively nurture a national identity. Functionally, nationalism is simply the integrative dynamic that fosters national solidarity based on shared cultural traditions, common values, and shared hopes. While nationalism can become destructive when it disregards the interests of other peoples, civic nationalism is beneficial in that it fosters social cohesion and nurtures national solidarity.

The Emergence of Nations

From the beginning of time, people have lived in communities. Because people are not isolated individuals but rather social creatures whose fulfillment depends upon social engagement with others, their flourishing occurs within families, groups, tribes, clans, villages, and related communities. In time, as groups become more integrated, they develop shared traditions, cultural values, and common communication patterns. These social groups provide the genesis for a nation. Because there are tens of thousands of people groups, nations reflect a composite of a variety of peoples sharing common interests and cultural values. Given this reality, Archbishop Roland Minnerath defines a nation as "a voluntary bond of citizens who wish to share a common destiny."[1] Similarly, political scientist Jack Snyder defines a nation as a people who are "found together in solidarity, fate, and common political aspirations."[2] According to political philosopher David Miller, "Nations are communities that do things together."[3]

Originally, nations were nurtured through functional cooperation. In time, political and religious leaders emerged to facilitate coordination and cooperation on security, social, and commercial concerns. When sovereignty emerged in the seventeenth century, political communities were held together chiefly through powerful rulers. With the rise of the industrial state and economic growth through commerce, the cohesion of political communities increased significantly as people became more integrated socially and economically. Andreas Wimmer argues that national integration contributed to social solidarity and the development of a national identity. "Political integration and national identification," writes Wimmer, "form two sides of the nation-building coin."[4] This shared identity was often supported by a common language, shared cultural traditions, and a dominant religion. This integrative dynamic, known as nationalism, is the multidimensional force that fosters and celebrates membership in a particular political community.

The cohesion and unity of communities is important in developing and maintaining peace and prosperity. It is also essential to providing a fundamental social order that facilitates economic and social interactions among community members. While such order can be established through different levels of coercion, the most desirable expression of community order is one that is rooted in trust—or what scholars call "social capital." The *Oxford Dictionary* defines the concept as, "the networks of relationships among people who live and work in a particular society that enable the society to exist and be successful." Although scholars define social capital in various ways, I refer to the concept as the norm that facilitates and promotes understanding and cooperation among people in a particular community. Communities that have a high level of social capital will have a high level of trust and function more predictably and harmoniously than those with less social capital.

Robert Putnam, who coined the term in his landmark study *Bowling Alone*, distinguishes between two types of social capital: bonding and bridging.[5] Bonding social capital is based on the cohesion arising from shared ethnicity, interests, religious beliefs, and similar traits. Such bonding, which is limited to those persons who share traits of a group, is expressed by people who are members of a gun club, of an immigrant community, or of a particular religion. A specific example of bonding capital is the identity politics based on race and gender that is currently practiced in the United States. Bridging social capital, by contrast, is based on shared values and ideas that bring together ("bridge") diverse groups of people. Such capital seeks to integrate different groups and communities by emphasizing a shared vision or common purpose. Examples of bridging social capital include ecumenical religious organizations, the civil rights movement, and pro-life movement. Whereas bonding social capital is exclusive and inward-looking, bridging social capital is inclusive and outward-looking.

While both types of social capital contribute to communal solidarity, the development of a tolerant, inclusive, and pluralistic nation can only be realized through social networks that bring together different groups and interests. Bonding capital can play an important role in fostering solidarity and trust among the subgroups of society. But if a nation is to foster openness and pluralism, it must pursue social solidarity through a political morality that champions diversity and inclusiveness.

The Rise of State Sovereignty

The state, which is as old as civilization itself, is responsible for maintaining social life in political communities. In ancient times, ruling authorities maintained order through a variety of institutions, such as city-states, empires, and feudal kingdoms. Following the Peace of Westphalia in 1648, however, the dominant political community became the sovereign state, that is, a political community where rulers had supreme power within the territorial boundaries of a given community. The Thirty Years' War had been fought among European powers over the right to determine a community's religion and ended with the settlement at Westphalia. This agreement dictated that rulers, not religious leaders, had supreme power within their territories, not only over political life but also over religion. As defined by Jean Bodin, sovereignty is the supreme power to make and enforce rules within a specific territory.

Although the sovereign state evolved in the succeeding centuries, the defining attribute has remained unchanged—namely, the ability to enforce decisions through the threat of coercive power. Sovereignty has two dimensions, internal and external. Domestically, sovereignty implies the ability to maintain order and enforce rules within a community's territorial boundaries. Internationally, sovereignty is the ability to ensure a community's autonomy and independence. This means that sovereign states are the final decision-making authority within global society. No other state or nonstate actor has the right to impose its will on the people of a sovereign state.

With the increased consolidation of nations and the growth in power of sovereign states, the increased fusion of nations and states resulted in the emergence of the nation-states. In the early nineteenth century, there were fewer than twenty nation-states, but by the beginning of World War I that number had increased to more than fifty-five. Following World War II, the number of nation-states rose dramatically as former colonies demanded political independence. And with the end of the Cold War, the number of nation-states again increased by more than twenty states. Currently, the world is comprised of close to two hundred independent states. As specified by the UN Charter, these nation-states are entitled to equality and autonomy, and serve as the foundational pillar of the international community.

The Responsibilities of States

What are the fundamental duties of a state? According to John Campbell and John Hall, modern states do three things: they provide political order, protect its people from foreign states, and instill a sense of belonging and solidarity among its inhabitants.[6] Noted historian Tony Judt offers a succinct definition: "keeping citizens safe is what states do."[7] Fundamentally, nation-states bear two types of responsibilities: those toward their own people and those toward other nations. The first responsibility concerns providing security, protecting human rights, and ensuring the economic welfare of people within its territorial boundaries; the second concerns the peace and prosperity of the world. The first task is domestic; the second is international.

Some thinkers argue that the basic duty of the state is to provide justice to its people. Others argue that the most important task is to ensure political order. Not surprisingly, one of the perennial issues in political philosophy is how to reconcile the demands of justice with the demands of order. From a Christian perspective, both social order and individual freedom are important. Government must ensure a stable order so that society can carry out its functions, and it can do so only if it has the power to make and enforce decisions. At the same time, government must be constrained by law and provide justice to its citizens by protecting people's basic rights. The challenge in statecraft is how to ensure a strong government that is also benevolent. Finding the balance between order and freedom is thus an ongoing task—for new regimes as well as established governments.

Henry Kissinger once said, "If I had to choose between justice and disorder, on the one hand, and injustice and order, on the other, I would always choose the latter."[8] In expressing this view he was paraphrasing the eighteenth-century German philosopher Johann Wolfgang von Goethe, who had declared that if forced to choose between injustice and disorder he would prefer injustice. He would do so because injustice was temporary and reparable while disorder made society impossible.

Political writer Robert Kaplan writes that people who have always lived in stable, orderly communities are unlikely to understand and appreciate the imperative of political order. In *The Tragic Mind*, he explores the insights of ancient Greek thinkers because they understood the dangers of anarchy.

Kaplan writes: "Anarchy was the ancient Greeks' greatest, most fundamental fear. The Greeks were too rational to ignore the power of the irrational that lay on the other side of civilization. They saw no moral equivalence between order and disorder."[9] Based on the insights of ancient Greek writers along with his experiences as a wartime correspondent, Kaplan concludes: "Order comes before freedom, since without order there can be no freedom or liberty for anyone."[10]

Besides maintaining order, the state must also ensure justice for its subjects. Justice is typically defined as giving each person their due—that is, what each deserves. But how can we determine what a person is due? There are two ways of doing so. First, by ensuring that the procedures used in making decisions are impartial and fair. This approach is known as procedural justice. The criminal justice systems typically are based on this conception. But since procedural justice is concerned with the processes and not outcomes, it is possible that such an approach can result in outcomes that appear unfair. Substantive justice, the second way, is therefore an approach that focuses on the fairness of results. The contemporary approach to social justice and equity are manifestations of this approach.

But both the procedural and substantive approaches are unlikely to provide a satisfactory conception of justice, for in the final analysis justice demands a transcendental conception of the good. Without an abstract conception of justice, politics becomes a contest of wills, not a search for the good.

Historically, most societies pay lip service to the idea of political justice, even when they fail to provide a functional definition of the concept. Since each society must work out concretely the definition and application of the abstract notion of justice to its specific environmental conditions, there is no universal conception of political justice. Notwithstanding the absence of an agreed operational conception of political justice, the late Paul Henry, a Michigan congressman, argued that the quest for justice involved four instrumental values: order, freedom, equality, and participation. Henry observed that while the presence of these four values did not provide an adequate definition of political justice "it is safe to say that they will always be marks of a just society."[11] In chapter 4, I briefly discuss the role of justice as it relates to the international community.

What are a state's responsibilities in the international community? According to the UN Charter (Article 2), member-states must settle interstate disputes peacefully and avoid threatening or using force against another state. Historian Dorothy Jones argues that there is widespread agreement about the fundamental rights and duties of states, a consensus that she terms "the code of peace."[12] According to Jones, the code is based on the UN Charter and multiple treaties and conventions, and includes such norms as political independence of state, self-determination of people, nonintervention in the internal affairs of other states, abstention from the threat or use of force, and respect for human rights.

In recent years, political leaders have questioned whether the sovereignty norm should protect regimes that abuse human rights. After the Rwanda genocide of 1994, scholars developed "the responsibility to protect" principle (R2P), which calls on the international community to intervene to protect human rights when a state is unwilling or unable to do so.

Richard Haass, the former president of the Council on Foreign Relations, the most influential nongovernmental organization on foreign affairs in the United States, has suggested that, given the increased interdependence of the international community, the concept of sovereignty as political autonomy is inadequate. In his view, "the world is too small and too connected for borders to provide cover for activities that by definition can affect adversely those who live outside those borders."[13] To address the need for greater concern for global affairs, Haass argues that sovereignty should involve obligations beyond the boundaries of nation-states. He calls the change "World Order 2.0."

THE DEVELOPMENT OF THE INTERNATIONAL COMMUNITY

In one of his poems, John Donne, the famous sixteenth-century cleric and writer, observes, "no man is an island." Since humans are social by nature, the flourishing of individuals must always be carried out within the context of society. Similarly, "no nation is an island." If nations are to develop and thrive, they can only do so in the context of relations with other nations. The international community is simply the byproduct of international relations among states. States pursue global interactions because their economic, political, and security interests are achieved through relationships with other states. Although theoretically possible, national self-sufficiency (autarky) is self-defeating since it impairs the security and welfare of people. Global society emerged because states needed to interact with other states to advance their national interests.

The Emergence of Global Society

States pursue their national interests in the international community through foreign policy. International relations scholars typically define foreign policy as the pursuit of a state's vital interests in terms of the interests of other states. While the most fundamental interests of nations are national security and prosperity, states also pursue common global interests, such as international peace, a stable international economic system, environmental protection, and nuclear nonproliferation. The creation of international organizations like the United Nations, the European Union, and the North Atlantic Treaty Organization (NATO) emerged not from the initiatives and work of one country but from the collaboration of multiple states. In the same way, the emergence of the international community arose not from the desires of an imperial power but from the ongoing interstate relations among states. When states have collaborated in preventing war, advancing economic prosperity, and addressing regional and global issues, they have established networks that provide the foundation of an emerging global society.

The fundamental problem in creating a global society out of distinct sovereign states is how to establish and maintain international order. An international community can exist only if a fundamental order is prevalent. No order, no global society. Historically, order has been configured in a variety of ways ranging from dominance to balance. In ancient times, order was maintained among various kingdoms, city-states, and other forms of community through imperial rule, with the Roman and Ottoman empires being prime examples. After nation-states emerged in Europe, international order was maintained through a *balance of power* among leading states. This system was institutionalized in the Congress of Vienna in the early nineteenth century. When the multilateral, balance-of-power system failed to prevent World War I, diplomats adopted a system of collective security to inhibit war. *Collective security* was based on two core principles: first, states needed to be as committed to communal solidarity as to their own national interests; and second, states had to be willing to punish aggression through collective action. As a peacekeeping theory, collective security failed because states were unwilling to abide by its core principles.

Some theorists argue that moral values and ideas are a chief determinate of global order. Others suggest that global institutions are the major source of peace and order in the world. Although principles, moral values, and institutions contribute to global order, most international relations scholars believe that *power* is a principal determinant of international relations and the fundamental source of world order.[14] According to foreign policy scholar Robert Kagan, "International order does not rest on ideas and institutions alone. It is also shaped by configurations of power."[15] He suggests that a major fallacy of the contemporary era is that belief that "a liberal international order rests on the triumph of ideas and the natural unfolding of human progress."[16]

Although many political observers think the United States remains the most powerful nation, the significant rise of China and Russia along with the continued influence of European nations and rising influence or other nations like Japan, Iran, and Brazil suggest a broader, more complex configuration of power. Given the significant changes in the distribution of global power in the post–Cold War era, the challenge for the leading states is how to manage global politics to ensure international order. According to Henry Kissinger, an effective and stable world order is sustainable only if nations view it as legitimate—that is, acceptable to their people. Kissinger writes, "any system of world order, in order to be sustainable, must be accepted as just—not only by leaders, but also by citizens."[17]

Since global order is based on the quality and actions of member-states, the challenge in advancing prosperity domestically and a peaceful international order will depend in great part on the quality of leadership from powerful constitutional states and on the ability of member-states to collaborate jointly in establishing norms and rules that foster order and prosperity. As noted earlier, not all member-states of the international system are strong and capable of fulfilling the legal and political responsibilities required by the UN Charter. Some states are unable or unwilling to fulfill the tasks of a responsible, legitimate government, resulting in human rights abuses, violence, and regional instability. In facing the suffering and chaos resulting from failing regimes, the challenge for developed countries is how to assist such regimes in alleviating domestic suffering and reducing regional instability.

The reform and political healing of failing nation-states is an especially difficult task. Foreigners can offer material aid and provide recommendations, but the repair of nation-states is necessarily a domestic undertaking. The intractability of political renewal is illustrated by Haiti, a country that has received billions of dollars in economic assistance and military aid but remains unstable and impoverished. Even the introduction of UN peacekeepers failed to contribute to the nation's political healing. Currently, Port-au-Prince, Haiti's capital, is governed chiefly by gangs, not by the country's fragile government. The foreign interventions in Iraq and Libya, for example, succeeded in toppling two despotic regimes but have struggled to establish a more humane domestic political order.

The Rise of International Organizations

Advancing a stable and prosperous world also demands that member-states cooperate in building and sustaining a humane global order. One of the important twentieth-century developments that contributed to the integration of international relations was the rise of intergovernmental organizations (IGOs). IGOs are organizations in which states, led by the major powers, establish rules and norms to facilitate interstate cooperation. The most important IGO is the United Nations, whose chief purposes are to prevent war and foster peace and prosperity. Currently, the world has more than three hundred IGOs. Some of the most important are regional organizations like the European Union and the Organization of American States, security organizations like NATO and the Southeast Treaty Organization, specialized organizations like the World Health Organization and the Food and Agriculture Organization, and economic organizations like the Inter-American Development Bank and the World Trade Organization.

International organizations have contributed significantly to improved living conditions worldwide. I next describe their important role in promoting economic growth. To a significant degree, the world's prosperity was made possible by the establishment of a liberal international economic system, which facilitated international trade and increased foreign investment. In the late 1940s, the United States, supported by allies, established three major IGOs that facilitated global economic growth. The three institutions, collectively known as the Bretton Woods system, are the General Agreement on Tariffs and Trade, the International Monetary Fund, and the International Bank for Reconstruction and Development (World Bank). The General Agreement on Tariffs and Trade, subsequently replaced by the World Trade Organization, establishes fair, equitable, and reciprocal commercial rules to facilitate international trade. The International Monetary Fund provides large loans to countries when facing major financial distress. Since financial crises can spread to other countries because of the interconnected nature of global finance, the stabilization of a country's monetary system is vital in maintaining a stable international monetary system. Finally, the World Bank assists developing nations by providing large loans to nurture economic growth.

Although all three organizations continue to carry out important functions in the global economy, two informal groups have emerged to strengthen international economic cooperation and to address other shared concerns. The first group, known as the Group of Seven (G7), is comprised of the seven leading democratic economies (Britain, Canada, France, Germany, Japan, Italy, and the United States). The G7 has no formal organization but holds a summit at least once a year.[18] The second group, the Group of Twenty, includes the G7 plus thirteen other leading economies. Established in 1999, the forum meets periodically to discuss pressing economic and related global issues. Since the G7 and the Group of Twenty are informal associations, they supplement more established organizations and formal diplomatic channels in facilitating international cooperation.

The liberal economic order, which is responsible for much of the world's economic prosperity, is facing a significant backlash. To a significant degree, the criticism of trade is due to the alleged loss of industrial jobs to China by the major economies, especially the United States. Additionally, the COVID-19 pandemic highlighted the vulnerability of countries who depend upon supply chains for essential products. As a result, some countries have begun to adopt a managed industrial policy that seeks, with government assistance, to redirect economic enterprise back to the home country.

SOURCES OF DISORDER AND INJUSTICE

Most human suffering in the international community is caused by domestic political oppression (such as genocide), international developments (such as interstate wars), or environmental catastrophes.

Domestic Sources

Domestic sources are responsible for even more human suffering than international wars and pandemics. Undoubtedly, the most destructive and harmful actions are those carried out by autocratic regimes when they seek to destroy a segment of their people or when they devise ill-conceived programs that result in famine or related catastrophic failures. Whereas the two world wars were responsible for more than seventy-five million deaths, the experiment in totalitarian communism was responsible for even more deaths. In 1997, a group of European and American scholars compiled a postmortem of communist atrocities and concluded that the total human cost in genocides, deportations, extrajudicial killings, and artificial famines exceeded ninety-four million deaths.[19]

Not all authoritarian regimes are the same. Some military governments, for example, may be content with controlling governmental power by prohibiting political activity. Such regimes may allow, however, a significant degree of economic and social freedom, while prohibiting basic civil liberties.[20] During the era of military rule in Chile, for example, the government allowed a significant degree of social, religious, and economic freedom, but placed strict limits on political freedom. People were free but had no voice on political affairs. I observed this strict enforcement of order while serving briefly at the US Embassy in Chile in the late 1980s. One day, while going to lunch in Santiago, I was given a leaflet as I walked across the city's central plaza (known as Constitution Plaza). Soon after receiving the leaflet, which announced a human rights gathering later that day, I noticed two plainclothesmen grab the man and force him into a nearby van.

After Fidel Castro took control of the Cuban government, he instituted comprehensive restrictions on human freedom, establishing a pervasive spy network through neighboring watchdog committees to monitor people's everyday lives. While totalitarian governance was modified over time, freedom was still severely restricted on the island four decades later. I personally witnessed the cost of these restrictions while leading a short-term academic program in 2003 for some fifteen college students. One night, after walking through the historic center of Old Havana, I decided to use a bike taxi to go back to my hotel. Soon after getting on the taxi, a plainclothesman stopped it and asked the young driver for his license. Since his license authorized him to take only Cubans, not foreigners, he was charged with a crime. He told me that he would be unable to work for the next month and that the fine would cost him some twenty dollars, a sum equal to his monthly wages.

The deliberate killing of peoples through genocide has also resulted in millions of deaths. In 1915 to 1917, the Ottoman Empire, while fighting in World War I, carried out a campaign against some 2.5 million Armenians living in the eastern areas of Anatolia, what is now Turkey. The campaign involved mass deportations, forced marches, and mass killings. As a result, some six hundred thousand to one million Armenians perished.[21] The Nazi genocide of Jews during World War II, historically the most destructive mass killing of a people, is responsible for more than six million deaths, most of which occurred in detention camps. In Rwanda, an ethnic conflict in 2004 was precipitated by the ruling Hutus against the Tutsi, resulting in more than eight hundred thousand deaths in two months. Most of the killings were carried out with machetes and involved people who were neighbors.

Another domestic source of human suffering is the collapse of a state. Weak and failing states are a major source of injustice because the absence of political order fosters instability, corruption, and criminality. For example, Afghanistan, Libya, South Sudan, Syria, and Yemen are deeply fractured countries and are unable to fulfill the responsibilities of states, as set forth in the UN Charter. Because of the frailty of their governmental institutions, human suffering is widespread.

The absence of effective governance has similarly impaired human welfare in Haiti. As of 2023, Haiti, despite having received billions of dollars in economic assistance in the previous thirty years, remains an unstable, corrupt, and violent country. Even the introduction of two UN peacekeeping missions (the first in 1993–1996 and the second in 2004–2017) contributed little to the restoration of political order. Given the fragility of the central government, criminal gangs are largely in control of Port-au-Prince, Haiti's capital. It is not an exaggeration to say that life in the capital in 2024 is "nasty, brutish and short," to use Thomas Hobbes' famous description of a society without government.

Widespread human suffering from war and oppression frequently leads people to flee their homelands and seek asylum in a foreign country. Unlike economic migrants, who move because they seek a better standard of living, refugees are people who move to stay alive. As of 2023, close to thirty-five million people had fled their own countries because of war or persecution, while another sixty-three million were internally displaced persons—individuals that had fled their homes but remained in their own countries.[22]

International Sources

Historically, international wars have been the most destructive and harmful cause of human suffering in the world. World War I was essentially a European conflict that resulted in the deaths of some twenty million military personnel and civilians. World War II, which involved countries in Europe and Asia, was far more destructive, resulting in the death of more than fifty-four million people. Although major international wars have not been fought between major powers since 1945, political wars within states have resulted in millions of deaths and resulted in mass migration to neighboring states. Such conflicts include wars during the Cold War in Korea, Vietnam, and Bosnia-Herzegovina and post–Cold War wars in Kosovo, Syria, and Yemen. Kalevi Holsti, a political scientist, calls these latter domestic conflicts "wars of a third kind." Because many new states are weak and deeply fragmented, he argues that "the major sources of war in the future will derive less from the character of relations between states than what goes on within states."[23]

While such domestic conflicts involve violence chiefly within the boundaries of a state, such civil wars are facilitated, expanded, and intensified by military and economic assistance from foreign states. For example, the ongoing war between the Yemen government and Houthi rebels has been facilitated and sustained by Saudi Arabia, a neighboring Sunni Muslim state, and Iran, a Shia Muslim state. Similarly, the 2023 war between Israel and Hamas fighters in Gaza has been facilitated in part by Iran's military support of Hamas. Since Israel limits ties between Gaza and neighboring countries, the Hamas governing authorities can provide its two million residents only limited benefits through the ongoing financial support of Muslim states like Qatar and Iran. And the continuing threat of Hezbollah fighters in southern Lebanon against Israel is similarly sustained by the continuing military and economic support that Iran provides the Muslim fighters.

In addition to such domestic conflicts, the rise of terrorist groups also poses a major threat to global order. Following the terrorist attack on New York City's World Trade Center on September 11, 2001, for example, the United States viewed the terrorism threat as global and undertook military operations against radical groups regarded as a threat to US security. While such initiatives may have improved American national security, they had a profound impact in other countries, especially Afghanistan and Iraq.

Another source of international disasters involves the spread of diseases. The rapid escalation of HIV in Africa in the 1980s and 1990s, for example, demonstrates the enormous social, economic, and personal costs that a global virus can inflict on society. Because African countries had limited medical resources, the disease caused millions of deaths on traditional communities. And since the virus was transmitted sexually among adults, children were left without parents or grandparents. The disease was not contained until Western countries, led by the United States, began to provide information and significant medical assistance in 2002 to 2004. It is estimated that the US initiative to contain AIDS helped to save the lives of some twenty-five million Africans. As of 2023, the HIV/AIDS pandemic is believed to have killed an estimated thirty-six million persons worldwide, most of them in Africa.[24]

The recent COVID-19 pandemic, which continues to threaten societies worldwide, has killed millions of persons. The virus surfaced in Wuhan, China, in mid-December 2019. Given the integrated nature of the world, the virus spread rapidly to other countries. According to the World Health Organization, developed countries in North America and Europe experienced more COVID-19–related death because of their high levels of globalization than poorer countries in Africa that were less integrated into the global economy.

Environmental Sources

A final systemic source of suffering is environmental catastrophes, such as earthquakes, wildfires, and global diseases. Recent examples of highly destructive earthquakes are the Indian Ocean earthquake and tsunami of 2004, the Haitian earthquake of January 2010, and the Turkey-Syria earthquake of February 2023. The first event resulted in the death of more than 230,000 persons, most of them on the Island of Sumatra, Indonesia. The second devastating earthquake left more than 1.5 million people homeless in Haiti and caused the death of nearly 220,000 people.[25] The third earthquake damaged more than 280,000 buildings, left more than 2.3 million people homeless, and caused the death of more than fifty-three thousand persons—forty-eight thousand in Turkey and six thousand in Syria.[26] Another illustration of the devastating effect of natural disasters was the wildfire that destroyed the town of Lahaina on the Hawaiian island of Maui in August 2023. The sudden fire, which was fueled by severe drought conditions and hurricane-level winds, engulfed the town, trapping people and animals alike. It is estimated that close to one hundred people perished and destroyed most buildings in the historic town.

GOVERNMENTAL RESPONSES TO DISORDER AND INJUSTICE

Fundamentally, states are chiefly responsible for the welfare and needs of their own people. But as I have already suggested, many states are incapable or unwilling to provide for their people's needs. If global peace and prosperity are important, how should strong, beneficent states respond? Should they stand by and allow people to suffer or should states, working through the United Nations or a coalition of concerned states, confront the abusive regime or intervene militarily to protect human rights? Additionally, how should the international community respond to aggression? Since international wars are a source of much suffering and destruction, how should major powers respond to systemic violence inflicted on civilians?

According to the UN Charter, member-states are obligated to pursue peaceful conflict resolution and to avoid threats to peace. Aggression is strictly prohibited. But what do these norms mean when a state claims that it is using force in defense of a vital interest, such as when Argentina used military force in 1982 to take control of the Falkland Islands. According to Argentina, it resorted to force because the islands (known as "Las Islas Malvinas") were viewed as Argentina's sovereign territory, acquired when it gained independence from Spain in the early nineteenth century.

More recently, the Russia-Ukraine war contests the legitimacy and boundaries of the Ukrainian state. According to Vladimir Putin, Russia's president, Ukraine is a part of Russia and should not be an independent state. In 2014, Russia used its superior military power to take control of Crimea, a peninsula in southern Ukraine, and commenced military operations in the eastern areas of the country next to Russia. The war escalated in 2022 when Russian military forces sought to topple the elected, pro-Western government of Volodymyr Zelensky in Kiev. Surprisingly, Ukrainian forces were able to repulse the attack, but the war has resulted in enormous destruction and suffering in Ukraine, including more than six million refugees fleeing the violence. As of 2023, the Ukrainian forces, supported militarily and economically by Western nations, have been able to thwart Russia's aggression and have inflicted enormous costs on its forces. It is unclear, however, how or whether the conflict will be resolved in the near future.

Domestic violence can be even more destructive and devastating than war. In 1994, for example, a genocide in Rwanda resulted in the massacre of more than eight hundred thousand people over a three-month period. Given the speed and enormity of the slaughter, the genocide deeply affected leaders and people worldwide. How could such an event have occurred? Why did peace-loving nations not halt the killing? Why was the small UN peacekeeping force not expanded and urged to restore order? Upon leaving office, President Bill Clinton said that he regretted that the US government had not done more to halt the mass killing. Similarly, Kofi Annan, who was head of UN Peacekeeping at the time of the genocide, also regretted having reduced the United Nation's presence in Rwanda precisely when its force could have helped to contain the atrocities. After Annan became UN Secretary General, he called on the international community to investigate how state sovereignty could be reconciled with the need to protect human rights. An international commission was established in 2000 to explore this issue and published its report a year later.[27]

The Responsibility to Protect

In 2001, the commission issued its report. The study, titled "Report of the International Commission on Intervention and State Sovereignty," concluded that sovereignty should be reconceived as "the duty to protect" rather than as the right to independence. Based on the commission's work, leading powers began to support an emerging doctrine called R2P. The fundamental claim of the doctrine is that when a state is unable or unwilling to protect human rights, the imperative of protecting human rights can override the duty of nonintervention. Based partly on the commission's work, the UN Security Council adopted a resolution in 2005 that affirmed the essential elements of R2P. Nevertheless, some major powers, including China and Russia, have voiced concern over R2P because of the potential diminution of the sovereignty and nonintervention norms. It is important to stress that while R2P has become part of the lexicon of international relations discourse, the principle is not international law. Rather, it provides a framework for assessing the inherent conflict between state sovereignty and human rights.

Perhaps the clearest application of R2P was the UN Security Council–authorized intervention in Libya in 2011. In the aftermath of the Arab Spring, major conflict had developed between the government of Muammar Gaddafi and anti-regime forces. When Gaddafi threatened mass slaughter against the rebels, Western governments called for the international community to protect Libyan civilians. As a result, the UN Security Council adopted a resolution authorizing military intervention to protect people in the Libyan conflict. NATO military operations against the Libyan state began almost immediately, and within a couple of months, the powerful Libyan military had been destroyed. Ironically, while the UN-approved action had been designed to protect civilians, foreign intervention helped the rebel forces take control of the country. More importantly, while the R2P action prevented wartime atrocities and eventually destroyed an autocratic regime, the opposition forces have been unable to establish a humane and effective government. Libya remains deeply divided by religion and tribal affinities, and as of 2024, the country is a weak, failing state.

CONFRONTING GLOBAL CHALLENGES

Since states are part of a global community of states, not all obstacles to human dignity, social order, prosperity, and individual welfare are solely domestic concerns. Many issues—such as economic prosperity, climate change, the spread of diseases—are transnational in character and can be addressed effectively only through interstate collaboration. Isolation and economic self-sufficiency may seem a short-term solution to avoid the competition and conflict endemic among member-states. But in the final analysis, global engagement is the only viable strategy that can provide nations with economic prosperity, human flourishing, and national security. Since governments are tasked with ensuring political order and caring for their people's welfare, states will necessarily give precedence to the pursuit of national interests. But this task can succeed only if leaders incorporate the interests of other states.

The global common good thus emerges out of the competing and conflicting interests of states as they seek to advance shared interests and confront common concerns. Whether cooperation is undertaken bilaterally or multilaterally, the peace and prosperity of the world will continue to depend upon the capacity of states to work together in identifying shared concerns and undertaking initiatives to address common problems and help resolve international conflicts.

Given the decentralized nature of global order, the most basic threat to global peace and prosperity is war. Although it is easy to assume that the relative stability of the current global system will continue indefinitely, the history of the twentieth century is a brutal reminder of destructiveness of war. It is important to remember, then, that peace is not a natural byproduct of international relations but a human creation. This is the central claim of Donald Kagan's impressive study *On the Origins of War*.[28] Prosperity, too, is a human creation and can only be advanced if people establish the preconditions and institutions that facilitate productive enterprise.

In addition to the ongoing challenges of maintaining international peace and promoting global economic prosperity, the world continues to face numerous major transnational problems that impair peace, prosperity, and human rights. The following is a list of issues that are currently regarded as important global concerns: proliferation of weapons of mass destruction, civil wars and violence, weak and failing states, religious persecution, gender discrimination, growth of refugees and irregular migrants, economic inequality within and among states, environmental degradation and abuse of the commons, climate change, the threat of pandemics, and financial crises. While some of these problems are chiefly domestic in nature, such as gender inequality or irregular migration, others, like the threat of pandemics or the challenge of climate change, are chiefly global in nature, demanding multilateral cooperation.

A major obstacle to confronting global issues is the difficulty of achieving consensus on the nature and causes of major problems. More significantly, once states have achieved significant agreement about the issues, an even greater obstacle looms: how to generate a shared commitment to costly and difficult reforms. The problem is especially acute because of the widely different capabilities between rich and poor nations, large and small states, and other significant variables. Additionally, cooperation is challenging because of the temptation among some actors to make promises without the firm commitment to fulfill them. The temptation to "ride free" is especially acute in collective action initiatives.

In conclusion, the world is comprised of almost two hundred nation-states, each of them responsible for the welfare of their own people but also responsible for the peace and prosperity of the international community of which they are a part. Since nation-states are sovereign and independent, the wellbeing of citizens will depend to a large extent on a government's capabilities to craft and enforce policies that are conducive to domestic order and prosperity. But because of the interconnected nature of states in global society, the peace and prosperity of the world can only be realized through effective interstate collaboration. In advancing human rights and economic prosperity domestically, states must have capable institutions and pursue wise policies that advance the general wellbeing of society. At the same time, member-states must cooperate in pursuing global order and maintaining an environment conducive to economic prosperity.

NOTES

1. Archbishop Roland Minnerath, "Nation, State, Nation-State and the Doctrine of the Catholic Church," The Pontifical Academy of the Social Sciences (PASS), www.pass.va/en/publications/acta/acta_22_pass/minnerath.html (July 29, 2024).

2. Jack Snyder, "The Broken Bargain: How Nationalism Came Back," *Foreign Affairs* (March/April 2019), 54.

3. David Miller, *On Nationality* (New York: Oxford University Press, 1997), 24.

4. Andreas Wimmer, *Nation Building: Why Some Countries Come Together and Others Fall Apart* (Princeton: Princeton University Press, 2018), 1.

5. Robert D. Putnam, *Bowling Alone* (New York: Simon & Schuster, 2000), 22–24.

6. John L. Campbell and John A. Hall, *The World of States* (London: Bloomsbury Academic. 2015), 5.

7. Tony Judt, *Postwar: A History of Europe since 1945* (New York: Penguin Press, 2005), 797.

8. Walter Isaacson, *Henry Kissinger: A Biography* (New York: Simon & Schuster, 1992), 76.

9. Robert D. Kaplan, *The Tragic Mind: Fear, Fate, and the Burden of Power* (New Haven: Yale University Press, 2023), xii–xiii.

10. Kaplan, *The Tragic Mind*, 32.

11. Paul B. Henry, *Politics for Evangelicals* (Valley Forge, PA: Judson Press, 1974), 82–84.

12. Dorothy Jones, *Code of Peace: Ethics and Security in the World of Warlord States* (Chicago: University of Chicago Press, 1992), 163–64.

13. Richard Haass, *A World in Disarray: American Foreign Policy and the Crisis of the Old Order* (New York: Penguin Press, 2017).

14. Although power can be expressed in a variety of configurations, theorists have classified world systems based on the number of major powers. The three systems are called unipolar, bipolar, and multipolar. The Cold War era, where two superpowers competed, was classified as bipolar, while the immediate decade follow the collapse of the Soviet was viewed as unipolar because of the dominant global role of the United States.

15. Robert Kagan, *The Return of History and the End of Dreams* (New York: Alfred A. Knopf, 2008), 96.

16. Kagan, *The Return of History*, 102.

17. Henry Kissinger, *World Order* (New York: Penguin Press, 2014), 8.

18. After the Soviet Union collapsed and Russia was rebuilding its institutions, it was invited to join the G7. But after Russia annexed Crimea, it was expelled from the forum in 2014.

19. Stéphane Courtois, et al., *The Black Book of Communism: Crimes Terror, Repression* (Cambridge: Harvard University Press, 1999).

20. The noted political philosopher John Rawls calls such regimes "decent hierarchical peoples." In his view, while such societies are undemocratic, they respect human rights and are nonaggressive in global society. See John Rawls, *The Law of Peoples* (Cambridge: Harvard University Press, 1999).

21. The government of Turkey has never acknowledged the Armenian Genocide. It claims, instead, that while thousands of Armenians were killed and forced to move from homes and villages, there was never a governmental campaign to exterminate the Armenian people.

22. UN High Commissioner for Refugees, "Global Trends Report 2022," www.unhcr.org/global-trends-report-2022 (July 29, 2024).

23. Kalevi J. Holsti, *The State, War, and the State of War* (Cambridge: Cambridge University Press, 1996), 216.

24. World Health Organization, "The Global Health Observatory," 2023, www.who.int/data/gho/data/themes/hiv-aids#cms (July 29, 2024).

25. Much of the death and destruction in Haiti was attributed to the inadequate infrastructure and substandard building codes. Some six weeks later, Chile, a much more economically developed country, suffered an earthquake of greater magnitude but resulted in far fewer deaths (about seven hundred). The much lower loss of life is attributed to the strict building codes in Chile.

26. UN Development Programme, "Türkiye-Syria Earthquakes," www.undp.org/turkiye-syria-earthquakes (July 29, 2024).

27. Global Center for the Responsibility to Protect, "Report of the International Commission on Intervention and State Sovereignty," 2001, www.globalr2p.org/resources/the-responsibility-to-protect-report-of-the-international-commission-on-intervention-and-state-sovereignty-2001/ (July 29, 2024).

28. Donald Kagan, *On the Origins of War: And the Preservation of Peace* (New York: Anchor Books, 1996).

Chapter 2

A Christian Approach to Global Politics

The Christian religion is expressed in three major traditions: Roman Catholicism, Protestantism, and Orthodoxy.[1] The first rupture in the church occurred in 1054 when the Western church, headed by the Catholic Pope in Rome, and the Eastern church, headed by the patriarch in Constantinople, agreed to part ways. The schism between Orthodoxy and Catholicism was partly over doctrine and over clerical traditions and practices. The third tradition, Protestantism, emerged in the early sixteenth century in response to teachings and practices of Catholic priests. In particular, the challenge was led by Martin Luther, who sought to make Scripture, not church traditions and teachings, the foundation of the Christian faith. Since I am chiefly concerned with the impact of the Christian church in the West, I focus only on the teachings of the Catholic and Protestant traditions.

The Bible is not a manual on what political actions should be undertaken by government. Nor does the Bible serve as a guidebook on how to think about the state and the international community. Instead, Scripture is a source of divine revelation on how persons should be related to God, to fellow human beings, and to the world itself. Nonetheless, the Bible, and more generally the Christian faith, provides a general approach to how Christians should live as well as how they should view social and political life. John C. Bennett, a mid-twentieth-century theologian, argued in *Foreign Policy in Christian Perspective* that the Christian faith provided an approach to international affairs by offering "ultimate perspectives, broad criteria, motives, inspirations, sensitivities, warnings, moral limits rather than directives for policies and decisions."[2] More recently, the National Association of Evangelicals' 2009 statement on immigration declares that the Bible "can serve as a moral compass and shape the attitudes of those who believe in God."[3]

A biblical framework does not emerge from specific Bible texts but rather arises from a general interpretive overview of biblical revelation. Such an overview will involve important insights and perspectives but also principles that can structure analysis and action. Since Christians have historically interpreted the demands of discipleship from a variety of theological perspectives, there is no single compendium of principles relevant to domestic and international political concerns. Different Christian traditions emphasize different principles based on how they define the relationship between spiritual and temporal life, the church, and the political community. For example, Christians following Anabaptist theology give priority to issues of peacekeeping and conflict resolution and avoid issues of war and coercive power, while Christians of a Reformed theological persuasion regard government as a divine creation and emphasize public order and the legitimacy of governmental force in restraining evil. For their part, Catholic thinkers emphasize public justice and the pursuit of the common good. They have also developed an elaborate framework, known as just war theory, to advance justice in wartime.

In this chapter, I begin by sketching core theological principles common to both Catholicism and Protestantism. I then explore some distinctive features of Protestantism followed by core social and political teachings of the Catholic Church. In the third section, I examine the challenges involved in integrating faith and politics and provide a framework for doing so.

BASIC PRINCIPLES OF CHRISTIANITY

Although biblical revelation is the basis of the Christian religion, there is no consensus on the fundamental teachings relevant to social and political life. Nevertheless, the teachings of Catholicism and Protestantism have emphasized several basic theological principles. These include God's sovereignty, human dignity, the universality of God's love, the pervasiveness of sin, caring for the poor and vulnerable, and the demand for justice.

God's Sovereignty

God's sovereignty means that all creation lives under the providence and judgment of God. Although humans have discretion in how they live, the world is under an omnipotent and omniscient God. Abraham Kuyper, a late-nineteenth-century Dutch theologian and politician, argued that God's sovereignty was expressed through the lives and service of Christian believers. He once declared, "There is not a square inch in the whole domain of our human existence over which Christ, who is sovereign over all, does not cry 'Mine!'"[4]

Human Dignity

Christians believe that persons, who are created in God's image, have infinite worth and are entitled to dignity and respect. Although people vary in gender, race, nationality, and levels of education and wealth, Christians believe that all persons are morally equal. As Paul notes in Romans, "there is neither Jew nor Greek for we are all one in Christ." This means that Christians comprise one people, where all persons are of equal worth and dignity. Political theorist Glen Tinder, a Lutheran, argues that a central contribution of the Christian faith is the notion "of the exalted individual."[5] This idea has provided the foundation for modern human rights and is the basis for claims of individual moral autonomy. Liberty is essential to authentic personhood because moral agency is only possible when people are responsible for their own thoughts and actions.

The Universality of God's Love

The Bible declares that God loves the world and especially the people He created. Scripture states that God "gave His only begotten Son" so that those who believe in Him can enjoy "eternal life" (John 3:16). Jesus expressed the priority of love by declaring that the first commandment was to love God with all one's heart, soul, mind, and strength, and that the second commandment was to love one's neighbor as oneself (Mark 12:30–31). For the Christian, love offers the foundation for building peaceful families, churches, and human communities. But loving others is especially difficult because of the propensity of self-love. Ethicist Reinhold Niebuhr argued that using love as a political ethic was insufficient for guiding political action because people are unwilling and unable to follow this ethic. For him, the Christian faith was not simply about love but also about redemption from sin through God's mercy and forgiveness.[6] In short, Christians are called to love their neighbor but also to repent of their sin for being unable to do so. Finally, since God's love is universal, this principle calls attention to the transnational nature of human responsibilities. In an essay "Who Is My Neighbour?" Rowan Williams, a former Archbishop of Canterbury, argues that a biblical response to this question demands that we ourselves must live as neighbors. Global ethics should not be concerned simply with who is and is not a neighbor; rather, it must focus on how we ourselves become more lovable, more involved with strangers.[7]

The Pervasiveness of Human Sin

According to the Bible, all persons "have sinned and fallen short of the glory of God" (Romans 3:23). For Christians, sin is not simply thinking and doing evil deeds but is the condition of exalting ourselves and making ourselves independent of God. For Reinhold Niebuhr, sin is rooted in self-love and pride, leading individuals to replace God's authority with the self.[8] While Glen Tinder argues that humans are created in God's image, he also claims that they are "fallen." For him, sin is occasioned by the propensity to exalt ourselves rather than allowing God to exalt us.[9] For Protestants, sin is universal and comprehensive, affecting all persons and all aspects of human life, including one's interests, thoughts, and morals. Where the Catholic faith emphasizes the role of reason and tradition, Protestants are much more skeptical of reason as they start from the assumption that sin taints reason, rendering it an unreliable instrument of justice.

In addition to these four fundamental theological tenets, Scripture also emphasizes two additional norms that are important in social and political life. These two additional principles are caring for the poor and vulnerable and the need for justice in human communities.

Caring for the Poor and Vulnerable

Although Scripture acknowledges that poor and vulnerable people will continue to be a part of social and political communities, the Bible is clear that we ought to care for the poor and seek to alleviate their destitution. Caring for those who are weak and vulnerable is a manifestation of our love of God. Not surprisingly, Christian churches have historically been at the forefront of providing compassionate care to the poor and the sick. Catholic orders have regarded medical care and education as vital services of the church and have therefore built thousands of hospitals, clinics, schools, and universities worldwide. Similarly, Protestant missionaries have also emphasized the care of the poor by building clinics and hospitals and establishing schools to encourage literacy. The renewal of Christian faith has often been accompanied by the establishment of charitable organizations that distribute food and provide medical care. The Salvation Army, created in nineteenth-century Britain, played a crucial role in meeting basic human needs and reducing crime and oppression in London soon after it was established.

The Need for Justice

One of the major themes of the Old Testament Prophets, especially Isaiah, Ezekiel, Jeremiah, and Amos, is the demand for justice. From a biblical perspective, justice is not simply an individual virtue but a communal or social expectation. When God established a covenant with the Jewish people, divine protection and blessings were conditional on people fulfilling their covenantal responsibilities, especially to treat others well. When the people failed to abide by God's demands for justice, God used the Prophets to warn his people that their greed, abuse, exploitation, and injustice would result in a harsh judgment. Rabbi Benjamin Scolnic writes that the Prophets were important because they "exhort the people to be charitable and merciful to the poor and to help those who were defenseless and needy, widows and orphans, oppressed people, strangers and those without legal rights. They stipulate impartiality in justice, and fairness. They insist on respecting the property of others. They demand respect for every human life."[10]

From a Scriptural perspective, justice is associated with the impartial administration of the law, supporting the poor and vulnerable, defending the oppressed, and caring for strangers. Scripture frequently associates justice with righteousness. Philosopher Nicholas Wolterstorff argues that the vision of *shalom*, or right relationships, best captures the Old Testament notion of justice. While shalom is often translated as "peace," the term entails a much broader conception of human wellbeing. According to Wolterstorff, shalom occurs when people are at peace "with God, with self, with fellows, with nature."[11] Political theorist Daniel Philpott has similarly argued that biblical justice involves a broader, more comprehensive account that goes beyond the typical emphases on individual rights and duties, fairness, and retribution. He calls this more holistic approach "justice as right relationship."[12]

The biblical conception of justice also involves the ethical demand of love. In exploring the relationship of love to justice, theologian Emile Brunner notes that love is greater than justice and more demanding. In his view, "Justice is nothing but the form of love which has currency in the world of institutions."[13] Given human nature, Biblical justice is a demanding ethic, requiring righteous living, loving relationships, and a fair and equitable distribution of resources. Although human efforts are likely to fall short of this biblical norm, justice provides an important ideal by which to judge individual and collective behavior.

PROTESTANT TEACHINGS

The Protestant Reformation emerged in the early sixteenth century when religious leaders began to question the primacy of clergy and the institutional role of the church. The Reformers claimed that the Bible is the sole source of authentic religious faith and that individuals can understand God's revelation without the assistance of clergy. Additionally, Reformers asserted that salvation in Christ is not mediated by priests but is a gift that is received by faith, not works. Finally, since Protestantism viewed the Christian faith fundamentally as a personal relationship between God (in Christ) and an individual, the

Reformation represented a major challenge to the institutional power of the Catholic Church.

The Reformation spawned a wide variety of different church groups. Early on, the two dominant Protestant groups were the Lutherans and the Calvinists, comprising the main branches of Reformed believers. In time, however, other church groups emerged, such as Anglicans, Puritans, Presbyterians, Mennonites, Methodists, and Brethren. While the governance of these denominations varied, Protestant churches continued to affirm the tenets of the classical faith—namely, the authority of Scripture, personal salvation through faith in Christ, and the priesthood of believers.

Because of the diverse manifestations of Protestantism, it is not easy to synthesize its political ethics. I therefore highlight principles that have been considered important by major Protestant and Evangelical churches. These norms include the dual nature of citizenship, the legitimacy of government, the priority of individual responsibility, stewardship, the need to manage government power, and the primacy of spiritual life.

The Dual Nature of Citizenship

Following Martin Luther's teaching on the distinct functions of the church and the state, Protestants believe that Christians have citizenship in two separate societies: the Kingdom of Man and the Kingdom of God. The first is represented by our temporal participation in political society; the second is represented by our spiritual participation in the church, the body of Christ. The first is a political community where the coercive power of government ensures order and the enforcement of laws in a specified territory. The church, by contrast, is a universal society governed by love of Christ and of neighbor. The classic statement of dual citizenship framework is set forth by Saint Augustine in *The City of God*. Augustine argues that two competing worldviews give rise to two alternative societies or ways of living. The earthly realm, or "City of Man," is guided by self-love and requires coercive power to maintain order and foster some level of justice. The alternative spiritual realm is the "City of God," which includes Christ's followers and is guided by divine love. Although all persons are citizens of temporal political societies, only Christians are citizens of the heavenly kingdom. Christians frequently face a tension between the demands of the two cities. Although Christians are called to give precedence to the Kingdom of God, there are no simple guidelines for how to determine the responsibilities to church and state, the spiritual city and the temporal city. When the Pharisees asked Jesus whether it was lawful to pay taxes to Caesar, he replies cryptically that we should "render to Caesar the things that are Caesar's and to God the things that are God's" (Matthew 22:21). Although Scripture calls on persons to obey legitimate governmental authority, the state's power must always be subservient to God's authority.

The Legitimacy of Government

Protestants believe that government is part of God's created order. Paul declares in Romans that people should be "subject to the governing authorities." Given the "fallen" status of human beings, social life in human communities necessitates public authority to ensure order and some degree of justice. Nicholas Wolterstorff argues that government is divinely instituted "as part of God's providential care" for human beings.[14] Although the Bible affirms the legitimacy of government, it does not specify how government should be constituted or what political form should be used in structuring a political community. Although a good case can be made for a limited government based on consent, a biblical approach to politics must focus on the most important moral dimensions of political society—namely, human dignity, human freedom, political order, and justice.

The Priority of Individual Responsibility

Another important principle of Reformation religion is the priority of the individual. Because sin is personal, redemption from sin involves an individual's acceptance of God's grace through Christ. Unlike the Roman Catholic Church, which emphasizes the role of the priest in mediating salvation, Protestants emphasize the personal relationship of God to the individual believer. In his classic book *The Cost of Discipleship*, theologian Dietrich Bonhoeffer emphasizes the radical individualism of being a Christian. He writes, "Through the call of Jesus men become individuals. . . . It is no choice of their own that makes them individuals; it is Christ who makes them individuals by calling them. Every man is called separately, and must follow alone."[15] Moreover, since people are sinful, an important emphasis of Protestantism is the need for individual confession and repentance. Not surprisingly, a key element in Protestant worship services is the confession of sin. Since spiritual life is conceived chiefly in personal terms, Protestants have historically emphasized the responsibility and accountability of individuals not simply in religious life but also in fulfilling temporal responsibilities.

Stewardship

Closely associated with the principle of individual responsibility is the notion of stewardship. Stewardship has two important dimensions. First, because the earth is God's creation, humans are responsible to protect and manage resources in a responsible manner. The principle of *creation care*, which calls for careful use and management of the earth's resources, is a manifestation of stewardship. Second, because God has created persons in his image and given them gifts and abilities, they have a responsibility to develop and use those gifts in the service of others. For Christians, work is not simply a means of earning a living but also a means of advancing God's Kingdom on earth.

The Need to Manage Government Power

Although Protestants acknowledge the important role of the state, they also emphasize the need to constrain government power to avoid excessive centralization. This claim is rooted in four truths—that God is sovereign, that the responsibility to care for the temporal world has been entrusted to people, that people are God's special creation, and that human sin is pervasive and universal. The first truth means that government should not encroach on the spiritual dimensions of life. The second truth acknowledges the state is a distinct political institution responsible for maintaining order and enforcing the law. Because people have been entrusted with distinct, separate callings (e.g., church, family, state), the state is simply one area in which people serve God.[16] Since the state must respect the autonomous, nongovernmental areas of life, the state's responsibilities are limited to its sphere of legal-political affairs. The third and fourth truths call for a limited government to avoid tyranny and protect human rights. Given human nature, the centralization of governmental power can result in political oppression. Lord Acton, the nineteenth-century British politician, captured the moral danger of political power with his famous aphorism: "Power tends to corrupt and absolute power corrupts absolutely." The Founding Fathers of the US Constitution were aware of the need to manage government power. As a result, they crafted a constitutional system in which the power of the federal government was shared by three distinct branches of government: the executive, the legislative, and the judiciary. In addition, by establishing a federal structure, the power of government was shared by national and subnational (i.e., state) institutions.

The Primacy of Spiritual Life

Although Protestants claim dual citizenship in the temporal and spiritual realms, they also believe that the Kingdom of God is primary. This means that spiritual life is the foundation for a moral life. Accordingly, the creation of humane and just societies is only possible when individuals are rightly related to God and to each other. Whereas secular politics focuses on the temporal demands of life, Christians believe that spiritual faith is the foundation for a good society. According to Timothy Shah, whereas Western political theory sought to improve the human condition by calling on the state to foster human virtues, Protestants have emphasized individual spiritual renewal as a foundation for a good society.[17] Indeed, the moral transformation of persons is the precondition for authentic political development. The primacy of faith has been stated eloquently by Richard Neuhaus. In his statement on "Christianity and Democracy." Neuhaus declares, "the first and final assertion Christians make about all of reality, including politics, is 'Jesus Christ is Lord.'" Since the primary task of the church is to proclaim the gospel, it must maintain a critical distance from all temporal initiatives. As a result, "Christians betray their Lord . . . if they equate the Kingdom of God with any political, social or economic order of this passing time."[18]

CATHOLIC TEACHINGS

Among Christian traditions, the Roman Catholic Church has developed the most elaborate and sophisticated body of political and social teaching based on Scripture and reason. This body, called *Catholic Social Thought* (CST), is expressed in core principles, such as personalism, common good, subsidiarity, participation, and social solidarity. Whereas Protestant principles are chiefly theological propositions, CST is focused on common issues and challenges in temporal life. To be sure, while Catholics affirm such Protestant norms as human dignity, justice, and caring for the poor, they also are likely to diverge from Protestant thought by decreasing the priority of some principles, such as individual responsibility, the need for a limited state, and the priority of spiritual life.

The teachings of the Catholic Church are rooted not solely in Scripture but also on reason and tradition. This three-legged stool provides the foundation for CST. Unlike Protestants, who think that each believer can understand and apply biblical truth individually, Catholics believe that the church, under the direction of bishops and priests, provides an authoritative interpretation of Scripture. Reason is also regarded as an important element in church teaching. Since God created a rational world, humans apprehend and enjoy creation through rational reflection, which can illuminate important moral principles. Although revelation is primary, reason provides an important supplement to understanding God's creation. Whereas Protestants are skeptical of the tradition of natural law, Catholics accept it as an important element in building and sustaining a humane world. To a significant degree, just war theory, which is rooted in principles of natural law, provides norms to constrain violence and limit human suffering in war. Finally, Catholics emphasize the role of tradition, defined as the collective teachings and practices of the church. Since the Roman Catholic Church is a hierarchical organization, papal encyclicals, official church declarations, and pastoral letters provide a wealth of resources that sustain Catholic teachings.

CST is not a fixed body of principles but a dynamic tradition that is continuously updated as Catholic leaders respond to changing circumstances in national and global life. Despite the different ways that scholars and theologians approach the body of social and political teachings of the Catholic Church, there is general agreement that the following principles comprise essential elements of CST: personalism, common good, subsidiarity, participation, and solidarity. I briefly explain each of these in the following.

The central idea of *personalism* is that humans are the central actors of social and political life. This principle, which was first given special prominence in the teaching document *Gaudium et Spes* (Joy and Hope) in 1965, was a theme repeatedly emphasized by Pope John Paul II. According to Jeffrey Kirby "the personalist principle insists on placing the human person in the centre of the social order and using his divinely-given dignity to judge and coordinate policy and efforts of and for the community."[19] Like the Protestant idea of human dignity, this principle assumes that people are made in God's image and therefore entitled to dignity. Because human life is sacred, the foundation of political and social life is rooted in the wellbeing of people.

The *common good* principle calls for the overall wellbeing of a community. Since human beings are social by nature, their own welfare and dignity can only be assured when they are in association with others. The social good of a community demands that each person's basic needs should be met. This concept applies not only to local and national communities but also to the international community itself.

Subsidiarity is the belief that decision-making should be carried out by individuals who have the greatest stake in the issues. This means that a decentralized structure is desirable because it is conducive to responsible decision-making and empowering to its participants. The general aim of this principle is to strengthen local ownership and participation by avoiding excessive overcentralization in organizations. According to US Catholic bishops, "The principle of subsidiarity reminds us that larger institutions in society should not overwhelm or interfere with smaller or local institutions, yet larger institutions have essential responsibilities when the more local institutions cannot adequately protect human dignity, meet human needs, and advance the common good."[20]

The principle of *participation* means that individuals must be involved in caring for their own needs as well as with those of others. According to this principle, each person has an important contribution to make in caring for the common good of society. Practical manifestations of this idea include participating in local elections, paying property taxes, obeying laws and regulations, voting in elections, and serving in politics and nongovernmental organizations.

Solidarity is understood as a fraternal love and civic friendship among community members. Since people pursue their own interests at the expense of, or in disregard of, the welfare of others, solidarity is the call to care for the needs of others, whether near or far. Since people are morally equal, solidarity involves extending concern for others at the familial, local, national, and international levels.

In addition to these core principles, CST also has stressed in recent years additional principles, such as creation care, the preferential option for the poor, and the preferential option for nonviolence.

Creation care is concerned with environmental protection, including the threat of climate change. A Catholic nongovernmental organization describes this principle as follows: "Care for the earth is a requirement of the Catholic faith. We are called to protect people and the planet, living our faith in relationship with all of God's creation."[21]

The *preferential option for the poor* seeks to give priority to the needs of the poor and the vulnerable. The principle emerged in the late 1960s as Latin American bishops struggled to respond to rampant poverty and egregious economic inequalities in the region. Whereas the common good norm embraces all members of a community, the preferential option focuses on the need to care for the weak and the vulnerable. According to a US Catholic Bishops document, "A basic moral test for our society is how we treat the most vulnerable in our midst."[22]

The *preferential option for nonviolence*, which is a more contested principle because of the church's historic support for just war theory, seeks to emphasize the importance of pacific conflict resolution. The norm became more important with the increased influence of pacifism as a response to the growing threat of nuclear conflict.

Like Protestant norms, CST principles do not provide readymade answers to contemporary political and social challenges. Instead, they offer a framework to help structure moral reasoning on important moral issues, including war, human rights, migration, environmental protection, nationalism, and the like.

THE CHRISTIAN FAITH AND POLITICS

Based on the biblical principles and church teachings examined earlier, a Christian approach to national and international politics should seek to apply foundational norms to the specific issues and challenges than confront contemporary public affairs. The following is a partial list of key moral norms that should guide the political analysis and action of believers: a) since each person is unique and of infinite worth, politics must uphold human dignity; b) people are fundamentally equal; c) since people are social creatures, social solidarity is imperative and requires the quest for developing and sustaining humane communities; d) Christians are dual citizens, with responsibilities to God and to temporal authorities; e) when conflict arises between the demands of faith and politics, the former take precedence over the latter; f) government is essential in maintaining order and pursuing justice; g) because of sin, the rule of law is essential in affirming human dignity and protecting human rights; h) because of sin, government power needs to be managed by ensuring that different institutions participate in decision-making; i) since people matter, individuals and institutions should pursue the common good at the local, national, and international levels; j) caring for the poor and vulnerable is a responsibility of both individuals and political communities; k) because peace is a moral priority, states should pursue peaceful conflict resolution; and l) political communities should make justice a priority.

In addressing national and international political issues, Christians have relied on two strategies: separation and integration. The separatist strategy seeks to maintain a clear separation between politics and religion but is expressed in two different ways. One approach emphasizes the supremacy of faith over temporal affairs. For such believers, the Christian faith is chiefly about an individual's relationship to God—to serve God by living in accordance with the demands of authentic discipleship. Since the demands of the Kingdom of God must take precedence over the responsibilities in the Kingdom of Man, religion must necessarily focus on spiritual concerns, especially people's relationship to God and to others. This approach has been expressed by pietist Christians, who seek to minimize engagement with the temporal concerns. The most radical expression of such pietism is manifested by Amish believers who are committed to pacifism and nonparticipation in secular society. For them, the only way to live an authentic Christian life is to avoid engaging in the secular institutions of society.

The alternative manifestation of the separatist strategy is rooted in the belief that Christians have dual citizenships and must maintain distinct responsibilities for each sphere. Since the spiritual and temporal realms place different demands and responsibilities, political effectiveness can only be realized when political responsibilities are undertaken based on political considerations, not the demands of the church. Since applying spiritual and moral truths can impair political calculations, Christians must respect the autonomy of the political sphere and support compliance with governmental decision-making. Despite the increasing political repression pursued by Germany's Nazi regime in the 1930s, the state Lutheran Church continued to support the government, to the great consternation and opposition of Christians like

Dietrich Bonhoeffer. Essentially, this approach reflects the theology of dual kingdoms advanced by Lutherans.

The second basic strategy that Christians have used in relating faith and politics is integration. According to this approach, Christians can fulfill simultaneously the obligations of dual citizenship by carefully reconciling competing and conflicting demands between religion and the state, faith and politics. Such reconciliation is challenging but feasible. It simply requires that believers allocate their responsibilities following Jesus' admonition that Christians are "to render to Caesar the things that are Caesar's and to God the things that are God's." This requires a judicious and prudent analysis of how Biblical demands should be applied to specific national and international political issues. This book is based on the appropriateness of this integrative approach to faith and politics.

The Bible and Politics

Although the Bible does not specify what types of political communities or governments are desirable, Scripture provides, as I noted earlier, principles and perspectives that help guide political analysis. In addition, church teachings on social and political life can help structure the moral analysis of public policy issues. But how should biblical principles and church teachings be applied to political issues? How should Scripture be used in confronting temporal concerns? Some Christians, for example, use general principles, such as social justice or peacekeeping, to advance public policies. Other believers attempt to use Scriptural texts to justify political concerns and advance specific public policies on issues such as Israel, migration, or climate change. Some Christians claim, for example, that the fundamental biblical message on migration is to "welcome the stranger," thereby undermining the need for border control.[23] Other believers use the Bible (specifically, the Old Testament) to justify Israel's sovereignty over all of Palestine.[24] When the Speaker of the House of Representatives, Republican Mike Johnson, was asked how he approached contemporary issues, he replied, "Well, go pick up a Bible off your shelf and read it. That's my worldview."[25] But the Bible is not a self-revealing text but one that requires interpretation in understanding and application. Consequently, the simplistic use of principles and biblical texts to justify political choices and policy prescriptions is both unwise and possibly counterproductive.

The approach taken here is that the Bible is God's revelation and provides guidance on how to find meaning and purpose in life. While Scripture provides a foundation for a Christian approach to politics, it does not provide specific guidance on governmental issues or public policy concerns. The Bible does not specify, for example, criteria for electing government officials or specify whether Congressional term limits are desirable. And, as I have stressed earlier, the Bible does not prescribe how the international community should be organized and governed. More specifically, Scripture does not offer specific policy guidance on such issues as national debt, nuclear energy, foreign aid, and irregular migration. In my book *Evangelicals and American Foreign Policy*, I describe the problem of faith and politics as follows:

> If the Bible is regarded as a direct guide to foreign policy issues, believers are likely to define global issues . . . in simplistic ways. On the other hand, if the Bible is viewed not as a manual on international relations but as a source of foundational principles that must be applied skillfully and judiciously to intractable interstate problems, then Evangelicals are likely to interpret problems pluralistically and devise multiple strategies for addressing them.[26]

Given the complexity of modern problems confronting governments and the general nature of biblical revelation, it is evident that there are no "Christian" answers to the major public policy concerns facing contemporary democratic states. Christians should also be skeptical of any individual or group that seeks to use religious authority to advance political initiatives or public policies. Periodically, religious leaders have sought to influence governmental decisions based on what they perceive to be God's will. Such efforts have rarely helped political leaders in making morally prudent decisions. More often, such initiatives can undermine the authority of the church and call into question the clergy's moral authority.

Such was the case when leaders of the National Council of Churches sought to influence the Iraq-Kuwait conflict. As noted in the introduction, the dispute began when Iraq invaded Kuwait in August 1990. In response, Western democracies, supported by UN Security Council resolutions, demanded the withdrawal of Iraqi military forces from Kuwait. When economic sanctions and Western political pressure failed to redress Iraq's aggression, the allies undertook military preparations to use force to compel Iraq's withdrawal from Kuwait. Church leaders declared their opposition to war and called for more time to allow sanctions to become effective. The clergy's condemnation of war was undoubtedly fueled by a pacifist orientation coupled with a desire to limit the destruction and death accompanying war. But what the clergy failed to appreciate was that the existing conditions in early January were inflicting gross human rights abuses and much human suffering on Kuwait's people. And the call to continue sanctions on Iraq were imposing great suffering on Iraqi people, especially children. As theorist Michael Walzer observed at the time, the opponents of war who supported a prolonged blockade of Iraq "seem not to have realized that what they were advocating was a radically indiscriminate act of war, with predictable harsh consequences."[27]

Nearly a century and a half earlier, clergy had similarly sought to influence presidential decision-making. A delegation of Presbyterian clergy visited President Abraham Lincoln and called on him to emancipate slaves immediately. Although Lincoln thought emancipation was a desirable goal, he believed that such action was premature. Lincoln's view was that for an emancipation proclamation to be effective, the Union government needed to be more successful in the war. In facing the dilemma of how to respond to religious voices, Lincoln penned an insightful reflection about faith and politics:

> I am approached with the most opposite opinions and advice, and that by religious men, who are equally certain that they represent the Divine will. I am sure that either the one or the other class is mistaken in that belief, and perhaps in some respects both. I hope it will not be irreverent for me to say that if it is probable that God would reveal his will to others, on a point so connected with my duty, it might be supposed that he would reveal it directly to me: for unless I am more deceived in myself that I often am, it is my earnest desire to know the will of Providence in this matter. And if I can learn what it is I will do it! These are not, however, the days of miracles, and I suppose it will be granted that I am not to expect a direct revelation. I must study the plain physical facts of the case, ascertain what is possible and learn what appears to be wise and right.[28]

If politics were simply a conflict between good and evil, integrating faith in public life would be a simple, straightforward task. But most problems and issues in national and international politics do not involve simply binary choices between the good and the bad, the just and the unjust. Indeed, political action is difficult because public policy issues typically involve multiple moral norms and demand trade-offs among competing goods.

Political Engagement Principles

Based on the overview of Christian norms discussed previously, how should believers integrate a Christian perspective with important national and international political issues? To aid the reader in this task, I offer the following guidelines to structure reflection and analysis. The framework has five elements.

The first requirement for a competent political engagement is knowledge of the issues. While some concerns can be defined simply, most political issues are problems precisely because they are complex and involve a variety of different ways of defining and approaching them. Nuclear energy, for example, is difficult because experts themselves are uncertain about the risks involved in nuclear fission, especially about how to dispose of nuclear waste. Nuclear energy has benefits over fossil fuels since the former does not contribute to greenhouse emission and can therefore help reduce global warming. But nuclear power plants, while costly, pose significant dangers, as the disaster at the Japanese nuclear power plant at Fukushima demonstrated in 2011. Climate change is similarly a complex issue, not so much because of global warming but because of divergent analyses of how to reduce greenhouse emissions by replacing fossil fuels with alternative energy sources.

Second, Christians should identify relevant moral issues. Many political problems are instrumental and do not raise fundamental moral concerns. Examples of nonmoral issues include whether to build a two-lane or a four-lane bridge, whether to grant temporary protective status to Venezuelans or to Colombians, or whether US foreign aid should be given in products or loans and grants. Many contemporary public policy issues, however, involve significant moral concerns that require trade-offs between competing goods. For example, should the United States give immigrant visas to family relatives or to skill-based workers? Should the United States continue to penalize Venezuela for its abuse of human rights or lift sanctions and import more Venezuelan petroleum in the hope that increased government revenues will reduce poverty and curb the exodus of citizens leaving the country? How much military assistance, and in what form, should the US government provide Ukraine in its war of self-defense against Russia?

The third element involves applying a Christian worldview to relevant political issues. This means that believers must discern which biblical principles are relevant and integrate them into the moral assessment of the issues. Most political issues will necessarily involve multiple biblical principles and core Christian norms. For example, if political order and justice are in conflict, which principle should take precedence? And while Scripture enjoins believers to be peacemakers, justice may require military action to halt aggression and restore a humane political order. Further, should a Christian give priority to environmental protection (creation care) over caring for the poor and the vulnerable, if the shift to renewable energy sources increases unemployment and harms the poor? Which Christian norms should guide US decision-making in deciding immigration policies, and in determining which refugee groups should be given priority over migrants requesting asylum?

In carrying out this task, it is important to avoid using specific Scriptural texts to address issues. In identifying key biblical norms, it is vital to apply the totality of God's revelation rather than a single text. The problem of using a single text is illustrated by a sermon preached by an influential preacher in Florida in the mid-1980s. Using a specific text (Neh. 2:17) that called for the building of the wall of Jerusalem, the preacher used Scripture to support

President Reagan's Strategic Defense Initiative, which aimed to destroy incoming missiles in the event of nuclear conflict.

Fourth, in confronting political issues, it is important to differentiate between the basic policy goals and the different ways that the problem might be alleviated—that is, between ends and means. Although many political disputes are focused on defining the purposes and goals of problems, the more common source of conflict is over the different ways to address an issue. For example, in seeking to reduce hunger in developing nations, should the West transfer food aid (the short-term solution) or support the infrastructure necessary for sustained economic growth (the long-term solution)? Similarly, in seeking to advance human dignity worldwide, should the US government restrict imports with tariffs to strengthen domestic employment or should it maintain relative free-trade policies to facilitate economic growth in developing nations and therefore contribute to poverty reduction in those countries? In short, in addressing the moral dimensions of public policy concerns, it is important to clarify goals and specify alternative means of pursuing the desired goal.

Finally, Christian political engagement demands an ethic of humility. Because political issues are complex and involve multiple moral dimensions, most concerns are not subject to a binary, good/bad response. Additionally, because most policy making is probabilistic, there is no certainty that the desired goals will be realized. Indeed, much policy making results in unanticipated outcomes. The late sociologist Peter Berger observed: "It is the easiest thing in the world to proclaim a good. The hard part is to think through ways by which this good can be realized without exorbitant costs and without consequences that negate the good. This is why an ethic of responsibility must be cautious, calculating a perennially uncertain mass of means, costs and consequences."[29] Given the complexity involved in addressing national and global issues, Christians seeking to advance human rights and justice should proceed in their political engagement with humility and tentativeness. As H. Richard Niebuhr noted long ago, God's strategy in the world was in the mind of the Creator and not in the minds of his lieutenants.[30]

In conclusion, the Christian faith provides important principles to guide political and social analysis and action. The Bible, however, does not offer specific guidance on the many difficult and complex problems facing nation-states and the international community. Instead, it provides a moral compass to guide in the development of moral, prudent public policies. Churches can help in this task if they focus on teaching political ethics and avoid direct public policy advocacy—a task left to political interest groups. Individuals can contribute to domestic justice and global order by using a Biblical worldview to assess and guide public policy concerns.

NOTES

1. These traditions, especially Protestantism, are subdivided into many different denominations based on competing and conflicting theological issues, diverse governing principles, and social and economic concerns.
2. John C. Bennett, *Foreign Policy in Christian Perspective* (New York: Charles Scribner's Sons, 1956), 16.
3. National Association of Evangelicals, "Resolution on Immigration," 2009, www.nae.org/immigration-2009/ (July 31, 2024).
4. Quoted in Richard J. Mouw, *Abraham Kuyper: A Short and Personal Introduction* (Grand Rapids, MI: Eerdmans, 2011), 4.
5. Glen Tinder, "Can We Be Good Without God?" *The Atlantic Monthly*, December 1989, 71–72.
6. Reinhold Niebuhr, "Why the Christian Church Is Not Pacifist," in *The Essential Niebuhr: Selected Essays and Addresses*, edited by Robert McAffee Brown (New Haven: Yale University Press, 1986), 111.
7. Rowan Williams, "The Ethics of Global Relationships," in *Who Is My Neighbour? The Global and Personal Challenge*, edited by Richard Carter and Samuel Wells (London: Society for Promoting Christian Knowledge, 2018), 15–29.
8. Reinhold Niebuhr, *The Nature and Destiny of Man*, volume 1, "On Human Nature" (New York: Charles Scribner's Sons, 1964), 16.
9. Tinder, "Can We Be Good Without God?" 77.
10. Rabbi Benjamin Scolnic, "The Prophets and Social Justice," www.ibjewish.org/wp-content/uploads/2014/10/Scolnic-Prophets-and-Social-Justice.pdf (July 31, 2024).
11. Nicholas Wolterstorff, *Until Justice and Peace Embrace* (Grand Rapids: Eerdmans, 1983), 70.
12. Daniel Philpott, "There Is a Wideness in God's Justice," *Nova et Vetera*, English edition, 18, no. 4 (2020).
13. Emile Brunner, *Justice and the Social Order* (New York: Harper and Brothers, 1945), 72.
14. Nicholas Wolterstorff, "Theological Foundations for an Evangelical Political Philosophy," in *Toward an Evangelical Public Policy*, edited by Ronald J. Sider and Diane Knippers (Grand Rapids: Baker Books, 2005), 160.
15. Dietrich Bonhoeffer, *The Cost of Discipleship* (New York: Macmillan, 1961), 84.
16. Abraham Kuyper, a late-nineteenth-century Christian politician, coined the term "sphere sovereignty" to emphasize that God's sovereignty is manifested by believers serving in distinct areas of life, such as church, state, family, and business.
17. Timothy Samuel Shah, "Some Evangelical Views of the State," in *Church, State, and Citizen: Christian Approaches to Political Engagement*, edited by Sandra Joireman (New York: Oxford University Press, 2009), 136.
18. Richard John Neuhaus, "Christianity and Democracy: Statement of the Institute on Religion and Democracy," Washington, DC: Institute on Religion and Democracy, 1981, 1.

19. Jeffrey Kirby, "'Personalism' in the Social Teaching of John Paul II," https://frkirby.com/wp-content/uploads/2014/01/Personalism.pdf (July 31, 2024).

20. US Conference of Catholic Bishops, "Forming Consciences for Faithful Citizenship: A Call to Political Responsibility from the Catholic Bishops of the United States," Washington, DC: US Conference of Catholic Bishops, 48, www.usccb.org/issues-and-action/faithful-citizenship/upload/forming-consciences-for-faithful-citizenship.pdf (July 31, 2024).

21. Catholic Community Services and Catholic Housing Services of Western Washington, "Catholic Social Teaching," https://ccsww.org/about-us/catholic-social-teaching/ (July 31, 2024).

22. "Forming Consciences for Faithful Citizenship," 50.

23. See, for example, Matthew Soerens and Jenny Hwang, *Welcoming the Stranger: Justice, Compassion and Truth in the Immigration Debate* (Downers Grove, IL: IVP Books, 2009); and M. Daniel Carroll, *Christians at the Border: Immigration, the Church and the Bible* (Grand Rapids: Baker Academic, 2008).

24. For an overview of different approaches that Evangelicals have used in addressing the status of Israel, see chapter 6, "Evangelicals and U.S. Foreign Policy Toward Israel," in Mark R. Amstutz, *Evangelicals and American Foreign Policy* (New York: Oxford University Press, 2014).

25. Quoted in Peter Wehner, "The Polite Zealotry of Mike Johnson," *The Atlantic*, October 31, 2023, www.theatlantic.com/ideas/archive/2023/10/polite-zealotry-mike-johnson/675845/ (July 31, 2024).

26. Amstutz, *Evangelicals and American Foreign Policy*, 125.

27. Michael Walzer, "Justice and Injustice in the Gulf War," in *But Was It Just? Reflections on the Morality of the Persian Gulf War*, edited by David E. DeCosse (New York: Doubleday, 1992), 3.

28. Quoted in Hans Morgenthau, *Politics Among Nations: The Struggle for Power and Peace*, seventh edition (Boston: McGraw-Hill, 2006), 268–69.

29. Peter Berger, "Moral Judgment and Political Action," *Vital Speeches of the Day* 56 (December 1, 1987), 120.

30. H. Richard Niebuhr, *Christ and Culture* (New York: Harper & Row Torchbooks, 1951), 2.

Chapter 3

Strengthening Nation-States

The nation-state is important because it provides a foundation for membership in established political communities. People need a political home—a community that provides the social and political structure that enables human flourishing. Although people can find belonging in families, churches, clubs, and similar organizations, the nation-state is the basic political community of global society, providing the foundation for national identity. According to Paul Collier, such shared identity is important because it provides the basis for "reciprocal obligations."[1] Since a nation-state seeks to provide for the common welfare by producing and distributing goods and services, beliefs and practices based on reciprocity enable the state to collect and distribute resources.

In modern nation-states, communal identity is legally acknowledged in citizenship, which is the formal relationship between an individual and the state. Whether acquired at birth or through naturalization, citizenship ensures the protection of rights and imposes communal obligations. Contrary to the notion that the state is simply a market that facilitates economic activity,[2] a nation is a people sharing common values, aspirations, expectations, and mutual obligations. Citizenship is important because it establishes formal ties between an individual and a political community.

I have written this book in the belief that belonging matters. And because social and political solidarity is important, we need to acknowledge the important role of both the nation-state and the global society of states. While citizenship in states matters, global sentiments and universal obligations are also important. This chapter explores the continuing importance of the sovereign state, while chapter 4 explores the role and importance of the international community.

Even though the global society of nation-states creates instability and conflict, the state remains the fundamental political community for ensuring human rights and advancing economic prosperity. The state is the sole institution with the authority to undertake decisive action in national and transnational life.

In our contemporary world, the nation-state is facing significant challenges, including increasing division and polarization and a decline in governmental authority. It would be wrong, however, to assume that the current challenges facing nation-states are new. What is unprecedented, however, is the loss of confidence in the capacity of nation-states to address important domestic and international concerns. Clearly, humans need a just political and social order to flourish. The question is how to advance a humane and beneficent state that nurtures civic life and individual freedom. If human rights are to be protected and economic prosperity to be advanced, national governments need to be both strong and legitimate. Strength is necessary to ensure compliance with governmental decisions, but if governments are to have the authority to rule, they must have the public's support—that is, they must be perceived as just. To the extent that a government is not considered legitimate, it will necessarily rely on coercive power to implement its decisions.

This chapter examines the nature and role of the nation-state and explores how the Christian faith relates to such a political community. Since one of the major contemporary problems in global affairs is the fragility of many states, the chapter also explores how states might be renewed and strengthened.

THE NATURE AND ROLE OF NATION-STATES

Nation-states vary in their ability to meet human needs and to fulfill interstate obligations. States that can fulfill domestic and global responsibilities typically have a strong national identity, significant physical resources, and capable institutions.

The Nature of Nation-States

From a standpoint of governance, the strength of government is crucial. A government's capacity to maintain order and make binding decisions for society is dependent on its ability to ensure compliance with its decisions. Fundamentally, a state's strength is dependent on two sources: the political capabilities (strength) of governmental institutions and the habits and disposition of people's voluntary compliance. Governing is therefore partly dependent on the power and coercive capabilities of the state, and partly on the willingness of people to accept voluntarily the decisions of government.

One of the key aspects of governmental capabilities is the notion of authority. According to political scientists, authority is the state's capacity to command obedience without coercion. Authority is not based on force but on the rightful acceptance of the individuals and institutions issuing commands. Although democratic participation is the most widely used method of generating political legitimacy, compliance is not solely rooted in political consent. Much of life is carried out following social mores, cultural traditions, institutional rules, and community practices through habits of voluntary compliance. This explains why moral values, reason, and cultural traditions play an important role in contributing to social order and supporting governmental decision-making.

Kalevi Holsti has argued that the effectiveness of a state is dependent upon its legitimacy—that is, the level of voluntary approval of citizens. According to Holsti, legitimacy has two dimensions: horizontal and vertical. Horizontal legitimacy refers to the level of national cohesion among groups and peoples, whereas vertical legitimacy refers to the strength of relationship between rulers and citizens, government and people.[3] Both horizontal and vertical legitimacy are essential if a nation-state is to provide essential services to its people and fulfill its obligations to other member-states of global society.

Strong governments are those that enjoy both horizontal and vertical legitimacy, which is often expressed by a high degree of compliance with governmental decision-making. Typically, strong states are those that provide vital services, have little corruption, maintain institutional accountability, and maintain trust in its institutions. Weak or failing states have little authority to make or enforce rules, and are plagued by high levels of corruption, widespread crime, and limited political order. Failing states like Eritrea, Libya, Syria, and Yemen not only have limited vertical legitimacy but also little horizontal legitimacy.

Developing and sustaining a strong, competent, and humane state is a never-ending challenge. According to Fukuyama, state building involves two fundamental issues: determining the *scope* of government and second, determining its *strength*.[4] The first involves defining the breadth of governmental responsibilities—that is, determining the tasks the government should undertake. The second, and the more important issue, is determining the power and capabilities of government. Although the strength of government is often associated with centralized power, the effectiveness of government is ultimately dependent upon authority, not brute power. This explains why participatory regimes can be as strong as dictatorships.

States vary widely in the range of tasks that governments assume. Communist states like Cuba and North Korea have relatively small private sectors since the state is responsible for most production and distribution of goods and services. By contrast, liberal states, like Australia and the United States, assume that private enterprise should assume the major responsibility for producing and distributing goods and services. Between the extremes of totalitarian dictatorships and liberal free-enterprise regimes are a variety of states that balance political order and economic freedom in different ways. Social democracy is the most common expression of this middle position between excessive state control and the liberal market society.

Finally, nation-states vary according to their political structure. For much of history, political communities were maintained through the superior power of rulers. Following the Enlightenment, the independent role of persons increased, eventually giving way to the rise of democratic institutions based on popular sovereignty and periodic elections. In the second half of the twentieth century, the number of democracies increased significantly. Currently, close to 45 percent of the world's almost two hundred states are democratic. Despite the growth of democracies, however, autocratic regimes and dictatorships are still prevalent. The rise of China and Russia in the new millennium has given renewed strength to the forces of authoritarianism.

The Role of Nation-States

The nation-state is the primordial political unit in global society because it alone has the ability, based on communal solidarity and state power, to make and enforce public decisions and to pursue effective international cooperation. According to economist Paul Collier, politics is primarily national because public policy is predominantly national. And it remains primarily national because only the nation can provide a shared identity that can sustain "far-sighted reciprocity."[5] To be sure, such social solidarity can rise and fall over time and therefore impair governmental decision-making.

People who live in stable and prosperous societies, however, are likely to take for granted the important role of the state in providing order and protecting human rights. Since most developed democratic countries provide ample security and welfare to its citizens, people in modern societies tend to assume that order and prosperity are simply natural byproducts of social life. Historically, however, the creation of a strong, beneficent state is not an inevitable result of communal politics but a deliberate human creation. Indeed, the development of nation-states involves a long and difficult journey in state building and nation building.

The importance of the nation-state in fostering a humane international system is emphasized by the noted political philosopher John Rawls. In *The Law of Peoples*, Rawls seeks to uncover the principles that can advance a just international order.[6] He argues that the foundation for a humane global system are societies that are well-ordered and that protect human rights.[7] Rawls's theory is significant because it grounds the order and prosperity of global society on the nature of the political communities comprising the world. Admittedly, Rawls focuses on peoples, not states, but he does so to highlight the pivotal role societies play in fostering international justice and global order. For Rawls, international justice can be secured only if two conditions are met: first, states need to protect human rights, and second, states need to respect the autonomy of other states and cooperate in ensuring a stable and prosperous international community.

Despite the pivotal role of the nation-state in national and international politics, an increasing number of people in Western societies have begun to question its legitimacy. For them, the important task of the new millennium is to shift allegiance from the nation to the international community in the belief that by undermining state sovereignty the competition and conflict common to contemporary international politics will dissipate. For political scientist Francis Fukuyama, however, the decline of the state would result in widespread harm. He writes: "For individual societies and for the global community, the withering away of the state is not a prelude to utopia but to disaster." In his view, the nation-state will continue to be a central actor in the international community because only a sovereign government has the capacity to make and enforce law. "What only states and states alone are able to do," he notes, "is aggregate and purposefully deploy legitimate power. This power is necessary to enforce a rule of law domestically, and it is necessary to preserve world order internationally."[8]

Shortcomings of Nation-States

While many nation-states have succeeded in building and sustaining strong, efficient, and accountable governments, there are many societies that have been unable to establish an effective state. Indeed, one of the major problems in global society is the weakness of some states. Although the causes of state failure are many, three sources are especially important in accounting for governmental incapacity.

First, governments fail because of increased political fragmentation. When ethnic, religious, and political groups pursue their own interests in disregard for the common good, national solidarity is compromised. The rise in political fragmentation weakens a state's horizontal legitimacy, which impairs, in turn, a government's authority.

A second source of a state's weakness results from the failure of a government to provide essential public goods, such as security, health care, and education. When a state fails to care for the basic needs of people, vertical legitimacy declines, calling into question the government's authority. Dictatorships may be able to retain power in the short term through their monopoly of power, but, ultimately, they will be unable to retain the public's support if they fail to provide essential public goods.

Third, states fail when they undertake misguided projects. For example, Stalin's collectivization of farming in the 1930s not only failed to increase agricultural production but led to the destruction of Ukraine's private farms and to widespread famine. Similarly, President Julius Nyerere's compulsory "villagization" in Tanzania was an abysmal failure, leading to much human suffering. Political scientist James Scott has examined the reasons for the failure of these and similar schemes to improve the human condition and concludes, "the progenitors of such plans regarded themselves as far smarter and farseeing than they really were and, at the same time, regarded their subjects as far more stupid and incompetent than they really were."[9]

The rise of destructive ideologies in the twentieth century is responsible for the greatest human suffering in modern times. And of all the misguided ideologies, the most harmful was the rise of totalitarian Communism, which inflicted millions of civilian deaths as a means of political control.[10]

Despite its imperfections and shortcomings, the nation-state remains the foundational political community of global society. Although the structure of the political world could change in the future, the nation-state currently is the chief community for citizens. According to Paul Collier, "nations and their citizens are the essential frame for public policy and will remain so for the foreseeable future."[11]

IS THE NATION-STATE IN TROUBLE?

Although the nation-state continues to be the chief actor in world politics, the modern state is under severe pressures. Several developments have contributed to the loss of faith in the nation-state. To begin with, increased domestic political polarization has undermined the coherence of states. Such polarization has emerged not simply because of deep political conflicts within society but also because of major religious and ethnic conflicts. For example, the deep ongoing political and religious disputes in Libya, Syria, South Sudan, and Yemen explain the continuing political weaknesses of these states.

The state is also being undermined by the rise of individualism and identity politics. Although social media is not responsible for such developments, modern technology has greatly intensified them. The US motto—*e pluribus unum* (from many into one)—is a reminder that what matters is not the celebration of difference but the transformation of diversity into communal solidarity.

Third, the inability to meet the growing demands from citizens has also weakened confidence in the nation-state. Fundamentally, the problem is that the public's political demands exceed the capacity of government to meet them. John Micklethwait and Adrian Wooldridge argue in *The Fourth Revolution* that modern states have tried to do too much. In their view, governments should undertake fewer tasks but excel in those tasks that they undertake.[12] But even making modest reforms can also present major challenges in the face of well-organized political opposition. The difficulty of making a modest change in the French retirement system (raising the retirement age from sixty-two to sixty-four) in the face of major labor opposition, for example, involved several years and significant resolve from the government of President Emmanuel Macron.

Fourth, globalization has also weakened states by undermining state sovereignty. While increased international trade and capital flows have contributed to the prosperity of many countries, globalization has undermined the ability of government to control borders and regulate financial transactions. Additionally, because of increasing mobility of investment capital, governments have less influence over business enterprise. As a result, the urban labor class in developed countries has suffered significant losses, exacerbating domestic economic inequalities.

Fifth, the nation-state is also being undermined by the changing values and beliefs of citizens in postmodern societies. According to Robert Inglehart, modern societies are chiefly concerned with material values, such as improved living conditions. Once a country becomes stable and prosperous, however, people shift their concerns from objective, instrumental values to subjective, postmaterialist values.[13] This shift occurs because people have the resources and leisure to reflect on the meaning of life. As a result, rather than seeking further economic wellbeing, they give priority to subjective, individual concerns. This explains, in part, the growing individualism in modern societies.

Finally, the nation-state is weakened by the postmodern shift in political allegiance from the nation to global society. This development is noticeable among prosperous, well-educated elites, who seek to identify with transnational, global issues rather than with national concerns. David Goodhart has called persons who identify closely with a particular community as "Somewheres," whereas those who identity with transnational concerns as "Anywheres."[14]

The weakness of nation-states is a serious problem because it compromises a state's ability to fulfill its domestic and international responsibilities. Fukuyama notes that "weak governance undermines the principle of sovereignty on which the post-Westphalian order has been built. It does so because the problems that weak states generate for themselves and for others vastly increase the likelihood that someone else in the international system will seek to intervene in their affairs against their wishes to forcibly fix the problem."[15]

The US interventions in failing states in the post–Cold War era illustrate this development. Michael Mandelbaum writes that in seeking to strengthen states, the US government did not simply contain domestic political conflicts but sought to transform societies as well. The effort to build nations and strengthen states, however, failed because such tasks are not easily undertaken by foreign powers, even one that is as powerful as the United States.[16]

IS NATIONALISM IMPORTANT?

Michael Ignatieff defines nationalism as "the belief that the world's people are divided into nations and that each of these nations has the right to self-determination, either as self-governing units within existing nation-states or a nation-state of their own."[17] When I taught international relations, I would define nationalism as the theology of the nation and patriotism as the worship of the nation. The first emphasizes the beliefs, practices, and traditions that are important in building and maintaining a nation; the second emphasizes public affirmation of the nation through service in the armed services, respecting the authority of police, and displaying loyalty through symbolic actions. Such symbolic actions include celebrations on Independence Day, flying the country's flag, singing the national anthem, and reciting the pledge of allegiance.

Despite these simple assertions about nationalism, the concept remains a highly contentious topic. To a significant degree, the disputes over this subject arise from the different ways that the concept is defined. Some scholars view it as the process of national integration that results in a common language, increased social and economic interaction, and a shared culture. Karl Deutsch, for example, claims that nations emerge through a process of social integration. Such integration fosters the development of a people or community that have interlocking habits of communication.[18] Other observers regard nationalism simply as love of a people and its land. Rich Lowry and Ramesh Ponnuru, for example, argue that nationalism "includes loyalty to one's country; a sense of belonging, allegiance, and gratitude to it. And this sense attaches to the country's people and culture, not just to its political institutions and laws."[19] Michael Lind argues that scholars and observers have provided four different ways of defining American nationalism: racial, creedal, multi-ethnonational, and cultural. Each roots American identity in how it views race, creed, ethnicity, and culture. For Lind, the only plausible basis for a widely shared identity is culture.[20]

Still others view nationalism as the result of shared political ideals and values. Yael Tamir, for example, argues that benign nationalism emerges from liberal values, such as the priority of freedom, individual rights, and equality. She claims that "nationalists can appreciate the value of personal autonomy and individual rights and freedoms, as well as sustain a commitment for social justice between and within nations."[21] But democracy and democratic institutions alone will not ensure community. Anatol Lieven argues, correctly I believe, that democracy alone cannot sustain a given state indefinitely if that state is deeply divided internally. He therefore claims that a deeper source of legitimacy is necessary. And for him this source is a common sense of national belonging. He writes: "In the modern world, the greatest and most enduring source of this feeling and this state legitimacy has been nationalism."[22]

Some scholars and political leaders regard nationalism as harmful, viewing it as an ideology of supremacy that involves hatred toward other peoples. Those who view nationalism this way argue that international wars are fueled by toxic nationalisms. Not surprisingly, those who view nationalism this way argue that patriotism is a preferable term to convey loyalty to the nation. Steven Smith, for example, argues that nationalism is competitive and exclusionary and therefore destructive to global order. He observes that although patriotism and nationalism are related, the latter is harmful because it is divisive and contemptuous of others, while the former is "a sentiment of gratitude and appreciation."[23] Paul Miller similarly views nationalism as harmful. In his view, nationalism is a destructive ideology because it is inconsistent with the universalism of liberal democracy. For him, the history of nationalism has been one of "idolatry and oppression."[24]

Andreas Wimmer observes that nationalism has gotten a bad reputation because it can be aggressive and divisive. As a result, some observers seek to replace the concept of nationalism, which is thought to be harmful, with patriotism, which is assumed to be peaceful and desirable. But the efforts to disparage nationalism have not been successful. Indeed, nationalism has contributed to many positive developments, including the nurturing of popular sovereignty, fostering equality among people, and providing the foundation for the modern welfare state. Wimmer writes: "Nationalism is not an irrational sentiment that can be banished from contemporary politics through education; it is one of modern world's foundational principles and is more widely accepted than its critics acknowledge."[25]

One of the dangers of nationalism is that unscrupulous political leaders can manipulate and misuse it. They can do so by using nationalism to foster fear and suspicion of outsiders—such as domestic minorities or foreign migrants. *The Economist*, a weekly magazine, calls such manipulation of national sentiments "paranoid nationalism."[26] A growing number of political leaders, such as Tunisia's Kais Saied, Russia's Vladimir Putin, Hungary's Viktor Orban, and America's Donald Trump, have resorted to stoking fear to consolidate domestic power. Such manipulation not only harms democracy but corrupts institutions. Still, the harm of negative nationalism should not detract from its positive effects when a nation is threatened, as was the case when Russia invaded Ukraine in February 2022. In response to this aggression, the Ukraine people have responded by strengthening their loyalty to the nation and rallying around their government.

To be sure, unconstrained nationalism can foster conflict and division. But most goods, when taken to extremes, are harmful and counterproductive. Individual freedom, for instance, when made an absolute value and taken to an extreme, results in anarchy. Authentic freedom, like nationalism, requires boundaries. The boundaries of nationalism are those of global society, where the national interest must also involve the interests of other nations. A beneficent nationalism is a part of the global common good. It is possible to reconcile the love of country with participation in the international community.

Given the elusive, abstract promises of global governance and the populist demands of autocratic leaders, the political challenge in the present age is how to reconcile the national interests of states with the global welfare of the international community. John Judis observes that political leaders must attempt to reconcile the demands of nations with the needs of global society. This is difficult because nationalism can be misused by leaders. He writes: "nationalist sentiments can be the basis of social generosity or of bigoted exclusion. Nationalism is an essential ingredient of political democracy; but it can also be the basis for fascist and authoritarian regimes. What direction these sentiments take depends very much on the interplay between historical circumstances and the appeals that a country's parties, politicians, and officials make."[27] A responsible nationalism must therefore integrate the needs of both nations and global society.

Since the primary task of a state is to advance the interests and welfare of its citizens, foreign policy is typically defined as the pursuit of a country's national interests while taking into account the interests of other states. The challenge is to advance a country's interests within the context of the international society of states. Former Harvard President Lawrence Summers observes that "the basic responsibility of government is to maximize the welfare of citizens, not to pursue some abstract concept of the global good."[28] While the slogan "America First" is frequently derided by critics of nationalism, it is important to recognize that a government's primary task is to provide security and prosperity to its citizens. This does not mean the state disregards the interests of foreign states, but that citizens have priority over non-citizens.

In sum, nationalism is desirable insofar as it nourishes the rights and duties of members in a particular political community. A feeling of belonging will contribute to loyalty and trust among members and foster reciprocity among them. At the same time, nations have a moral responsibility to care for peoples in foreign societies since they, too, are entitled to dignity and respect.

CHRISTIANITY AND THE NATION-STATE

How should Christians view the nation-state? How should they conceive of the world? Is the nation-state as well as the global society of states consistent with Christian political principles described earlier? Should believers emphasize membership in their nation-states or shift allegiance to the international community?

As noted previously, the basic pillar of the international community is the sovereign state. Scripture does not specify what type of political organization should be normative. But as noted in chapter 2, both Protestants and Catholics have developed theological principles and social norms that can guide reflection on both the state and global society. Protestant principles are especially helpful in considering the legitimacy of the sovereign state, while Catholic principles provide important insights about the importance of transnational relationships.

Scripture teaches that government is a divinely sanctioned institution. Because people matter, and since sin is pervasive, government is instituted by God to punish evil and preserve the good. According to ethicist Nigel Bigger, the Old Testament supports the notion of a "chosen nation" because Israel is the vehicle of God's redemption. In the New Testament, by contrast, religion is no longer confined to the Jewish people but is expanded to all nations. St. Paul declares that "there is neither Jew nor Greek, for you are all one in Christ Jesus." Accordingly, Bigger observes that "a properly Christian view . . . insists that every nation is equally accountable to God for its service of the human good. No nation may pretend to be God's chosen people."[29] Adrian Hastings similarly argues that the Christian faith encourages both national and transnational sensibilities, the first rooted in the Old Testament and the second based on the New.[30]

Some Christians have questioned the division of the world into states and have advocated a borderless world. According to this view, borders impair human community and unnecessarily divide humanity into competing, conflicting societies. Such divisions not only encourage conflict but exacerbate inequalities among people. William Cavanaugh, a professor of religion, declares, "A world without borders is a peaceful world, a world where all may be one."[31] Mark Tooley writes that borders are not ungodly. In his view, the advocates of a borderless world want to overturn the human story and return to Eden. But humanity fell from the Edenic peace and harmony and now awaits redemption. Tooley writes: "Borders, properly understood, are gracious gifts to fallen humanity. Borders can be ugly but they can also be lovely. Fences may imprison or fortify. But they also can be friendly markers over which neighbors converse in between tending their own gardens."[32]

Others have questioned the importance of the nation-state. Cavanaugh argues that the nation-state, while providing desirable social goods and services, is not a vital human community. It cannot ensure the common good. It is, rather, "a large bureaucratic provider of goods and services that never quite provides value for money."[33] He suggests that the state is not unlike a telephone company, which offers important services to customers. Since the nation-state is not the keeper of the common good, Cavanaugh argues that "we need to adjust our expectations accordingly." In his view, this requires that the church must reject its focus on the nation-state. He declares: "The church must break its imagination out of captivity to the nation-state; it must not simply rely on the nation-state to be its social presence."[34]

Gary Chartier, a legal philosopher, similarly calls into question the moral legitimacy of the nation-state from a Christian perspective. He argues that states are both illegitimate and dangerous. They are illegitimate because "they lack consensual foundations," and they are dangerous because "of the power they place in the hands of the venal, the hubristic, and the self-righteous."[35] Chartier argues that, instead of the state, a model community more conducive to human diversity is "radical consociationalism." Such a structure emphasizes a plurality of nonterritorial associations, each with its own rules based on consent. In his view, the consociational approach has the advantage of encouraging human flourishing while moving away from the violence fostered by the state. Chartier, who is opposed to world government, thinks that applying this approach to the international community would help foster the global common good.[36]

In assessing the legitimacy of the state, Christian anthropology is important. The Christian perspective on human nature involves two attributes: the universality and equality of human dignity, and the pervasiveness of human sin. Given the inherent worth of every person, a legitimate sovereign state must ensure the dignity of each member of society. The guarantee of human dignity and equality (human rights), however, is only possible if the ruling authorities have the capability to ensure such rights through legitimate public authority. Since human sin is pervasive, political power can be corrupted and misused, resulting in oppression rather than liberation. As a result, the principle of constrained or limited government is essential.

A constitutional democratic system of government is especially desirable in securing human rights. Democracies—that is, governments based on popular sovereignty, political participation, limited government, and the rule of law—are fragile and prone to cumbersome decision-making. Winston Churchill once noted, "democracy is the worst form of government—except for all other systems that have been tried." Despite the inherent shortcomings of democratic government, ethicist Reinhold Niebuhr makes a compelling case for such a system. In *The Children of Light and the Children of Darkness*, he writes: "Man's capacity for justice makes democracy possible, but man's inclination to injustice makes democracy necessary."[37]

In short, while the contemporary nation-state is not divinely ordained, a constitutional regime is consistent with core social and political principles of Christianity. These norms include the priority of people, the pervasiveness of sin, the call for justice, the need for limited government, and the importance of communal life. At the same time, because all nations are a part of God's creation and because all people bear the image of God, the global society of states is also a priority for Christians. How believers reconcile their responsibilities to their nation and to the international community is a never-ending quest.

THE CHALLENGE OF CHRISTIAN NATIONALISM

When the Puritan settlers came to America in the seventeenth century, they believed that they had a "covenant" responsibility to establish a model settlement—a "city upon a hill." They believed that faith should guide them in building a Christian nation that would serve as an example to the world. Ever since its founding, political leaders have integrated Christian values with the functioning of the state. Christian nationalism (CN) is the byproduct of the fusion of religion and politics, of the sacred and the secular. Whereas the early manifestation of a Christian nation emphasized political and religious ideals, the more recent expressions of CN have been defensive in nature, focusing on the threats posed to America by secularism, materialism, and globalization.

A recent Pew Research Center survey found that 45 percent of respondents believe that the United States should be a "Christian nation." The survey also found that 60 percent of the respondents believe that American Founders "intended the United States to be a Christian nation."[38] But what do people mean when they support the idea of a Christian nation? Does it mean that the laws should be consistent with Scripture or that the institutions should privilege Christianity? Or does it mean that Christian values should inform the decisions and policies of government? Or is the concept simply a way of declaring that most people in American society should be Christians? Since the term is undefined, it is difficult to draw any conclusions about the role of religion in American society.

The uncertainty about how to define a Christian nation affects how to conceive of CN. Andrew Torba and Andrew Isker, both staunch supporters of CN, for example, define the concept as "a spiritual, political, and cultural movement comprised of Christians who are working to build a Christian society grounded in a Biblical worldview."[39] In *The Case for Christian Nationalism*, Stephen Wolf defines CN as "a totality of national action, consisting of civil laws and social customs, conducted by a Christian nation as a Christian nation, in order to procure for itself both earthly and heavenly good in Christ."[40]

While some observers view CN as simply the fusion of religion and politics, critics of the concept tend to view the concept as an ideology. In their book *Taking America Back for God*, the sociologists Andrew Whitehead and Samuel Perry define CN as an ideology "that idealizes and advocates a fusion of American civil life with a particular type of Christian identity and culture."[41] Paul Miller similarly regards CN as an ideology that is rooted in symbols and emotions rather than ideas. In his view, CN views "America as a Christian nation and it wants the government to promote a specific Anglo-Protestant cultural template as the official culture of the country."[42] In his view, CN is inconsistent with democratic values. Nilay Saiya, who is also critical of CN, defines it as "a political ideology and cultural framework advocating for the fusion of a particular form of Christianity with a country's civic life and political institutions and for the privileging of Christianity in the public realm."[43]

The problem with these and similar definitions is that they rely on nebulous conceptions of religion and nationalism. For example, Whitehead and Perry do not tell us what the beliefs and practices are of CN advocates.[44] Miller's analysis similarly suffers from lack of conceptual clarity. In his view, CN is an inclusive movement of three forces: White Evangelicals, the Christian Right, and Trump supporters. Not surprisingly, Miller views the history of nationalism as "overwhelming one of idolatry and oppression."[45] The most significant shortcoming of contemporary CN is that the religion that is integrated with nationalism isn't an authentic faith but a tribal religion. The prevalent integration of nationalist rhetoric and with religious symbols among political conservatives has contributed to a folk religion that is experienced far more viscerally than it is intellectually or theologically. Thomas Kidd, a history professor, agrees, arguing that it is important to distinguish between its theological expression and its emotional variant. Kidd suggests that what is prevalent in the United States is not a rational set of beliefs but rather a visceral stance.[46] This is why columnist David French suggests that, as Americans continue to wrestle with CN, the debate will not focus on the nationalism of ideas, but rather on the nationalism rooted "more in emotion and mysticism than theology."[47]

There can be little doubt that the integration of crude nationalism with simplistic Christian symbols and language has resulted in a phenomenon that is inconsistent not only with the Christian faith but also with civic nationalism. As Daniel Strange observes, CN is "a heretical form of Christianity paired to an idolatrous form of nationalism."[48]

While I am strongly opposed to crude CN, I remain convinced that a legitimate case can be made for the application of faith to national political affairs. An authentic Christian faith, guided by love of God and love of neighbor, will necessarily ensure the priority of the Kingdom of God over temporal political concerns. Although love of nation is legitimate, such support is always conditional to the demands of the Kingdom of God. Accordingly, Christians should not support CN if it inverts or subverts Christian teachings and values. On the other hand, the Christian faith calls on believers to serve the common good by caring for the welfare of others and to advance justice, both domestically and internationally. A nationalism that is inspired and guided by Christian norms can contribute to the common good of both states and global society.

STRENGTHENING NATION-STATES

I have suggested that nation-states suffer from a variety of deficiencies that impair their functioning. Some states have limited integration, while others suffer from insufficient governmental authority. Other states suffer from excessive authoritarian control, thereby impeding individual liberties and human rights. Still other states have capable governmental institutions but because of deep divisions among its citizens, find it difficult to address vital national concerns. Given the variety of problems and limitations facing nation-states, reforms or remedies will necessarily reflect the specific environmental context that each state faces. No common strategy of nation and state building will suffice.

Efforts to strengthen nation-states involve two dimensions. The first seeks to foster increased national solidarity, while the second seeks to strengthen governmental institutions. Because state building is more amenable to external assistance, foreign aid programs have often sought to strengthen governance and governmental institutions. The first task, however, is essentially one that must be undertaken by domestic political initiatives.

State Building

State building involves the strengthening of government institutions, such as courts, legislatures, and state agencies. The capabilities of government are not based solely on power but on legitimacy—that is, the people's willingness to voluntarily accept the authority of government. People pay their taxes not simply because they fear the consequences of unlawful behavior but also, and more importantly, because they accept the legitimacy of the tax and desire to voluntarily contribute to the nation. But if people are to view government as legitimate, people must regard the state institutions as fair, impartial, and trustworthy.

Social scientists agree that nurturing strong institutions is imperative in building and sustaining a strong state. Unlike organizations, institutions are a broader set of rules, norms, and codes of conduct that constrain and prescribe decision-making in public affairs. The rules, whether formal or informal, create incentives that influence human behavior. Since the 1990s, the World Bank has emphasized the importance of building capable, efficient, and accountable institutions as a basis for fostering social and economic development.

Another important requirement in strengthening states is nurturing an honest, accountable, and democratic political culture. Since government is the visible one-ninth of the submerged iceberg, an effective, beneficent state cannot exist apart from a moral political culture. A responsible government cannot be constructed on a society where lying, stealing, and bribes are commonplace. The impact of widespread distrust is evident in many developing nations where metal barriers on windows and high fences are common. By contrast, a Dutch or Danish town is likely to have few territorial barriers and no fences around homes because of high levels of social trust.

Since government rests on the prevalent traditions and cultural values of society, strengthening governmental institutions is possible only when the social and cultural fabric of society is strengthened. Weak states typically suffer from two corrosive cultural problems: corruption and institutionalized political hypocrisy. Corruption is the abuse of public power for private gain. It typically involves dishonest or fraudulent behavior. Political hypocrisy, by contrast, is the widespread acceptance of a gap between law and behavior, theory and practice.

Corruption takes many forms, including bribery, nepotism, extortion, embezzlement, kickbacks, and money laundering. Although corruption is prevalent in the private sector, it can have devastating impact on the state. When citizens lose confidence in governmental institutions because of the misuse of public resources, governmental authority declines. Like a cancer, corruption is difficult to eradicate. The World Bank and other leading intergovernmental organizations have emphasized the need to combat corruption and make financial transactions as transparent as possible. Transparency International, a leading nongovernmental organization committed to reducing corruption, has developed a "Corruption Perception Index," ranking countries on the level of corruption in the public sector. In 2022, the most corrupt countries were Yemen, Libya, North Korea, Haiti, and Burundi; the least corrupt were Denmark, Finland, New Zealand, Norway, and Singapore.[49]

Since corruption is like a disease, confronting it will require time, persistence, and moral courage. Christians can play an important role in this task by demanding accountability and transparency in financial transactions and policy making.

The other major impediment is the prevalence of a gap between the formal/legal institutions of government and the behavior of people. This institutionalization of a gap impedes the effectiveness of the state because people presume that government rules are designed as ideals rather than regulatory norms. In Latin America, this gap, which emerged from the Spanish regulations made for the colonial territories in the New World, is expressed in the phrase "*obedezco pero no cumplo*" (I obey but I do not comply). To be sure, hypocrisy—the failure to live in accord with one's proclaimed beliefs and values—is a problem afflicting all people and societies.[50] But when hypocrisy becomes widespread and institutionalized throughout society, it is corrosive on public life, leading people to assume that political life is not about serving the common good but pursuing one's personal interests.

Sustaining a strong state is essential to the work of government. Without strong institutions, the making and enforcing of laws is impossible. And without a strong, capable government, maintaining social and political order is impossible. As Thomas Hobbes noted long ago in *Leviathan*, political order is a precondition for peace, security, and prosperity. The challenge is how to create and sustain a political order that also ensures liberty and other basic rights. During the heyday of communism in the Soviet Union, there was little crime. While directing an overseas college program in the mid-1980s, I recall running late at night in Leningrad (now Saint Petersburg) with a student. We were in a foreign country and although it was dark, we felt totally safe because of the pervasive and intrusive role of the state. While too much government regulation is a problem, as was the case under Soviet communism, the weakness of the state is also a problem. When the state is unable to protect property and people, as is the case in Haiti and Libya, lawlessness and crime are prevalent. Clearly, the challenge in state building is to foster a strong government that is constrained through the rule of law. While periodic elections are important, maintaining a limited, constitutional state is even more so.

Nation Building

Nation building involves building common bonds that override narrow allegiances. Like the development of shared traditions and cultural values, the building of a national identity is a long-term process that proceeds slowly over time. Unlike state building, nation building is a much more difficult and elusive challenge. Essentially, the strengthening of national solidarity is a process that must be carried out indigenously with limited or no external assistance. The difficulty of foreign powers in fostering national integration was evident in the failed efforts by the United States and Britain to rebuild Iraqi society after the destruction of the Baathist regime headed by Saddam Hussein.

According to Andreas Wimmer, the success of building a nation is dependent on three conditions: a) the development of civil society organizations, b) the rise of a state capable of providing public goods, and c) the emergence of a shared medium of communication.[51] The problem with fragile or failing states is that civil society is weak or nonexistent. This means that nongovernmental institutions must be created and developed to foster shared social concerns. Second, if the state is to contribute to national integration, it must be able to provide essential public goods, like effective law enforcement, clean water, health care, and education. Providing such services is important since people will develop confidence in the state and thereby facilitate communal solidarity. Finally, the development of a common language or other shared means of communication is important since they provide a way by which people can communicate across different parts of society. National solidarity is nurtured by a more integrated communications network.

Fukuyama argues that since the developed nations have greater knowledge of how to strengthen government institutions than to build coherent nations, they should focus on strengthening government institutions. Fukuyama writes, "what is most urgent for the majority of developing countries is to increase the basic strength of their state institutions to supply those core functions that only governments can provide."[52]

In conclusion, strong, beneficent states are essential for providing domestic and global public goods. Human rights can be advanced and protected only if governments have the capacity to make and enforce rules. The task of building and sustaining a strong nation-state will necessitate a shared political identity. Sustaining national solidarity is a difficult, long-term task, especially in fragmented societies where people have deep psychological attachments to their religious, cultural, and ethnic communities. The central government can of course help foster integration by providing security and prosperity. While government can provide essential public services, the task of strengthening communal bonds is a never-ending responsibility among individuals, groups, and communities that will depend on the moral virtues of people. Communal solidarity is possible only when people exhibit compassion, tolerance, patience, and mercy. Finally, nongovernmental organizations and religious actors can also help foster a shared national identity by facilitating cooperation among associations and interest groups and demonstrating a commitment to the common good. Christian citizens have a special responsibility to foster communal solidarity by caring for neighbors and welcoming strangers.

NOTES

1. Paul Collier, *The Future of Capitalism: Facing the New Anxieties* (New York: HarperCollins, 2018), 212–13.
2. The idea of the state as a market is advanced by Philip Bobbitt, *The Shield of Achilles: War, Peace, and the Course of History* (New York: Anchor Books, 2002).
3. Kalevi Holsti, *The State, War, and the State of War* (Cambridge: Cambridge University Press, 1996), 84–90.
4. Francis Fukuyama, *State Building: Governance and World Order in the 21st Century* (Ithaca, NY: Cornell University Press, 2004), 6–14.
5. Collier, *The Future of Capitalism*, 212.
6. John Rawls, *The Law of Peoples* (Cambridge: Harvard University Press, 1999). Although Rawls refers to societies, not nation-states, his analysis is fundamentally about the existing international community of nation-states.
7. Two types of regimes are essential in building a peaceful global society: "liberal peoples"—constitutional, democratic regimes that protect human rights domestically and fulfill international obligations—and "decent hierarchical peoples"—nondemocratic regimes that respect human rights and are nonaggressive toward other states.
8. Fukuyama, *State Building*, 120.
9. James C. Scott, *Seeing Like a State: How Certain Schemes to Improve the Human Condition Have Failed* (New Haven: Yale University Press, 1998), 343.
10. The terror that Communist regimes imposed resulted in an estimated 20 million deaths in the Soviet Union, 65 million deaths in China, 2 million deaths in Cambodia, 2 million deaths in North Korea, and 1.5 million deaths in Afghanistan.
11. Collier, *The Future of Capitalism*, 212.
12. John Micklethwait and Adrian Wooldridge, *The Fourth Revolution: The Global Race to Reinvent the State* (New York: Penguin Press, 2014).
13. Ronald Inglehart, *Modernization and Postmodernization: Cultural, Economic and Political Change in 43 Societies* (Princeton: Princeton University Press, 1997).
14. David Goodhart, *The Road to Somewhere: The Populist Revolt and the Future of Politics* (London: Hurst & Company, 2017).
15. Fukuyama, *State Building*, 96.
16. Michael Mandelbaum, *Mission Failure: America and the World in the Post-Cold War Era* (New York: Oxford University Press, 2017).
17. Michael Ignatieff, *Blood and Belonging: Journeys into the New Nationalism* (New York: Farrar, Straus and Giroux, 1993), 5.
18. Karl W. Deutsch, *Nationalism and Its Alternatives* (New York: Alfred A. Knopf, 1969).
19. Rich Lowry and Ramesh Ponnuru, "For Love of Country," *National Review*, February 6, 2017.
20. Michael Lind, "The Case for Cultural Nationalism," *National Review*, September 11, 2017.
21. Yael Tamir, *Liberal Nationalism* (Princeton: Princeton University Press, 1993), 6.

22. Anatol Lieven, *Climate Change and the Nation State: The Case for Nationalism in a Warming World* (New York: Oxford University Press, 2020), 66.

23. Stephen B. Smith, *Reclaiming Patriotism in an Age of Extremes* (New Haven: Yale University Press, 2022), 9.

24. Paul D. Miller, *The Religion of American Greatness: What's Wrong with Christian Nationalism* (Downers Grove: IVP Academic, 2022), 7.

25. Andreas Wimmer, "Why Nationalism Works: And Why It Isn't Going Away," *Foreign Affairs* (March-April 2019), 28.

26. "How Paranoid Nationalism Corrupts," *The Economist*, September 2, 2023.

27. John B. Judis, *The Nationalist Revival: Trade, Immigration, and the Revolt Against Globalization* (New York: Columbia Global Reports, 2018), 35.

28. Lawrence Summers, "How to Embrace Nationalism Responsibly," *The Washington Post*, July 10, 2016.

29. Nigel Bigger, *Between Kin and Cosmopolis: An Ethic of the Nation* (Eugene, OR: Cascade Books, 2014).

30. Adrian Hastings, *The Construction of Nationhood: Ethnicity, Religion and Nationalism* (Cambridge: Cambridge University Press, 1997), 187–203.

31. William T. Cavanaugh, *Migrations of the Holy: God, State, and the Political Meaning of the Church* (Grand Rapids, MI: Eerdmans, 2011), 70.

32. Mark Tooley, "Are National Borders Ungodly?" *Juicy Ecumenism*, October 23, 1918, https://juicyecumenism.com/2018/10/23/are-national-borders-ungodly/ (August 1, 2024).

33. Cavanaugh, *Migrations of the Holy*, 42.

34. Cavanaugh, *Migrations of the Holy*, 42.

35. Gary Chartier, *Christianity and the Nation-State: A Study in Political Theology* (Cambridge: Cambridge University Press, 2023), 171.

36. Chartier, *Christianity and the Nation-State*, 185–97, 276–77.

37. Reinhold Niebuhr, *The Children of Light and the Children of Darkness: A Vindication of Democracy and a Critique of Its Traditional Defense* (New York: Charles Scribner's Sons, 1964), xiii.

38. Gregory A. Smith, Michael Rotolo, and Patricia Tevington, "45% of Americans Say U.S. Should Be a 'Christian Nation,'" Pew Research Center, October 27, 2022, www.pewresearch.org/religion/2022/10/27/45-of-americans-say-u-s-should-be-a-christian-nation/ (August 1, 2024).

39. Andrew Torba and Andrew Isker, *Christian Nationalism: A Biblical Guide to Taking Dominion and Discipling Nations* (Gab AI Inc: 2022), xxii.

40. Stephen Wolfe, *The Case for Christian Nationalism* (Moscow, ID: Cannon Press, 2022), 9.

41. Andrew L. Whitehead and Samuel L. Perry, *Taking America Back for God: Christian Nationalism in the United States* (New York: Oxford University Press, 2020).

42. Miller, *The Religion of American Greatness*, 59.

43. Nilay Saiya, "Christian Nationalism's Threat to Global Democracy," *The Review of Faith and International Affairs* 22, no. 1 (2024).

44. Whitehead and Perry use survey data to identify people who support (or oppose) CN. Based on their data, they identify four groups: Rejectors, Resistors,

Accommodators, and Ambassadors. The last group are the "evangelists" for CN. Surprisingly, nearly half of all CN advocates are Evangelicals, while 6 percent have no religious affiliation at all.

45. Miller, *The Religion of American Greatness*, 7.

46. Quoted in David French, "One Reason the Trump Fever Won't Break," *The New York Times*, October 1, 2023.

47. French, "One Reason the Trump Fever Won't Break."

48. Daniel Strand, "A Better Christian Nationalism," *Providence* (January 14, 2021), https://providencemag.com/2021/01/better-christian-nationalism/ (August 1, 2024).

49. Transparency International, "Corruption Perception Index," 2022, www.transparency.org/en/cpi/2022/ (August 1, 2024).

50. The United States illustrates national hypocrisy by the gap between its declared ideals of freedom, equality, and the rule of law and the failure to fully fulfill those norms.

51. Andreas Wimmer, "Nation Building: Why Some Countries Come Together While Other Fall Apart," *Survival* 60, no. 4 (2018), 151–64.

52. Fukuyama, *State-Building*, 42.

Chapter 4

Strengthening Global Society

Periodically, political leaders refer to "the international community." What is this community? Does the international community exist? What does it mean to be a global citizen?

Ever since the rise of the sovereign state in the seventeenth century, the world has been governed by competing imperial powers and nation-states. As the number and strength of nation-states increased in the eighteenth and nineteenth centuries, world order was maintained through a balance of power among leading states. At the end of the Napoleonic Wars, major European powers met in the Congress of Vienna and established an informal system (known as the Concert of Europe) that maintained peace through a balance of power. In effect, peace was sustained through diplomatic negotiation among imperial powers. By the beginning of the twentieth century, the alliance system that had provided international order had collapsed, leading to World War I. When the war ended, it included a peace treaty, the Treaty of Versailles, that called for the establishment of an international organization to foster peaceful conflict resolution and war prevention. That organization, the League of Nations, was established in 1920, and contributed to increased global cooperation but proved ineffective in inhibiting war. In 1946, the League was replaced by the United Nations. Although the United Nations was more effective in managing international conflicts than the League, its major contribution has been in fostering multilateral cooperation in social and economic affairs.

In this chapter, I examine the political nature and emergence of global society. I first describe the rise of international organization, which emerged as a means of fostering global order and preventing war. I next explore alternative conceptions of the world. These alternative visions are significant since they influence how leaders view the world and how global problems are assessed.

In the third and fourth sections, I examine the role of the Christian faith and world order and the challenge of pursuing justice in global society. In the final part, I explore how global solidarity might be advanced. Given the structure of the international community, the key to strengthening global society will necessarily depend on whether leading states use their power to advance the world's common good and tend "the commons" of the global village.

THE EMERGENCE OF INTERNATIONAL ORGANIZATION

According to Inis Claude, Jr., the roots of international organization emerged in the nineteenth century from three developments: first, the Concert of Europe, a system of multilateral, high-level conferences among European powers; second, the Hague System, which involved two international peace conferences at The Hague in 1899 and 1907; and third, the rise of public international unions, which provided transnational cooperation in a variety of areas of common interest.

The Concert of Europe, a system of periodic multilateral conferences, was important because it illuminated the problems and challenges of international collaboration through diplomacy. The Hague system was significant because it involved small powers, thus emphasizing the need for universality in promoting shared interests. Although the Hague Conferences did result in treaties designed to regulate war and inhibit human suffering, their principal contribution was the development of international norms and principles governing behavior in wartime. Finally, public international unions, such as the International Telegraphic Union, the International Red Cross, and the Universal Postal Union, contributed to global order by demonstrating the importance of institutions in facilitating transnational cooperation in areas of common concern.[1]

These three multilateral initiatives provided a model for fostering cooperation through diplomacy and illuminated some of the limitations and shortcomings involved in seeking the common good among sovereign states. The promise of international organization is that it can inhibit war and facilitate economic prosperity. States pay the cost of such cooperation by limiting their freedom and independence. Claude writes, "Men and nations want the benefits of international organization, but they also want to retain the privileges of sovereignty, which are inseparable from international disorganization."[2]

As noted earlier, the League of Nations, the first major international organization of the twentieth century, emerged in the aftermath of World War I. Given the enormous destruction of the war, the allied powers sought to establish a global structure that would inhibit war and facilitate interstate conflict resolution. Many of the key principles of the League were set forth by US President Woodrow Wilson, who believed that global order could best be preserved through open diplomatic cooperation among peace-loving states. Major powers, led by the United States and the United Kingdom, were involved in the drafting of the "Covenant," the League's formal charter. The central premise of the new intergovernmental organization was that aggression should be prevented through *collective security*—that is, through collective punishment of an aggressor state by League member-states.

Since the collective security failed to keep the peace in the 1930s, political leaders sought to remedy its weaknesses by establishing a more robust global organization. Thus, following World War II, allied powers created a new organization, the United Nations. The United Nations was structurally similar to the League but instead of relying on voluntary actions of member-states to maintain peace, the new organization assigned responsibility for peacekeeping to the institution's Security Council, comprised of the world's five leading powers. In effect, the UN Charter sought to maintain peace and prevent aggression through the deterrent power of the most powerful nations. But such a system could only work if the five Permanent Members could agree on when aggression occurred and what action was required in response. Despite the improved structure, the United Nations has had limited influence in preventing wars and managing interstate conflicts. Instead, its major achievement has been to offer a forum for addressing common concerns and fostering cooperation on economic, health, environmental, scientific, and related issues.

The United Nations is based on the sovereignty and political independence of states, the formal equality of member-states, the inviolability borders, the prohibition of aggression, and the demand for peaceful conflict resolution. Although the United Nations' preamble emphasizes human dignity, the United Nations is agnostic about human rights. Fundamentally, the organization is a forum designed to foster global order based on the diverse values, cultural traditions, and ethnicities of its members. Although its members must be peace-loving, there is no expectation that regimes must ensure religious freedom, protect human rights, or maintain self-government rooted in consent. The promotion of values such as human liberty, religious freedom, and the rule of law must therefore be advanced by influential democracies, like the United Kingdom, Germany, and the United States. International organization is a means of promoting and sustaining international order, not a means to promote democracy and human rights.

ALTERNATIVE CONCEPTIONS OF GLOBAL SOCIETY

International relations scholars have developed two distinct approaches to global society. These two perspectives are communitarianism and cosmopolitanism, and they represent alternative visions of political community. The first reflects a realistic conception of politics while the second reflects an idealistic perspective. Communitarianism views the world as a society of states and emphasizes the role of the nation-state in securing prosperity and human rights for its people. Cosmopolitanism, by contrast, emphasizes the universality of human dignity be virtue of membership in global society. For the cosmopolitan, global citizenship takes precedence over citizenship in subsidiary political communities. Both perspectives affirm human dignity but do so in different ways: communitarianism by prioritizing rights within a nation, and cosmopolitanism by prioritizing human welfare within a global context.

Communitarianism

The communitarian perspective assumes that people have an inherent right to membership in a nation. Article 15 of the Universal Declaration of Human Rights expresses this basic truth by declaring that "everyone has the right to a nationality." A fundamental assumption of this perspective is that persons are social beings who want to belong to a community—family, neighborhood, church, city, country. Personal identity is viewed as inextricably tied to communal membership. The communitarian believes that sovereign nation-states provide a means of nurturing communal trust, fostering social and political order, and protecting human rights.

The communitarian perspective assumes that people flourish best within the proximate communities in which they live, work, and serve, such as families, churches, neighborhoods, civic associations, cities, and nations. Social bonds are not created and sustained with abstract principles but through tangible behaviors that nurture trust and social solidarity. While it is important to recognize the inherent dignity of all people, solidarity is best nurtured within the communities where people live and work. We can hope for a more just global order, but given human nature and political realities, sovereign governments provide the most effective institutions for securing order and proximate justice within nations.

While membership entails living in a particular community, membership involves more than mere residence. Instead, robust communal membership, formally defined as citizenship, involves rights and responsibilities within a nation. This explains why regulating membership and controlling borders is important. According to this conception, a sovereign political community can be sustained only if the government regulates entry. Political theorist Michael Walzer illustrates the importance of membership by comparing a political community with neighborhoods, clubs, and families. States are like neighborhoods, he argues, in that cohesion is based partly on shared cultural norms and are similar to clubs in that membership is a decision taken by the members. States also are like families in that they often extend refuge to persons in need.[3]

In *The Law of Peoples*, political theorist John Rawls argues that international peace and justice and human welfare can be advanced only through stable, humane political communities. Indeed, the foundation for a just global order is the stability provided by nations in caring for their own people and respecting the sovereignty of other nations.[4] Similarly, political ethicist Michael Ignatieff argues that the sovereign state is essential in securing and protecting human rights. He writes, "If we want human rights to be anchored in the world, we cannot want their enforcement to depend on international institutions and NGOs. We want them anchored in the actual practice of sovereign states."[5]

Cosmopolitanism

The cosmopolitan perspective views the world as a coherent global society where the transnational bonds of persons take precedence over nation-states. The cosmopolitan perspective was first expressed by Cynics in the fourth century BCE when they coined the term "cosmopolitan," meaning "citizen of the world." Stoics subsequently emphasized human equality by virtue of the universality of human reason. Because people matter and because people are equal, the wellbeing of the world's people is paramount. In such a world, the most important community is the society of humanity, where all persons are citizens of the world. According to the cosmopolitan worldview, states play an insignificant role in people's affairs. Indeed, the division of the world into nation-states is contrary to global welfare. Territorial borders are not only an impediment to human wellbeing but are also inconsistent with a just world.

For the cosmopolitan, the problems of hunger, war, inequality, and refugees are a direct byproduct of the decentralized system of nation-states. Although cosmopolitan scholars differ on what institutions are necessary to foster peace and justice in the world, there is significant consensus that international institutions must play an increasingly important role. If that is to be the case, then state sovereignty must necessarily decline. Some cosmopolitan thinkers call for stronger international organizations and the reduction or elimination of state sovereignty. In effect, they would like the United Nations, or some similar global organization, to assume a much more powerful role in regulating international relations and resolving interstate disputes.

Because of its idealistic nature, the cosmopolitan worldview is defended and promoted primarily by political theorists, moral utopians, and religious leaders. Political theorist Martha Nussbaum celebrates the cosmopolitan ethic because it focuses directly on the welfare and dignity of persons. She argues that we should shift our allegiance from the nation to global society, thereby nurturing a global society of all human beings.[6] Ethicist Peter Singer similarly argues for a shift toward cosmopolitanism. In *One World*, he writes that the rise of the "global village" demands a new ethic that can serve the interests all persons regardless of where they live. Using a utilitarian morality that seeks to advance "the greatest good for the greatest number," he writes that the "global village" requires that global responsibilities take precedence over the specific duties of fellow citizens. Whereas Rawls pursues justice through states, Singer argues for a world where sovereignty is no longer decisive. "A global ethic should not stop at, or give great significant to, national boundaries. National sovereignty has no intrinsic moral weight."[7]

While some cosmopolitans may long for world government, most cosmopolitans seem satisfied to define the international community as an ideal moral community. For example, Nussbaum argues that cosmopolitanism does not call for giving up memberships and associations in existing human communities. While claiming that people can continue to maintain their loyalty and affection to ethnic, religious, and other groups, cosmopolitanism, she declares, demands that "we should give our first allegiance to no mere form of government, no temporal power, but to the moral community made up by the humanity of all human beings."[8]

What are the implications for these two competing theories? For the communitarian, the challenge involves advancing international peace and prosperity through nation-states. This is best achieved by addressing shared concerns and resolving conflicts through negotiation and multilateral cooperation. For the cosmopolitan, a better world can be advanced by strengthening international organizations and expanding the role of global NGOs. However, since the root cause of many of the world's problems remains state sovereignty, a more peaceful, prosperous world can be realized only if state sovereignty gives way to global institutions.

JUSTICE AND THE INTERNATIONAL COMMUNITY

In order to assess the structures, policies, and informal political patterns of the international community, it is necessary to have a normative standard by which to judge institutions and policies. Political theorists and ethicists call this norm justice. While there is no widely accepted definition of justice, scholars have historically associated the norm with rendering what is due. It is also frequently associated with doing what is right and treating others with fairness. Fundamentally, justice is a relational concept that applies to persons as well as collectives. The biblical ideal of shalom and the ethic of love provide an ideal standard for individuals and political communities.

Although justice is a common topic in Western political philosophy, political thinkers have approached the concept from different perspectives. Two influential approaches view justice in either procedural or substantive terms. *Procedural justice* entails the rightness and fairness of rules and procedures and their consistent and impartial application. This type of justice is illustrated in the American judicial system, which seeks to resolve disputes based on "the rule of law"—that is, through the impartial application of laws. This type of justice is also expressed in international law, which specifies the rights and duties of states. A more specific example of procedural justice in the international community is the just war tradition. Just war theory sets forth procedures that can inhibit war and minimize human suffering in the event of war.

Substantive or distributive justice (frequently termed social justice in domestic affairs) concerns the rightness and equity of outcomes. The concern with international inequalities is an expression of this perspective. Similarly, the concern with equitable participation in greenhouse gas reductions is also the result of such a perspective.

Ideally, the two justice perspectives should reinforce each other. Regrettably, however, the two visions are frequently in conflict, yielding different results. For example, this occurs domestically when the results of criminal justice follow established procedures but yield results that appear unfair. But it also happens in international affairs among states and people when the pursuit of justice may be procedurally fair but leads to outcomes that are considered unjust. On the other hand, the quest for substantive justice may compromise procedural justice norms. This is illustrated by the arbitrary way wars settle territorial boundaries and disregard the legitimate claims of people who have lived for centuries in a particular place. After Germany was defeated in World War II, for example, the Germans who had lived in the Sudentenland of Czechoslovakia were forced to leave their communities and move to Germany. Similarly, after the state of Israel was established in 1948, some seven hundred thousand Palestinians were forced from their homes to make way for the new state.

In view of the inherent tension between these two perspectives, a Christian approach to the global community should seek, to the extent possible, to integrate elements of each of these traditions. Such an approach would seek to ensure fairness in how justice is advanced but also in the outcomes of such a process.

CHRISTIANITY AND THE INTERNATIONAL COMMUNITY

How should Christians regard the international community of some two hundred nation-states? As with the nation-state, there is no Christian conception of global society. But given Christian principles of human dignity, the universality of God's love, the common good, and transnational solidarity, a morally legitimate global order should seek to enhance human dignity by providing social order and individual liberty. A centralized world system has the advantage of maintaining order, but the disadvantage of limited liberty. By contrast, the existing system of nation-states has the advantage of empowering decentralized authority consistent with subsidiarity, but the disadvantage of facilitating conflict among states. Although Scripture does not provide guidance on which conception is preferable, the decentralized nation-state system provides a structure that allows human rights, prosperity, and justice to be advanced through the wise and cooperative action of member-states. To be sure, the existing international community has many limitations, but given realistic alternatives, it offers a means of fulfilling legitimate moral ends of political and social life.

Although Christians believe that "In Christ, there is neither Jew nor Greek," the belief in the universality of the Kingdom of Christ has not resulted in agreement about how to view the temporal world. For example, Catholics have been more supportive of an international community than Protestants. Historically, the Roman Catholic Church held a universalist conception of the world. When sovereign states emerged in the seventeenth century, the Vatican strongly condemned this development. Protestants, by contrast, contributed to the rise of sovereignty and supported the development of sovereign states. They did so not simply because the Treaty of Westphalia ended the bitter religious disputes among Christians, but also because the decentralized global order had inherent religious, political, and social advantages over an imperial order. These advantages included increased religious tolerance, separation of church and state, political self-determination, and popular sovereignty. In time, as the number and power of nation-states increased, the Catholic Church was reconciled to the notion of sovereignty. By the late nineteenth century, the Catholic Church had not only accepted the reality of state sovereignty, but also the importance of individual rights and democratic governance.

By the late twentieth century, there was widespread acceptance among Christian political thinkers that the global society of states was morally legitimate. Despite theological differences between Protestant and Catholic theologians, there was general agreement that the global society of states is consistent with core Christian principles, including human dignity, the need for justice, subsidiarity, and communal solidarity. At the same time, however, religious leaders, especially those with progressive dispositions, continued to emphasize global responsibilities over those toward nationals. For example, this globalist disposition was expressed in a May 2018 declaration titled "Reclaiming Jesus," authored by a group of Mainline Protestant leaders.

Ostensibly written to counter the toxic nationalism of the Trump presidency, the statement declares, "Our churches and our nations are part of an international community whose interests always surpass national boundaries. The most well-known verse in the New Testament starts with 'For God so loved the world' (John 3:16). We, in turn, should love and serve the world and all of its inhabitants, rather than seek first narrow, nationalistic prerogatives." Additionally, the declaration states, since Jesus calls on believers to go into all nations to make disciples (Matthew 28:18), "we reject 'America First' as a theological heresy for followers of Christ."[9]

The global international order that was established at the end of World War II involved the creation of political and economic institutions by Western democracies, led by the United States and the United Kingdom. This global order is regarded as "liberal" because it is based on principles of liberal political economy developed in England in the late eighteenth and early nineteenth centuries. Politically, the liberal order sought to support the creation of democratic governments and to nurture individual freedom. Economically, the order sought to foster economic growth through free enterprise and international trade. Despite challenges to its values from Communist states, the liberal order was responsible for a dramatic rise in the number of democratic governments and an unprecedented expansion of wealth in the second half of the twentieth century. Indeed, human welfare improved significantly throughout the world, resulting in increased longevity, a decline in infant mortality, and a rise in per capita income. The emergence of globalization in the 1980s was a direct byproduct of the institutionalization of a liberal economic system.

The editors of *Providence*—an online periodical that seeks to analyze global issues from a Christian perspective—have suggested that the work of maintaining a humane global order can be regarded as a contemporary version of the "creation mandate" to cultivate the Garden of Eden (Genesis 2:15). "Cultivating the garden of world order," they write, "means tending to the tasks that uphold public safety, execute justice, and promote human flourishing."[10]

As noted earlier, ethicists and political theorists have espoused alternative conceptions of global order. One school relies chiefly on moral ideals; the other relies on a realistic perspective of political life. According to ethicist Reinhold Niebuhr, the idealistic perspective of world community is propounded by "the children of light"—individuals who believe that moral ideals can inevitably "bring warring vitalities under their dominion." The alternative perspective—advanced by "the children of darkness"—assumes that the advance of order and justice in the world requires power. For Niebuhr, both perspectives are necessary in creating a humane world order because both moral ideals and power are essential in such an enterprise. Niebuhr writes that "the first task of a community is to subdue chaos and create order; but the second task is equally important and must be implicated in the first. That task is to prevent the power, by which initial unity is achieved, from becoming tyrannical."[11]

Elsewhere I have argued that a Christian approach to international affairs should be rooted in both the universal ambitions of cosmopolitanism and the concern for solidarity expressed in communitarianism.[12] In my view, focusing solely on the legitimacy and wellbeing of citizens in nation-states is not consistent with the global aspirations found in the universalism of the Kingdom of God. On the other hand, giving precedence to the global claims of the international community is unlikely to secure order and advance proximate justice in nation-states. Thus, the realities of power politics need to be integrated with universal moral ideals. How the idealistic and realistic perspectives are integrated will vary in time and place as Christians address the concrete challenges of transnational concerns.

In view of this, I believe that Christians should accept, provisionally, the existing international political system but continue to work for a more effective and just world order. In pursuing a more stable and just world, Christians should be guided by the need for peace and global solidarity while also accepting the need for limited government, accountability, and subsidiarity. Ideals will inspire the former, but existing political realities will demand realistic action. In short, if Christians are to contribute to peace and justice, their strategy should be influenced by both moral ideals and practical political realities.

CHRISTIANS AND GLOBAL PROBLEMS

Christians have a unique opportunity to share God's love through charitable assistance. Historically, Christian charities have played an important role in meeting human needs. The Catholic Church has built thousands of hospitals and clinics worldwide to provide medical care and established an even larger number of schools and universities to foster literacy and provide basic and advanced learning. Protestant organizations have similarly played a critical role in providing health care and education, especially in developing nations. For example, World Vision, the largest Christian charity in the world, works individually and collaboratively in mobilizing resources to address short-term disaster relief. Samaritan's Purse similarly uses its ties to Evangelical churches to mobilize humanitarian resources to address human suffering.

One advantage of private charities is that they can respond more quickly and more appropriately because they have fewer constraints governing their operations. Additionally, since churches and religious charities maintain close ties with local institutions, such networks facilitate distribution of resources through their offices, clinics, or warehouses. Christian charities like World Vision and Samaritan's Purse have been especially effective in distributing humanitarian relief because of their strong community relationships. Their effectiveness, however, lies not simply in the efficiency with which they can distribute resources but also in the reliable, trustworthy networks that they utilize. Because corruption is widespread in many poor, developing nations, the effectiveness of Christian charities will depend on the institutional capacity to distribute goods and services without graft. Whereas irregular and illegal societal norms in developing nations often constrain effective humanitarian aid, Christian churches can help nurture alternative behavioral patterns based on honesty, trust, and promise keeping.

While governmental aid provided the bulk of humanitarian assistance following Haiti's 2010 earthquake, Christian charities played a pivotal role in responding to the crisis. For example, Samaritan's Purse provided the following assistance to Haiti in the first three months following its 2010 earthquake: fourteen shiploads of emergency supplies, nine thousand tons of food, housing for 10,400 families, removal of ten thousand dump truck loads of rubble, and medical assistance to treat injuries and to contain the cholera epidemic. Samaritan's Purse then maintained its presence in Haiti through longstanding projects, in part, to be ready for future needs like those that arose during the devastating 2021 earthquake.[13]

Individual churches also play an important role either through their own humanitarian initiatives or by collaborating with established religious charities. Saddleback Church, a megachurch in Lake Forest, California, and Willow Creek Church, a megachurch in Barrington, Illinois, have similarly maintained relief programs to address not only short-term needs but also longer-term development. In the aftermath of Rwanda's 1994 genocide, Saddleback Church sought to assist Rwandan people in overcoming the wounds from the atrocities. It did so through an innovative program (called PEACE)[14] that resulted in some two thousand church members traveling to Rwanda to assist churches in strengthening education, health, and medical care. It is estimated that some three thousand Rwandan parishes were trained in "church health."

Besides contributing to the spiritual life of people, Christian churches also nurture values and dispositions that foster healthier, more peaceful human relationships. To be sure, religious faith is not automatically transferred into human dispositions and behaviors. But moral development is possible, and Christian institutions can play an important role in teaching and nurturing moral values and behaviors that are conducive to stronger interpersonal relationships and communal bonds. The importance of trust and promise keeping have been central to the success of national development. The significance of moral development is illustrated in the work of Opportunity International, an Evangelical relief organization that has pioneered in making small loans to women. Its financial services have been highly effective because they are closely associated with local churches, which nurture values of truth, fidelity, and promise keeping as an expression of authentic faith. As a result, the repayment of loans is above 95 percent. In effect, Christian borrowers turn out to be faithful customers, thereby facilitating future loans for others.

STRENGTHENING GLOBAL INTERDEPENDENCE

Given the existing problems arising from the decentralized international order, how can global society be strengthened? What initiatives might be undertaken to foster increased global integration? More specifically, what institutional reforms might be undertaken to strengthen international solidarity and thereby foster increased cooperation in protecting human rights and preventing interstate conflict?

Obstacles to Solidarity

There are several major impediments to global solidarity. In the contemporary world, major obstacles to international harmony and unity include the pursuit of national interests at the expense of global interests, the rising political conflict between democracy and autocracy, increased suffering and instability from failing states, the threat of extremist political violence, the harmful impact of social media, and the growing influence of individualism. While some of these impediments can be overcome through changes in the balance of power among leading states, others are less amenable to reform since they reflect patterns and traditions within the countries themselves.

The first obstacle—pursuing national interests in disregard for the general welfare of global society—can be addressed only when leaders seek to balance their national interests with the pursuit of the global common good. To overcome the limitations of national self-interest, leaders must make the quest for the global common good a priority. So long as states face a tension between immediate national interests and long-term global interests, states will be tempted to pursue their short-term interests in disregard of the interests of other states. This does not mean, however, that the common good cannot be pursued. Rather, if the global interests are to be advanced, an enlightened diplomacy must seek to reconcile the demands of national and global welfare.

The second impediment is the conflict between Western liberal democracies and authoritarian regimes. This dispute between liberalism and illiberalism, like the Cold War contest between totalitarian communism and democratic capitalism, is rooted in different conceptions of the role of the state and of the nature of global order. According to Robert Kagan, an international relations scholar, "the global competition between democratic and autocratic governments will become the dominant feature of the twenty-first-century world."[15] To a significant degree, the emergence of this conflict has resulted from the increased political influence of autocratic regimes, especially China and Russia, and the declining appeal of democratic values and institutions. The simplicity of authoritarian decision-making has offered an appealing alternative to the cumbersome process of democratic decision-making. A 2019 survey of thirty-four countries found that only 44 percent of the people were satisfied with how democracy was working in their countries; 52 percent were dissatisfied.[16] So long as leaders of major powers continue to be guided by alternative values and ideals, this dispute will likely persist.

A third obstacle to global integration is the instability resulting from weak and failing states. Failing states are a problem because they provide a haven for criminal gangs and terrorist groups. Foreign states can of course prevent a failed state's harmful effects from spreading, but the creation of a stable and prosperous nation-state is essentially a long-term, indigenous process. The recent efforts of foreign military intervention to prevent atrocities (e.g., Libya) or to help stabilize domestic political divisions (e.g., Bosnia-Herzegovina, Somalia, and Iraq), demonstrate the limited impact of such initiatives. As noted earlier, the task of nation building is essentially a domestic political task. Renewing and restoring a capable central government can only succeed through the establishment of effective and accountable institutions. This is a task that requires much time and moral leadership.

The fourth impediment—the rise of extremist armed groups—can be contained in the short term through military power, as was demonstrated with the allied defeat of the Islamic State of Iraq and Syria in 2019. But so long as authoritarian states continue to support radical groups, such as Hezbollah and the Houthi, the threat of terrorist groups will persist. The 9/11 Al-Qaeda attack on the World Trade Center and the 2023 attack by Hamas fighters on Israeli settlements demonstrate the danger posed by extremist nonstate actors on global order.

Fifth, the rise of social media poses another threat to global society. Although modern communications technology can facilitate communication, it can also foster fragmentation. Whether social media contributes to individualism and group fragmentation or to communal solidarity will depend on the prevalent cultural traditions of society and the way that such technology is utilized. For example, since the culture of the United States is far more individualistic than that of European countries, surveys indicate that social media is viewed more negatively in the United States than in Europe.[17]

Finally, increased individualism threatens social solidarity—at the local, national, and global levels. Although societies vary in their levels of communal solidarity, modernity has increased freedom and individualism worldwide. To a significant degree, the rise of individualism is a byproduct of the increasing standard of living in countries, but especially in the Western economies where most basic needs of people are satisfied. As sociologist Ronald Inglehart has shown, as countries achieve higher levels of development, people's values and orientations shift from material interests to more subjective, individualistic concerns.[18]

Strengthening Integration

Given these obstacles to global solidarity, how can global society be strengthened? To advance global harmony, numerous strategies are available. Six of these are a) strengthening international governmental organizations, b) strengthening international NGOs, c) empowering local grassroots organizations and national NGOs, d) increasing transnational integration through functional networks and transnational advocacy networks, e) strengthening social and political morality, and f) strengthening religious universalism.

As noted earlier, intergovernmental organizations have played an important role in facilitating multilateral cooperation. Despite its shortcomings, the United Nations continues to be an important forum for international dialog and cooperation. More specialized intergovernmental organizations like the World Health Organization, the North Atlantic Treaty Organization, and the Organization of American States contribute significantly to global order and prosperity through their more specialized and limited membership. Since the United Nations was established nearly seventy-five years ago, some scholars have called for modifications in the organization's structure. Observers note that the world is more diverse and multilateral than it was in 1945 and have called for increasing the size of the UN Security Council by adding influential countries like Germany, Japan, and Brazil. But this is unlikely to occur given the veto threat of existing permanent members, whose power would be diminished with the addition of additional members. Other more feasible reforms would entail making the UN bureaucracy more effective and efficient through improved management.

A second way to strengthen global society is to increase the number and influence of international NGOs—especially those involved in providing services to people. While advocacy NGOs can influence governmental action, direct-service NGOs can foster transnational solidarity as people and organizations from different nations collaborate on common causes. Direct-service NGOs can play a vital role in advancing many of the Sustainable Development Goals established by the United Nations in 2015. The advantage of local, small-scale initiatives over those of international organizations is that they nurture a strong bond between donors and recipients, between an organization and the people being served.

A third strategy involves strengthening national NGOs and local grassroots organizations. Although international NGOs are important, their work presupposes strong organizations at the local and national levels. The efficacy of NGOs is rooted in the voluntarism that is best nurtured and organized at the community level. Thus, as people become more involved in common health, social, and economic concerns, the shared concerns can be expanded from a city to a country to the world.

Fourth, global integration can be advanced through functional and advocacy networks. Rather that viewing the world as a chessboard of nation-states, this approach views the international community as a system of networks created in response to both transnational needs as well as global problems and threats. Given the desirability of international cooperation on issues such as information flows, health care, and scientific inquiry, people can develop even more effective and efficient functional networks. Such collaborative networks can address problems such as the regulation of cyberspace, money laundering, protection of water, and human trafficking. According to Anne-Marie Slaughter, global needs and problems arise because people are "too connected" internationally. Slaughter argues that in addressing global concerns, traditional interstate collaboration needs to continue, but must be supplemented by functional networks that are flexible and open.[19] Margaret Keck and Kathryn Sikkink similarly show the importance of advocacy networks in strengthening shared interests and in fostering transnational political action.[20]

Fifth, global society can be strengthened by a renewed commitment to nurturing social and political morality. Although the specific manifestations of such morality will vary among cultures, there is widespread agreement that an ethic of caring and generosity is essential to a thriving, productive community. Thus, if global solidarity is important, people must demonstrate that this ethic applies not only to family and neighbors but to all human beings, including those in foreign lands.

In *The Ordinary Virtues*, Michel Ignatieff examines whether globalization is fostering moral agreement among people. He does so by investigating the personal, social, and political ethics of various societies. He found that people's morality was best expressed in their everyday behaviors as they confronted poverty, unemployment, disease, and similar challenges. Ignatieff found that while abstract human rights rhetoric did not guide people's specific actions, such rhetoric contributed indirectly to global solidarity by providing a foundation for people's moral actions. He calls these moral behaviors "ordinary virtues," and they include trust, tolerance, forgiveness, reconciliation, and resilience. Whereas scholars have thought that globalization would strengthen international political morality based on abstract principles such as freedom, rule of law, and consent, Ignatieff argues that the "moral globalization" taking place is rooted in the acceptance of diverse values and behaviors based on the acknowledgment of human equality. Ignatieff writes: "The most striking feature of the ordinary virtue perspective is how rarely any of our participants evoked universal principles of any kind . . . and how frequently they reasoned in terms of the local, the contingent, the here and now, what they owed those near to them and what they owed themselves."[21] "What human beings share, everywhere," he continues, "is not a language of the good or a global ethic, but instead a common desire, in their own vernacular, for moral order, for a framework of expectations that allow them to think of their life, no matter how brutal or difficult, as meaningful."[22] If we accept Ignatieff's conclusion that people are likely to be influenced more through particular local initiatives than through programs of moral universalism, it is then vital that individuals cultivate morality in their neighborhoods and local associations. Strengthening the ethics of local communities provides a basis for a more harmonious nation and global society.

In *Thick and Thin*, Michael Walzer distinguishes between the political morality of nations and the political morality of the international community.[23] The first, he argues, is a "thick" morality characterized by specific, concrete norms, such as distributive justice, rule of law, and freedom of assembly. The second, the "thin" morality of global society, is diffuse, general, and theoretical, and characterized by such norms as truth-telling, promise keeping, and human equality. Both the "thick" and "thin" moralities are important. Indeed, since the "thick" morality fosters and sustains communal solidarity, the strengthening of global society will necessarily involve transnational moral values that emerge from the values and behaviors within local communities and nation-states.

Finally, religious values can contribute to global solidarity. This is especially the case for Christianity, which emphasizes the dignity and equality of persons and the need for compassion and forgiveness. The widespread support for Christian values, however, has not resulted in a call for a coherent, unitary global order. Rather, despite the shared belief in human equality, the Christian faith is expressed in different theologies and behavioral applications. Moreover, while different religions will necessarily compete for adherents, the fundamental norms of religions tend to share a basic moral vocabulary that emphasizes human dignity, caring for people in need, compassion toward the vulnerable, forgiveness, and interpersonal reconciliation. According to Ignatieff, "religious languages of human universality in general are the oldest, and they may prove to be the most enduring vernacular in which human beings recognize their common identity."[24]

THE PROBLEM OF WORLD ORDER

Having sketched initiatives for fostering global integration, will such actions advance global order? Does the strengthening of global solidarity contribute to global peace? While solidarity is essential in sustaining communal bonds, it does not guarantee peace. Global order can only be assured through legitimate power. The international community may be highly interdependent, but without strong governance, backed by power, competition and conflict will imperil peace, and disorder will persist. To paraphrase Robert Kagan, a liberal rules–based international system, like the one created after World War II, is like a garden that requires continual tending.[25] If leading democratic states are unable or unwilling to care for the fragile liberal order, the jungle of disorder will return. Gardening is essential in fostering and sustaining global order.

Journalist Bret Stephens argues that the liberal rules–based order (based on democracy, markets, and peace) that was established after World War II was successful because the United States served as the global policeman. It was American power—which he terms *Pax Americana*—that helped establish and enforce the rules and practices that maintained international stability.[26] Fareed Zakaria observes that the rules-based global political and economic order that the United States established was historically unprecedented in that it sought not simply to advance its national interests but also those of other nations. Whereas imperial powers in the past had used their power to increase their own national influence and wealth, the liberal international order that the United States helped to create in the late 1940s was undertaken in the belief that it would advance national and global interests. Zakaria writes: "The world order it proposed, created, and underwrote was good for the United States but also good for the rest of the world. It sought to help other nations rise to greater wealth, confidence, and dignity. That remains the United States' greatest strength."[27]

Kagan notes that "world order is one of those things that people don't think about until it is gone."[28] He suggests that global order is an ongoing responsibility for leading states. This is especially the case for the fragile international liberal order that was established in the late 1940s. Since such an order is based on democracy, free trade, and pacific settlement of disputes, the system has survived and prospered only because the United States, the world's leading economic and military power, has helped to sustain it.

Foreign policy scholar Walter Russell Mead observes that "states are imploding and the rule of law is disappearing across large parts of the world." As a result, world disorder is spreading rapidly. He writes, "Threatened by powerful and relentless adversaries from without, undermined by political decadence and institutional decay from within, the rules-based international order has not been this imperiled since the 1930s."[29] If Mead's assessment is valid, then the task of strengthening global order is a vital task. While strengthening global integration is necessary, it is unlikely to succeed without major impetus from powerful states. Accordingly, major democratic states must use their wealth and power to protect the values and institutions of the liberal international system. Given the significant improvements in human rights and economic prosperity that have been made possible by that liberal order, it would be tragic if leading democratic states allowed systemic disorder to return.

In conclusion, the decentralized international system has many limitations. The most serious shortcoming is the lack of harmony and unity arising from the competing and conflicting interests of member-states. Since many issues and concerns are of a transnational character, addressing problems requires cooperation. To facilitate such collaboration, states have created multinational organizations and specialized agencies. In addition, concerned citizens have established NGOs to address common transnational problems. Since it is unlikely that the structure of global society will be reformed soon, global solidarity can be strengthened in the meantime through increased functional cooperation. The global common good can be advanced through networks that address transnational needs and problems. Sovereignty will continue to divide states, but this does not mean that pursuing shared interests is not feasible. The challenge in advancing the global common good is to nurture collaboration in the face of continuing competition among states.

NOTES

1. Inis L. Claude, Jr., *Swords into Plowshares: The Problems and Progress of International Organization*, fourth edition (New York: Random House, 1971), 21–39.

2. Claude, *Swords into Plowshares*, 39.

3. Michael Walzer, *Spheres of Justice: A Defense of Pluralism and Equality* (New York: Basic Books, 1983), 35–42.

4. John Rawls, *The Law of Peoples* (Cambridge: Harvard University Press, 1999).

5. Michael Ignatieff, "The Return of Sovereignty," *The New Republic*, February 16, 2012, 28.

6. Martha C. Nussbaum, "Patriotism and Cosmopolitanism," in *For Love of Country: Debating the Limits of Patriotism*, edited by Joshua Cohen (Boston: Beacon, 1996), 7.

7. Peter Singer, *One World: The Ethics of Globalization*, second edition (New Haven: Yale University Press, 2002), 12.

8. Martha C. Nussbaum, "Patriotism and Cosmopolitanism," 7.

9. "Reclaiming Jesus: A Confession of Faith in a Time of Crisis," www.barmer34.de/files/Barmer_Erklaerung/Downloaddateien/Reclaiming_Jesus.pdf (August 1, 2024).

10. The Editors, "A Christian Declaration of American Foreign Policy," *Providence*, September 21, 2016, https://providencemag.com/2016/09/christian-declaration-american-foreign-policy/ (August 1, 2024).

11. Reinhold Niebuhr, *The Children of Light and the Children of Darkness: A Vindication of Democracy and a Critique of Its Traditional Defense* (New York: Charles Scribner's Sons, 1944), 178.

12. Mark R. Amstutz, "Two Theories of Immigration," *First Things* (December 2015), 37–42.

13. The outbreak of the cholera epidemic affected 7 percent of Haiti's population and led to the death of more than eighty-three hundred people in the immediate aftermath of the earthquake.

14. The PEACE program has these elements: *p*lant churches, *e*quip servant leaders, *a*ssist the poor, *c*are for the sick, and *e*ducate the next generation.

15. Robert Kagan, *The Return of History and the End of Dreams* (New York: Alfred A. Knopf, 2008), 72.

16. Pew Research Center, "How People Around the World See Democracy in 8 Charts," February 20, 1920, www.pewresearch.org/short-reads/2020/02/27/how-people-around-the-world-see-democracy-in-8-charts/ (August 1, 2024).

17. Pew Research Center, "Views of Social Media and Its Impact on Society," December 6, 2022, www.pewresearch.org/global/2022/12/06/views-of-social-media-and-its-impacts-on-society-in-advanced-economies-2022/ (August 1, 2024).

18. Ronald Inglehart, *Modernization and Postmodernization: Cultural, Economic and Political Change in 43 Societies* (Princeton: Princeton University Press, 1997).

19. Anne-Marie Slaughter, "How to Succeed in the Networked World: A Grand Strategy for the Digital Age," *Foreign Affairs* (November/December 2016).

20. Margaret E. Keck and Kathryn Sikkink, *Activists Beyond Borders: Advocacy Networks in International Politics* (Ithaca: Cornell University Press, 1998).

21. Michael Ignatieff, *The Ordinary Virtues: Moral Order in a Divided World* (Cambridge: Harvard University Press, 2019), 208.

22. Ignatieff, *The Ordinary Virtues*, 202.

23. Michael Walzer, *Thick and Thin: Moral Argument at Home and Abroad* (Notre Dame, IN: University of Notre Dame Press, 2019).

24. Ignatieff, *The Ordinary Virtues*, 19–20.

25. Robert Kagan, *The Jungle Grows Back* (New York: Alfred A. Knopf, 2018), 24

26. Bret Stephens, *America in Retreat: The New Isolationism and the Coming Global Disorder* (New York: Sentinel, 2014).

27. Fareed Zakaria, "The Self-Doubting Superpower," *Foreign Affairs* (January/February 2024), 53.

28. Kagan, *The Jungle Grows Back*, 24.

29. Walter Russell Mead, "World Disorder Is Spreading Fast," *The Wall Street Journal*, September 26, 2023.

Chapter 5

The Christian Faith and Migration

As noted earlier, the growth of globalization has resulted in a far more integrated global community. The rise of modern technology has not only facilitated the cross-border movement of goods, services, finance, and information, but has also increased the number of people moving across state boundaries. Although most transborder movement of people involves tourism or business, a significant number of people move to other countries permanently—either to increase their living conditions or to flee violence and persecution. According to the International Organization for Migration, the UN organization promoting humane and orderly migration, there were more than 281 million international migrants in 2022—that is, people living outside of their homeland.[1]

While most of these persons had moved voluntarily, many were refugees or asylum-seekers fleeing violence. It is estimated that in 2022 there were more than thirty-five million refugees, representing a significant increase because of armed conflict in Ukraine and the collapse of Afghanistan. Additionally, more than five million persons were seeking asylum in a foreign country.[2] Asylum-seekers differ from refugees in that a refugee is registered in a foreign country after fleeing their homeland, while asylees request protection after arriving in a host nation.

In this chapter, I describe why migration is an important issue in the international community. I begin by noting that a sovereign state has the sole right to decide the number and criteria for admission into their country. Under international law, people have the right to emigrate, but there is no right to immigrate. Such a decision is the prerogative of the admitting state. I next describe two alternative perspectives on migration based on competing visions of global society. I then address two major global concerns—the growth of refugees and irregular migration. The latter issue involves people who enter a foreign country without a state's consent or who enter a country lawfully but remain beyond the terms of their visa. The issue of refugees is a vital global concern because refugees are seeking safety away from their own homeland. The issue of unauthorized migration is important because it raises issues of distributive justice and how the claims of law-abiding migrants are reconciled with those who have avoided authorized admission procedures. In the chapter's final section, I explore how a Christian perspective can contribute to the moral analysis of this complex issue and provide guidance in developing humane, just policies.

THE IMPORTANCE OF INTERNATIONAL MIGRATION

Migration is an important global issue for several reasons. First, people flee their homeland because of civil wars, repression of ethnic minorities, and widespread societal violence. The persistence of weak and failing states is a major cause of the growth of refugees. And since the care of refugees is dependent upon the willingness of neighboring states to accept them, as well as the financial support from major developed states, the ongoing care of such people is a major international issue. While the refugee issue requires multilateral coordination through the UN High Commissioner for Refugees, caring for people is ultimately dependent upon the voluntary actions of member-states. Since refugees, like stateless persons, do not enjoy human rights protections from a state, their wellbeing is dependent upon voluntary support and assistance from other countries.

Second, the prevalence of people fleeing persecution and violence has led to a significant increase in the number of people requesting asylum. As noted earlier, an asylum-seeker is a person who requests protection from a host country. An asylee is essentially a refugee who is seeking protection after arriving in a safe country. In 2022, nearly one million persons applied for asylum in EU countries.[3] Most of these applicants were from Syria and Afghanistan. This number, however, does not include the four million Ukrainians granted temporary protection because of the Russian war against Ukraine.

In the United States, the demand for asylum increased significantly under the administration of President J. Biden because of more lax border controls. Migrants cross the long southern border with Mexico into the United States and then turn themselves in to border agents to petition asylum. Since asylum is a recognized international legal obligation, US government officials comply with international obligations by making a preliminary investigation to determine if the applicant has a credible claim. If the government determines that a credible threat exists, a migrant is allowed to remain in the United States and given a future court date to determine the legitimacy of the claim.

Because modern communications technology provides people with more knowledge about economic conditions in foreign lands, a growing number of people from poor countries attempt to move to more prosperous countries. Such international migration is difficult, however, since the demand for entry permits (visas) in developed nations is much greater than the supply. Because of the limited availability of visas, a growing number of migrants rely on smugglers to enter countries covertly. In effect, irregular migrants bypass established rules governing immigration, forcing them to live outside of the law.

Weak, failing states are another cause of international migration. When states are unwilling or unable to provide a stable and humane environment for work or a just government to ensure human rights, people may decide to emigrate to a more stable, prosperous state. Such migration is mostly voluntary and dependent upon the willingness of a host country to accept the migrant. The collapse of Venezuela under the rule of strongman Nicolás Maduro, for example, has resulted in rampant poverty, leading more than six million of its citizens to emigrate to neighboring countries to find work and sustain life. One organization has estimated that four million of these refugees are struggling to meet basic human needs.[4] The social and economic conditions in Haiti are even more dire since gangs have replaced the government as the ruling authorities in urban areas, especially its capital, Port-au-Prince. Unlike Venezuela, however, Haiti is an island and leaving the country is much more difficult because escaping poverty and lawlessness involves making a dangerous journey on small, ill-equipped boats.[5]

Undoubtedly, if member-states were stable, peaceful, prosperous, and democratic, international migration would be less of a global concern. But the international community is comprised of many failing and oppressive societies. The challenge for well-functioning states is how to assist those nation-states that are unwilling or unable to ensure the rule of law, foster job creation, and provide a humane political environment that protects human rights. Given the egregious inequalities among states, international migration will continue to be a central moral issue in global politics.

Finally, and most important, international migration has increased as an inevitable result of the world's economic development. As the world has become more interdependent and more modern, people's aspirations have increased. According to Hein de Haas, people are not moving to leave desperate poverty and lawlessness; rather, they are moving because they are drawn to the promise of a better future. Haas writes, "migrants actively seek to migrate because they see a clear benefit in doing so."[6] Thus, when President Joe Biden asked Vice President Kamala Harris to travel to Central America and uncover the "root causes" of migration, he was accepting the widespread belief that "emigration is a desperate flight from misery." Because of the prevailing acceptance of this view, European governments have launched numerous migration awareness campaigns to deter people from migrating. Such campaigns, which seek to alert migrants to the danger and cost of such travel, have been woefully unsuccessful, however. Regardless of their economic status, people are rational and will, after assessing the risks and potential gains from migration, pursue their own interests.

Despite its global significance, public opinion on international migration is mixed and varies considerably among countries. According to a Gallup poll, immigration has been the second most important noneconomic concern of the US public for many years.[7] In Britain, the public viewed immigration as the top public concern in the decade prior to Brexit but following Britain's withdrawal from the European Union, it became less important.[8] In France, a majority of the public view immigration negatively, perhaps in part because of the limited assimilation that has been achieved with its North African immigrants. A 2017 survey found that 40 percent of the French public regarded immigrants as a "threat" to the nation.[9] And in the United States, immigration became the top public policy concern in 2023, with 27 percent of the people identifying the issue as being most important.[10] In addition, polls in developed countries have found that the public tends to support existing levels of immigration but has deep reservations over unregulated migration. Indeed, a prevailing concern is that, despite a plethora of laws and regulations, governments have been unable to regulate migration.

INTERNATIONAL LAW AND MIGRATION

According to international law, people have an inherent right to leave their homeland. The Universal Declaration of Human Rights declares (Article 13): "Everyone has the right to leave any country, including his own." Although individuals have the right to emigrate, they do not have a right to immigrate to a particular state. This is because governments, not international organizations or the migrants themselves, determine admission into sovereign countries. While the Universal Declaration (Article 15.1) affirms the right to a nationality, this claim does not entitle a person to reside in a country of their choosing. The moral asymmetry between exit and entry, departure and arrival, is manifested in everyday social and economic life. For example, a worker can leave their job but they do not have a right to another position in another company. Similarly, a student can withdraw from a college or university but they do not have a right to be a student at another institution. That decision is the sole responsibility of the individual college or university to which application is made.

Are territorial borders morally legitimate? Do states have the legal and moral right to determine the number of and criteria for migrant admissions? Political theorist Michael Walzer argues that states have the right to regulate migration by controlling membership.[11] His analysis suggests that states have a right to protect their distinctive cultural, social, and political traditions by regulating admission. States, he argues, also have a moral obligation to care for strangers, especially those suffering from violence and persecution. Walzer's analysis is important because it provides an ethical justification for the contemporary international legal order and for the widespread practices of border control by sovereign states.

Myron Weiner, a political scientist, describes the consensus on immigration among industrial states as follows: "that no government is obligated to admit migrants, that migration is a matter of individual national policy, that most governments need more effective control over their borders, that more forceful measures are needed to halt illegal migration and to distinguish genuine asylum seekers and refugees suffering from persecution and violence from individuals who use these procedures to migrate, that 'temporary' guestworker policies do not work."[12] In addition, there is widespread agreement that states have a moral responsibility to care for refugees. This does not mean that states are obligated to accept refugees but that once they have arrived in a safe country they may not be returned to their homeland while danger persists. This last principle is called *non-refoulement* and is a basic rule of international law. This may explain why many states go to great lengths to avoid having asylum-seekers arrive on their soil.

ALTERNATIVE CONCEPTIONS OF MIGRATION

As noted earlier, scholars of international relations have developed two perspectives on the nature of global society: communitarianism and cosmopolitanism. Both perspectives affirm human dignity but do so in different ways. The communitarian emphasizes the role of states in securing human rights, while the cosmopolitan emphasizes the universality of human dignity by virtue of membership in a global society.

Given the divergent worldviews of communitarianism and cosmopolitanism, it is not surprising that they provide radically different perspectives on immigration. Since communitarians assume that nation-states are the basic communities of global society, they argue that honoring the sovereignty and political independence of states is vital to global order, and that regulating migration is an important task of sovereign states. As the saying goes, "No borders, no country." This does not mean that states should restrict immigration but that migration policies should be fair and reasonable by incorporating the interests of migrants with the interests of citizens of the receiving state. Since the needs and wants of refugees, economic migrants, families, businesses, citizens, and others will inevitably conflict, the challenge for policy makers is to make and enforce immigration rules that are fair and implemented with consistency. In sum, the communitarian view calls for effective border regulation and the establishment of a regulatory immigration regime characterized by justice, consistency, and effectiveness.

The cosmopolitan approach to immigration is essentially one of encouraging transnational migration. Since the fractured world of sovereign states is not conducive to human wellbeing, territorial borders are viewed as inimical to global welfare and an impediment to human flourishing. The priority is to meet human needs. The care of refugees and poor migrants must take precedence over the wants and needs of citizens. While some cosmopolitan thinkers may regard immigration restrictions as a temporary practical necessity, the long-term aim is to eliminate border controls altogether to facilitate the free, transnational movement of people.

Most international migration is short-term and temporary. Tens of millions of people use their national passports to travel for leisure, study, or business. In addition, millions of workers, especially from low-income countries, travel to foreign lands to work. Such legal cross-border travel is a part of a stable, humane global society. Migration becomes a global problem, however, under two conditions: first, when civic strife and wars lead to the collapse of states, resulting in people fleeing their homeland; and second, when people determine that developed nations offer a better environment for meeting their needs and wants, and seek to enter another country without the consent of the host state. The first problem gives rise to refugees; the second to irregular migrants. Refugees flee because they want to live; economic migrants travel to other countries because they want a better life. The next two sections address each of these problems.

CARING FOR REFUGEES

According to international law (the Refugee Convention of 1951), a refugee is a person with a "well-founded fear of persecution" because of race, religion, nationality, political opinion, or membership in a particular social group. Fundamentally, a refugee is a person who seeks safety outside of their homeland because of war, ethnic strife, religious persecution, political oppression, or other significant threats to personal security (such as membership in a social group). Typically, refugees flee to neighboring countries and are then registered by the UN High Commissioner for Refugees, the international organization responsible for refugees.

According to James Purcell, who served as the first director of the US Department of State's Bureau for Refugee Programs, the refugee regime established in the aftermath of World War II had these elements: first, the processing of refugees would be carried in a territory away from the conflict; second, temporary settlement would be provided near the home country, or what was termed "first-asylum" states; and third, if danger persisted in the home country and regional settlement was inadequate, a third-country resettlement would be a last-resort solution. The success of this regime was rooted in offshore processing and the reliance on first-asylum countries. For Purcell, the first-asylum system was the anchor to the refugee regime.[13]

This system has not been used in recent years, especially after the humanitarian crisis developed in Syria that resulted in more than five million refugees. Instead of addressing this complex humanitarian crisis comprehensively, leading states minimized the nature of the crisis and pursued ad hoc strategies to cope with the immediate needs of migrants arriving at their borders. According to Alexander Betts and Paul Collier, during the first four years of the Syrian war, European powers neglected the crisis, allowing neighboring countries to accept some four million refugees. Betts and Collier call this phase a "heartless head" strategy. When many refugees began entering Europe in 2015, however, some governments, led by Germany, decided to disregard their EU collective responsibilities and resorted to unilateral actions. This approach is called "headless heart" because the decision to allow migrants to request political asylum in a country of their choosing all but destroyed any hope of addressing the asylum challenge in a multilateral fashion.[14]

Both the number of refugees and the number of asylees have increased in the new millennium. As noted previously, there were about thirty-five million registered refugees in 2023 and about five million asylum-seekers. While caring for refugees is chiefly a multilateral issue, the disposition of asylum cases is a concern of the national state where the migrant is seeking protection. As a result, the media typically offers greater coverage of the asylum issues than the plight of refugees. This is especially the case in countries where the number of asylum-seekers is overwhelming state capabilities, such as in Britain, Germany, France, Italy, and the United States.[15]

From a moral perspective, refugees have the strongest claim to admission in foreign countries. Since refugees flee their homeland to save their lives, there is widespread consensus in global society that they are entitled to protection. The fundamental political issue in caring for refugees is who should provide safety. The claim of protection, however, does not mean that refugees are legally entitled to admission. Rather, it suggests that states should provide safety as a voluntary, humanitarian act. Such safety may be temporary or long term, with permanent resettlement considered the least desirable alternative.

Since the end of the Second World War, the United States has resettled more refugees than any other country. Based on procedures worked out between the Congress and the Office of the President, each year the government establishes a ceiling for total refugee admissions, specifying ceilings for different geographical regions. Although the number of refugees admitted per year varies, since 2000 the total number of refugees resettled in the United States has averaged about sixty thousand. This total, however, excludes migrants that are granted asylum or some type of temporary parole.

Another US migrant program is Temporary Protected Status (TPS). This program allows migrants to remain temporarily in the United States if conditions in their homeland pose a threat to their safety. TPS, which grants migrants the right to remain in the United States for up to eighteen months, allows them to work and protects them from deportation. Since most TPS holders continue to reapply for protection, many holders have lived in the United States for more than twenty years. As of 2023, sixteen countries had TPS status, providing protection to more than 600,000 persons, with the largest groups being from Venezuela, El Salvador, and Haiti. In 2023 the TPS designation was granted to migrants from Afghanistan and Ukraine residing in the United States.

Since President Joseph Biden assumed office in 2021, the number of migrants requesting asylum has increased dramatically. Of the 2.3 million migrants who were detained at the US border in 2022, approximately one-third had requested asylum.[16] The rise in the number of asylum-seekers is a direct result of the lax practices used by the government in making a preliminary determination about the credibility of the applicant's request. When a migrant's asylum application is viewed as credible, the migrant is released into the country while they await a court date—typically more than four years away. In the meantime, migrants can secure work if they receive approval from the government.

The Biden administration's lax approach to border control and asylum has been detrimental to the nation's legal immigration regime. First, it has undermined the historic priority given to registered refugees. Allowing persons who have traveled through other countries to request asylum at the US southern border undermines the distinction between refugees who are seeking safety and migrants who are seeking an improved standard of living. Arthur (Gene) Dewey, who held leadership posts on refugee issues in the Department of State and the United Nations, thinks that the current US approach to migration issues has contributed to America's loss of global leadership on refugee concerns. The unwillingness to distinguish between refugees and economic migrants has eroded the government's willingness and ability to care for refugees. According to Dewey, "When you let everyone come in, you lose the ability to discriminate and care for those who are fleeing persecution."[17] Second, the lax approach to asylum has greatly complicated the work of immigration courts. Although the government added one hundred more immigration court judges in the 2023 fiscal year, the total court backlog increased by more than a million during this time. By the end of 2023, the total court backlog was three million cases.[18] Additionally, the problem of processing asylum claims is complicated by the failure to deport persons who have been denied asylum.

Since the US government provides limited assistance to communities receiving asylees, such migrants pose a major social and economic burden on cities and other communities, especially if their number is large. This was especially the case in 2022 and 2023 when hundreds of thousands of asylum-seekers were given temporary protection. To dramatize the federal government's ineffectiveness in controlling its southern border, Florida and Texas began bussing migrants to major metropolitan centers, especially "sanctuary cities,"[19] such as Chicago, New York, and Philadelphia. As of mid-2023, some two thousand asylum-seekers were arriving every week in New York City, resulting in an unanticipated and unprecedented demand for housing and social services. The city's mayor declared that the cost over three years for these services would exceed twelve billion dollars.[20]

As noted earlier, asylum applications are adjudicated by immigration courts located throughout the United States. Although the percentage of asylum approvals has varied over time and among the different immigrant judges, the approximate overall rate in recent years has been about 40 percent.[21] Migrants whose requests are not approved can appeal the judgment to a higher court. Even if the migrant's request is ultimately denied and an order of removal is issued, the government's lax enforcement of deportation means that many unauthorized migrants continue living in the shadows. It is estimated that more than one million persons have refused a deportation order.

THE CHALLENGE OF IRREGULAR MIGRATION

As noted earlier, since the demand for visas to prosperous countries is much greater than the supply, many migrants seek to evade border regulations. They do this by entering a country without legal inspection or by entering legally and remaining in the host country after the terms of the visa have expired. Irregular migrants—also called undocumented or unauthorized migrants—have increased in number in recent years not so much because of declining economic and social conditions in their homelands but rather because of increased possibility of securing a better life in developed countries. The dreams of a more prosperous and humane life in a stable, economically developed country are facilitated by increased information from social media and travel assistance from smugglers.

The promise of a more prosperous standard of living explains why migrants risk dangerous sea voyages from northern Africa to Italy or from the French coast to Britain. It also explains why people trek through difficult jungle terrain in the Darien Gap of Panama to reach the southern border of the United States or hike through the arid Arizona desert to escape government agents patrolling the country's territorial borders. Such dangerous journeys have led to countless tragic deaths, as migrants perish when boats sink in the sea or when they die from dehydration or starvation as they journey in arid, deserted lands. Since most illegal migration is guided by smugglers, human rights abuses are prevalent in such journeys.

According to one estimate, between 3.9 and 4.8 million unauthorized immigrants were living in EU countries in 2017. Given Europe's population of about five hundred million, this means that roughly 1 percent of its people were unauthorized. Of this total, about 25 percent were in the process of seeking asylum. It has been estimated that about 70 percent of all irregular migrants were living in four countries: France—three hundred thousand to four hundred thousand, Germany—one to 1.2 million, Italy—five hundred thousand to seven hundred thousand, and the United Kingdom—eight hundred thousand to 1.2 million.[22]

According to recent government estimates, between eleven million and twelve million irregular migrants were living in the United States in 2023. A large percentage have been in the country for many years and have established roots in their local communities. They are employed in a wide variety of jobs, especially in the construction and agricultural sectors and service industries. Many irregular families have children who were born in the country and since the United States grants citizenship to all children born in the country, these children are US citizens. Other mixed-status families involve marriage between a US citizen and an irregular migrant. One of the difficult challenges is how to care for the persons who were brought to the country illegally as children. Since they are now adults, the moral issue is how to regularize their status. Despite legislative efforts to accommodate these so-called Dreamers, Congress has been unable to resolve their status.

The challenge of how to address unlawful migration in the United States is vexing. It is difficult because the resolution of this issue has implications for current and future immigration policies, especially since regularization without changes in existing laws could fuel additional illegality. Moreover, since US immigration law gives priority to family admissions, the regularization of irregulars could fuel an increase in family-sponsored admissions. In addition, granting amnesty could be viewed as unjust by migrants who had followed or were following established immigration procedures. The least problematic issue is how to resolve the legal status of children brought by irregulars years ago (Dreamers). To my mind, these young people should be granted legal status since they are not responsible for their own unauthorized entry.

There is no simple, easy solution to the issues arising from unauthorized migration. Since the principal parties concerned with irregular migration—workers, businesses, migrants, political parties, and the like—hold competing and conflicting interests, the only way to reconcile them is through compromise—that is, giving each group a portion of their interests. But since compromise will entail accepting elements that are deemed unsatisfactory to each of the parties, the strength of the resolution will depend, ironically, on their shared dissatisfaction with the final accord.[23] Ideally, such a compromise should entail, among other things, reform of existing law that shifts visa priority from families to jobs, increased enforcement of border security and employment law, and a five-year program of legal regularization based on security checks and payment of past fines and taxes. And since asylum claims are overwhelming the immigration system, it is also important to carefully redefine criteria for identifying a refugee. The current statute, which dates to 1951, needs to be amended to facilitate the distinction between asylees and economic migrants.

It is important to distinguish legal immigration from the challenges arising from unauthorized migration. The challenge for a constitutional government is to devise a just, fair, and consistent program of migrant admissions. This means that the government must determine the type and number of migrants it seeks to admit. Some countries, like Canada and Australia, emphasize skill-based immigration. The United States, by contrast, gives preference to family ties, with nearly 70 percent of all legal admissions based on family reunification. While the number of persons given legal permanent resident status is not fixed, since 2010 about one million migrants have received this designation annually. Given the liberal immigration policies that have been pursued since the Cold War and especially since its end in 1990, about forty-six million people born outside the United States are now living in the country. This total represents about 13.9 percent of the country's total population.[24]

THE CHRISTIAN FAITH AND MIGRATION

What contribution can Christians provide governments on migration? Since how the world is conceived will influence how one approaches the challenges of migration, I first explore competing visions of the world. I next examine how some denominations have sought to address contemporary migration concerns. Finally, I explore how a Christian worldview can be brought to bear on this issue.

How to View the World

Before addressing the challenge of immigration policy, however, it is important to ascertain how the Christian church should regard the world. As noted earlier, two competing worldviews of the world have been prevalent among scholars: a communitarian perspective and a cosmopolitan worldview. Since the Christian faith assumes the inherent dignity and equality of all persons, it is a religion that is universal in scope and one that disregards social, ethnic, gender, and economic distinctions. As noted in Scripture, the church—the Body of Christ—is a unitary community where differences among believers is unimportant. What is significant is the bond of love that unifies the Christian community. Since a biblical perspective is clearly consistent with the universalism of cosmopolitanism, Christians can approach migration concerns from this perspective. Such an approach can highlight core moral concerns, including the priority of persons, social solidarity, and the necessity to care for those suffering poverty and oppression.

The world, however, is not the church and is not coterminous with the Kingdom of God. Rather, the world represents the Kingdom of Man—the earthly, temporal world where the maintenance of order and the quest for proximate justice is dependent upon the authority of government. Whereas love is the ruling ethic in cosmopolitanism, justice is the prevailing ethic of the communitarian ethic. Given the conflicts, wars, and divisions in the existing world, the communitarian worldview provides a necessary corrective to the idealism of cosmopolitanism. Indeed, such an approach is necessary if we are to highlight people's social needs. Human beings are not solitary individuals whose identity is nurtured and developed in isolation. Rather, persons are social creatures who long to be a part of communities—to belong to a family, tribe, club, neighborhood, church, or nation.

In view of this, a Christian approach to migration should be rooted in both the universal ambitions of cosmopolitanism and the concerns of social solidarity found in communitarianism. How best to integrate these two worldviews in addressing immigration concerns will vary from one time and place to another. Some circumstances will call for giving priority to the political and social solidarity of states. In others, the need may be for greater concern to expand immigration and care for refugees and asylees. Given the migration pressures identified earlier and the challenges posed by failing states, communitarianism offers a necessary perspective.

Church Documents

Catholics and Protestants, however, have emphasized different aspects of faith in their social and political engagement. Roman Catholics, for example, following their well-developed tradition of Catholic social thought,[25] have emphasized such norms as human dignity, the common good, social solidarity, and the preferential treatment of the poor. The political and social ethics of Protestants, by contrast, have emphasized such norms as the dignity of persons, the universality of sin, the need for political order, dual citizenship, the responsibility of individuals, and need for justice. How such principles and insights are applied to the challenges of migration will, of course, vary among different denominations as they respond to specific national concerns. To illustrate how churches have sought to address migration issues in the United States, I briefly describe some church documents written to address them.

In 2003, Catholic bishops from the United States and Mexico issued a pastoral letter on immigration titled "Strangers No Longer."[26] The letter sets forth principles that Catholics should use in assessing bilateral migration concerns, such as the quest for work in a foreign land, and then offer policy suggestions to address specific concerns, such as giving priority to family relationships, legalization of irregular migrants, and increasing employment-based visas. Fundamentally, the document seeks to encourage a more expansive and flexible approach to Mexican migration. The principal shortcoming of the document is that it addresses a public policy concern as a political interest group rather than as a church. The comparative advantage of the Catholic Church is theology, not public policy. Instead of giving advice to government officials, it should seek to educate its parishioners on the fundamental moral issues involved in the policy debate.

In 2009, the National Association of Evangelicals adopted a two-page resolution on immigration.[27] The resolution, like the pastoral letter, is more concerned with reforming public policies than with educating its members on how to approach the issue biblically. While the National Association of Evangelicals' statement acknowledges that Scripture does not provide a blueprint for contemporary laws and policies, it nevertheless critiques the US immigration system. It declares that the rise in unauthorized migration is due to the government's failure to issue sufficient visas to meet the country's labor demands. It further calls on the government to offer a qualified amnesty to irregular migrants and to expand the number of family-based permits. In effect, the National Association of Evangelicals' statement was a call for a more flexible, expansive immigration system to meet migrants' demand for work and family unity.

The document that reflects the most careful integration of biblical and theological thought with the challenges of migration is "Immigrants Among Us"—a study issued by the Lutheran Church-Missouri Synod in 2012.[28] In my book *Just Immigration*, I stated that the report was "a model of how to assess a complex public-policy concern from a biblical perspective."[29] Rather than seeking to offer policy advice to government officials, the document offers biblical and theological insights relevant to the challenges of migration. It highlights the role of the church and the state and focuses on the imperatives of loving one's neighbor and obeying government authority. Since the report illuminates the inherent tensions between the dual imperatives of love and obedience and the dual kingdoms of temporal and spiritual life, it provides a theological framework to assess migration. Instead of seeking to advance public policies, the church statement does something far more important—namely, it provides an educational resource that can help church members assess the moral dimensions and challenges of migration.

Unlike the Lutheran document, many religious leaders approach migration from a cosmopolitan perspective that disregards the state and governmental responsibilities. For them, topics such as citizenship, rule of law, sovereignty, and human rights are of secondary importance. Instead, they prioritize making the immigration system more open and flexible—one which permits migrants from poor countries to move to more prosperous countries. A short book that reflects this progressive, cosmopolitan outlook is *The Bible and Borders* by M. Daniel Carroll R., a Bible professor. While Carroll avoids getting into specific public policy issues, his overall approach to migration is that Scripture calls for the welcoming of migrants. In his view, a biblical approach to migration must involve "a consistent ethic of hospitable welcome toward the outsider."[30]

A common motif of cosmopolitan believers is the call to "welcome the stranger."[31] While being kind, generous, and merciful are important personal attributes, such values are insufficient to guide the making of regulations and laws. How can the US Department of Homeland Security, which is charged with regulating national borders, utilize such values? Can such values determine how many refugees should be admitted and from what geographical regions? Given the enormous suffering in South Sudan, Haiti, and Yemen, should people from these countries receive priority over those from more developed and less dangerous countries in Central America? Should irregular migrants receive preferential treatment over migrants currently awaiting visas? Clearly, a welcoming ethic is important but insufficient to guide tradeoffs among competing and conflicting claims of worthy migrants. If immigration practices are to be consistent with justice, the hard work of assessing competing moral values and interests must be undertaken. Thus, if Christians are to contribute to a better, more just immigration system, they will have to go beyond principles of human dignity and compassion and undertake the intermediate work of policy analysis using biblical norms.

Applying Faith to Migration

Before seeking to apply Christian values and principles to migration, it is useful to highlight major moral issues relevant to the problems surrounding international migration. Without seeking to provide a comprehensive account of immigration concerns, the following moral issues illustrate the importance of ethical dimensions of immigration.

1. *Borders:* The first core issue is the legitimacy of borders. Is the existing global order of nation-states just? Although this issue is not immediately relevant to immigration policies, it is a foundational issue, since how the world is conceived will influence the analysis of migration.
2. *Human dignity:* Since human dignity is a central principle of the Christian faith, migration is important because people matter. The legitimacy of immigration policies is thus dependent on how people are treated.
3. *Caring for the poor:* Since the Bible calls for caring of the poor and the vulnerable, immigration policy should seek to give priority to "the least of these."
4. *Procedural justice:* Since procedural justice demands that government rules should be fair and enforced impartially, migrants following the law should have precedence over those that have sought admission by avoiding government controls.
5. *Moral precedence:* Since refugees are fleeing to find safety while economic migrants are seeking a better standard of living, refugees should have precedence over migrants.
6. *Common good:* Migration policies should seek the common good of both the nation-state and the world. Pursuing the nation's common good will necessarily require that migrants' desires are reconciled with those of citizens of the receiving state. Additionally, the quest for the global common good will require that the wants and interests of sending states are reconciled with those of the receiving state.
7. *Solidarity:* Since family, social, and communal relationships matter, protecting communal solidarity is important. This means that the allocation of visas must weigh the merits of family-based and skill-based visas. In addition, since mass migration is a threat to a nation's solidarity, regulating immigration and securing borders is imperative.

In applying biblical principles and insights to migration challenges, it is helpful to restate some of the core norms that were highlighted in chapter 2. These are human dignity (personalism), the universality of divine love, caring for the poor and vulnerable, the need for justice, the important role of government, and the importance of social solidarity and the common good. While each of these principles represents important values, they cannot be used in isolation to develop policies.

The principle of human dignity, for example, means that we must treat the world's eight billion people with equality and dignity. While treating every migrant with dignity is possible, treating everyone equally is impossible when crafting an immigration policy. The purpose of such a policy is to establish criteria by which to establish admission. Clearly, some migrants will be admitted while others will be denied admission.

Similarly, while the demand to love our neighbor is a vital moral imperative, it is unlikely to contribute to migration decision-making. Since the ethic is universal, it applies to all persons, and therefore is an insufficient criterion by which to judge admissions. Migration policies should of course be consistent with norms of equality, nondiscrimination, and human dignity, but such norms cannot alone be the basis of a government's immigration policy.

Justice, too, is an important biblical norm. But given the elusive nature of this idea, the quest for a just immigration policy will depend upon other elements. For example, if substantive justice requires that refugees and the poor and the vulnerable receive priority over family-based migrants, then the justice norm will be approximated when policies and their implementation fulfill these conditions. And if procedural justice requires that lawful migrants be given priority over irregular migrants, then the justice norm will be approximated when migrants following government rules are given precedence over those who have avoided government controls. While the ideal of justice provides a standard for judgment, it can be approximated only through incremental adjustments.

The existence of dual citizenships is also a reminder of the importance to differentiate the Kingdom of Christ from the Kingdom of Man. While some Christians seek to develop insights about global society and immigration concerns based on insights of the Heavenly Kingdom, we need to remember that citizenship in the state is based on law, coercion, and power. Christians seeking to advance a humane and just immigration regime need to address migration concerns using the instruments of temporal authority—the state, government, rule of law, and obedience to public authority—rather than relying on biblical principles alone.

Finally, since communal solidarity is important, immigration policies should not undermine existing nations by fostering mass migration. Protecting the integrity of existing nation-states is important to the human dignity of citizens. At the same time, nurturing global solidarity is also vitally important. The challenge in addressing immigration is to seek to nurture social solidarity both within nations as well as the world itself.

In sum, the Christian faith provides values and perspectives that can foster a humane, just approach to global migration. Christian ethics can remind decision-makers that all persons—refugees, legal immigrants, irregular migrants, and visitors—need to be treated justly and with dignity. While compassion and mercy can contribute to a welcoming perspective toward migrants, establishing admission criteria will inevitably involve the difficult task of making trade-offs among competing values. Christians can contribute to the moral analysis of trade-offs by illuminating important biblical norms. And once policies are established, believers need to support the enforcement of government rules unless those rules are viewed as inconsistent with biblical morality.

In conclusion, mass migration arising from failing states, civil wars, and environmental calamities is a global concern because it challenges states' capacity to regulate immigration. While the humanitarian needs of migrants are a global concern, the response is determined chiefly by each nation-state. The number of refugees and types of migrants that any state will admit is largely up to government officials, not some global institution. States and international organizations can highlight the moral and political challenge posed by mass migration, but it is states that determine how they will respond to humanitarian needs, the desire of migrants seeking a better standard of living, and the needs and wants of their own citizens. While international governmental organizations and nongovernmental organizations can help to guide public policy actions, the responsibility for regulating migration is in the hands of each member-state. Churches and religious organizations can play an important role in addressing this issue by highlighting the moral dimensions involved in migration policies and by emphasizing the need for compassion toward every human being.

NOTES

1. International Organization for Migration, "World Migration Report 2022," https://worldmigrationreport.iom.int/wmr-2022-interactive/ (August 1, 2024).

2. UN High Commissioner for Refugees, "Global Trends Report 2022," www.unhcr.org/global-trends-report-2022 (August 1, 2024).

3. Council of European Union, "Asylum Applications in the EU," 2023, www.consilium.europa.eu/en/infographics/asylum-applications-eu/ (August 6, 2024).

4. International Organization for Migration, "Over Four Million Venezuelan Refugees and Migrants Struggle to Meet Basic Needs Across the Americas," 2023, www.iom.int/news/over-four-million-venezuelan-refugees-and-migrants-struggle-meet-basic-needs-across-americas (August 6, 2024).

5. To control the number of persons fleeing Haiti, the United States, along with other countries, deters such travel by forcing boats with migrants to return. International Organization for Migration, "Over Four Million Venezuelan Refugees and Migrants."

6. Hein de Haas, *How Migration Really Works: The Facts About the Most Divisive Issue in Politics* (New York: Basic Books, 2023), 108.

7. Gallup, "Most Important Problem," 2023, https://news.gallup.com/poll/1675/most-important-problem.aspx (August 6, 2024).

8. Migration Observatory, "UK Public Opinion toward Immigration: Overall Attitudes and Level of Concern," 2023, https://migrationobservatory.ox.ac.uk/resources/briefings/uk-public-opinion-toward-immigration-overall-attitudes-and-level-of-concern/ (August 6, 2024).

9. European Conservative, "Poll: Only 13% of French Think Migrants Represent an 'Opportunity' for the Country," 2023, https://europeanconservative.com/articles/news/poll-only-13-of-french-think-migrants-represent-an-opportunity-for-the-country/?print-posts=pdf (August 6, 2024).

10. Pew Research Center, "Immigration Named Top U.S. Problem for Third Straight Month, 2024," https://news.gallup.com/poll/644570/immigration-named-top-problem-third-straight-month.aspx (August 10, 2024).

11. Michael Walzer, *Spheres of Justice: A Defense of Pluralism and Equality* (New York: Basic Books, 1983), 35–42.

12. Myron Weiner, "Ethics, National Sovereignty and the Control of Immigration," *International Migration Review* 30 (Spring 1996), 192.

13. James N. Purcell, Jr., *We're in Danger! Who Will Help Us? Refugees and Migrants: A Test of Civilization* (Bloomington, IN: Archway Publishing, 2019).

14. Alexander Betts and Paul Collier, *Refuge: Rethinking Refugee Policy in a Changing World* (New York: Oxford University Press, 2017), 73–92.

15. For a different perspective, see de Haas, *How Migration Really Works*. Haas argues that there is no real refugee "crisis."

16. TRAC, "A Sober Assessment of the Growing U.S. Asylum Backlog," 2022, https://trac.syr.edu/reports/705/ (August 6, 2024).

17. Interview with Mr. Dewey on January 5, 2024. Gene Dewey was assistant secretary of state for population, refugees, and migration from 2002 to 2005 and was assistant secretary general, UN Deputy High Commissioner for Refugees, from 1986 to 1990.

18. TRAC, "Immigration Court Backlog Tops 3 Million," 2023, https://trac.syr.edu/reports/734/ (August 6, 2024).

19. A sanctuary city is one that has passed ordinances prohibiting cooperation with federal enforcement of immigration statues and policies.

20. Jeffrey C. Mays, "Mayor Adams Says Migrant Influx Will Cost New York City $12 Billion," *New York Times*, August 9, 2023, www.nytimes.com/2023/08/09/nyregion/adams-nyc-migrants-cost.html (August 10, 2024).

21. TRAC, "Immigration: Asylum Decisions," 2023," https://trac.syr.edu/phptools/immigration/asylum/ (August 6, 2024).

22. Pew Research Center, "5 Facts About Unauthorized Immigration in Europe," November 2019, www.pewresearch.org/short-reads/2019/11/14/5-facts-about-unauthorized-immigration-in-europe/ (August 6, 2024).

23. I owe this insight to Henry Kissinger, the former US Secretary of State, who observed that negotiated settlements will always seem somewhat unjust and involve relative dissatisfaction. "The generality of this dissatisfaction," writes Kissinger, "is a condition of stability because were any one power totally satisfied, all others would be totally dissatisfied."

24. USA Facts, "How Many People Are Coming to the US and Where Are They Coming From?" 2024, https://usafacts.org/state-of-the-union/immigration/ (August 6, 2024).

25. Catholic social thought, a tradition rooted in Scripture, natural law, and church teachings, was developed over many centuries to structure moral reflection on social and political life.

26. Catholic Bishops of Mexico and the United States, "Strangers No Longer: Together on the Journey of Hope," 2003, www.usccb.org/issues-and-action/human-life-and-dignity/immigration/strangers-no-longer-together-on-the-journey-of-hope (August 6, 2024).

27. National Association of Evangelicals, "Resolution on Immigration," 2009, www.nae.org/immigration-2009/ (August 6, 2024).

28. The Lutheran Church—Missouri Synod, "Immigrants Among Us: A Lutheran Framework for Addressing Immigration Issues," November 2012, www.cui.edu/Portals/0/uploadedfiles/AboutCUI/Immigrants_Among_Us-FINAL_(English)%20(1).pdf?ver=mawv7apNkeNyf2rao3tj1w%3d%3d (August 6, 2024).

29. Mark R. Amstutz, *Just Immigration: American Policy in Christian Perspective* (Grand Rapids: Eerdmans, 2017), 208.

30. M. Daniel Carroll R., *The Bible and Borders: Hearing God's Word on Immigration* (Grand Rapids: Brazos Press, 2020), 117.

31. Matthew Soerens and Jenny Hwang Yang, two World Relief employees, have published a book on immigration reform with this title—*Welcoming the Stranger*.

Chapter 6

The Christian Faith and Development

Development is a multidimensional process by which society becomes more economically prosperous through increased productivity. Economic growth is important because it provides the means for improving the standard of living for people. Growth requires important economic inputs and a stable legal, political, and economic order. But development is not simply a technical process dependent upon technology and financial resources. Rather, it is a human process that relies on trust and promise keeping. Social scientists refer to these cultural preconditions as social capital. Since Christianity is a religion that is rooted in the love of God and the love of neighbor, the church has a unique role to play in fostering moral preconditions that contribute to productive enterprise or what might be termed "culture care."

Given the extraordinary global improvements in living conditions in recent decades, development may seem to be a lower global priority than other pressing concerns like climate change, gender discrimination, social and economic inequalities, and universal education. As noted earlier, more than one billion people have moved out of abject poverty in recent decades. As a result of greater economic modernization and the spread of modern medicine and technology, people are living longer and healthier lives. Still, tens of millions of people continue to suffer from malnutrition, disease, inadequate shelter, gender discrimination, and inadequate health care. Thus, despite extraordinary social and economic achievements since the end of the Cold War, much remains to be done to strengthen human dignity worldwide.

Before examining the contribution that Christians can make to development, I first explore the fundamental condition of economic and social life, namely poverty. I then examine the nature and importance of development and argue that economic growth is essential for improving living conditions and especially for reducing poverty. I then discuss why the Christian faith prioritizes poverty and provides inspiration to confront the plight of those suffering from destitution. The Christian faith does not provide a theory on how to address poverty. Rather, it provides a moral framework for structuring reflection on this problem.

THE BASIC CONDITION OF LIFE: PRIVATION

It is easy to forget that the conveniences of modern life did not exist a century ago. Homes in the United States did not have central heating, toilets were in an outhouse away from the house, and transportation was slow and cumbersome. In 1900, only 1 percent of homes had indoor plumbing. More significantly, longevity in 1900 in the United States was forty-seven years but by 2019 it had risen to seventy-nine years. Infant mortality was 157 deaths per one thousand live births in 1900 but by 2010 it had decreased to 7.1 per one thousand live births. What explains the dramatic rise in living conditions? The answer: economic growth.

In my lifetime, I have witnessed dramatic improvements in living conditions affecting communications, travel, and home comforts. As a young boy growing up in southern Chile, our home had no central heating, only cold water, and a wood-burning kitchen stove. Poverty in our town was widespread. In the winter, hungry children would come to our home to ask for bread. And when our family returned to the United States, we traveled by a freighter, which was the least expensive way of making the trip. The two-week journey was an exciting but slow trip. Today, I can make the same journey on an airplane in ten hours. I also recall making a telephone call from Chile to my grandparents in Kansas in 1952. The call, which involved waiting three to four hours while the telephone company found an available landline to the United States, was costly and had poor reception. In contrast, I am currently assisting an Afghan family that recently arrived in the United States. Their little boy told me that he talks to his grandfather in Afghanistan every day via smartphone. And the miracle of modern technology provides goods and comforts that would have been unimaginable fifty years ago. The revolution in electronics and media, for example, allow homeowners to watch movies on large television screens without having to go to a theater. Similarly, who would have anticipated electric automobiles even twenty years ago or having a telephone conversation with a telecom agent located in Bangladesh? And even more astounding, who would have anticipated the introduction of artificial intelligence at the beginning of the new millennium?

Since the fundamental condition of life in past centuries was poverty and deprivation, what needs to be explained is not poverty but rather the creation of wealth. One simple but erroneous theory is that wealth comes from resources. According to this theory, Spain and Portugal became rich in the sixteenth and seventeenth centuries because they found gold and silver in the Americas. Similarly, Saudi Arabia and Kuwait are rich because they have ample oil deposits. While natural resources can provide an important element in wealth creation, many countries with ample resources remain impoverished and backward because they rely excessively on a single source of income, whether it be tin, oil, copper, coffee, or some other basic product. Economist Paul Collier argues that natural resources are a "trap" that can impair development rather than facilitate it. It is a trap because resource surpluses tend to undermine political institutions and weaken political restraints.[1]

An alternative theory views wealth creation as the result of economic growth. Fundamentally, growth occurs when human beings produce goods and services through the creative and efficient integration of labor, capital, and technology. While resources are important elements in economic growth, this perspective views development as a dynamic, innovative process where people invest time and capital to produce goods and services that contribute to increased productivity. Wealth is not extracted; rather, it is made. Switzerland, a landlocked country, is rich not because of resources but because of the productive ingenuity of its people. The importance of human dispositions and habits was highlighted years ago by a Danish diplomat who visited a college class I was teaching. When a student asked the visitor why Denmark, a country with few natural resources, was rich, the diplomat responded as follows: "When the Good Lord made the earth, he gave the Danish people poor land and placed it far north, making winters long and dark. Because of the adversity imposed by weather, the Danish people had to plan carefully to survive the harsh winters. And because they learned to plan, they also learned to save. This disposition to plan and to save explains Denmark's modern wealth."

The importance of human ingenuity is also evident in the prosperity of The Netherlands, a nation known as a "low country" because most of its land is at or below sea level. While much of the country's land is naturally waterlogged, the Dutch have developed a complex system of dikes and drainage canals that allows the available land to be used for agriculture. Ironically, despite its limited arable land, The Netherlands has been a major exporter of flowers and vegetables in the post–Cold War years. Not only have the Dutch learned to control the sea, but they have also transformed the former Zuiderzee, a large, shallow bay south of the North Sea, into a freshwater lake. Moreover, through sophisticated engineering, the Dutch have transformed most of this lake into agricultural lands. Through a careful and lengthy process, engineers and scientists have been able to drain and desalinate these lands, known as polders, thereby transforming the former sea into arable land. It is estimated that roughly twenty-five hundred square miles of territory that were previously under water have been reclaimed. Because the Dutch people are proud of their achievements in containing and overcoming the sea, they brag, "God created the earth, but the Dutch made The Netherlands."

THE NATURE OF ECONOMIC GROWTH

The Problem of Inequality

What is more important, growth or equity? Should governments prioritize ensuring the fair distribution of existing resources, or should they focus on increasing the wealth of society? If reducing poverty is important, a government can pursue one of two options: provide resources for those in poverty or pursue economic development in the hope that such growth will impact the poor. The first strategy involves redistribution; the second involves establishing policies that foster wealth creation. Of course, governments can combine these two alternatives in a wide variety of mixed strategies. But the stark alternatives illuminate an important issue—namely, whether absolute or relative gains are more important.

To illustrate the tension between these two approaches, I would ask students in my third-world politics class which option they would prefer from the following two country scenarios. In the first scenario, the total value of resources was one hundred units and country A had thirty units (30 percent) and B had seventy units (70 percent). In the second scenario, total resources were 180 units, with A receiving only thirty-six units (20 percent) and B receiving 144 units (80 percent). Typically, a majority would prefer the second scenario, believing that the absolute rise in welfare from thirty to thirty-six units was more important than the relative decline from 30 to 20 percent. But there were some students who assumed that justice required an equitable distribution, and therefore preferred the first option even though it provided for less wealth for them. To be sure, the rise of inequalities is a problem that can threaten the social solidarity essential to maintaining a stable and prosperous society. This is especially the case in democratic countries.

Based on my international travels, I have witnessed the difference in these two development approaches. In the early 2000s, I visited Cuba on several occasions while directing a short-term study program for college students. Havana is a fascinating city, in great part because the city has changed little since the communist regime took control of the country in 1959. Since then, the government has prioritized equality over freedom, with the state regulating most social and economic activity. The government ensures primary education and basic health care for all people. However, since the state controls the production and distribution of goods and services, there is little innovation and private enterprise. There are comparatively few stores, and the number and variety of goods is limited. To ensure that people's basic nutritional needs are met, the government issues ration cards that entitle citizens to receive few basic goods, such as beans and rice, and to purchase other foodstuffs at subsidized prices. The ration centers that I saw, however, had few products and most shelves were empty. With few exceptions, Cuban people seemed frustrated with government-imposed limitations on political and economic freedom.

By contrast, when I visited Ho Chi Minh City in 2013, I found the Vietnamese city to be a dynamic, energetic, and thriving metropolis. Although the Communist Party controlled the state, the regime had adopted a market-based strategy at the end of the Cold War that had unleashed the creative and innovative energies of its people. Since private enterprise was now allowed, commercial life was thriving, with ample availability of goods and services. Unlike Cuba, the adoption of a market economy had increased investment and productivity, resulting in a dramatic rise in foreign trade. Because of increased economic growth, people's living conditions were improving significantly. Comparative data suggest that Vietnam is pursuing a strategy that is more conducive to people's wants than that of Cuba. According to one subjective index, the World Happiness Report, Vietnam ranked sixty-sixth out of 138 countries; regrettably, the report fails to include Cuba, undoubtedly since the government would not allow a poll to be taken of its people.[2] Another index, the Legatum Prosperity Index, which is based on social, political, and economic measures, ranks Vietnam seventy-third out of 167 countries, while Cuba ranks 104th.[3]

I have also witnessed the importance of economic growth in Chile, the country where I lived as a young boy. When I grew up in southern Chile in the 1950s, the town in which I lived, Temuco, was a small city of about fifty thousand people. The main streets were paved, but most side roads, including the street on which I lived, were covered with gravel. There was significant poverty in the region, and during the winter's rainy months children would regularly come to our home in the late afternoon and ask for bread. After Chile adopted a market-based economic strategy in the late 1970s, Chile experienced significant economic growth that greatly reduced the poverty rate. Today, the town in which I grew up is a thriving city of more than 350,000 people, with modern products and services widespread.

The Nature of Development

Development economists hold a variety of different theories and approaches on how to foster growth. Some economists stress savings and investment, while others emphasize technology and modernization. A growing number of social scientists emphasize the pivotal role of institutions,[4] while others call attention to the pivotal role of culture.[5] Still, there is broad consensus that growth is essential in reducing poverty[6] and that growth is a multidimensional process that is facilitated when social, political, economic, and cultural preconditions are present in society. External assistance can help in nurturing and fostering some of the necessary preconditions, such as strengthening education and building infrastructure. Ultimately, however, growth occurs when governments and their citizens use scarce resources to invest and produce goods and services that contribute to human welfare. But if such enterprise is to occur, certain environmental conditions must be present, including political order, rule of law, property rights, a culture of trust and promise keeping, and public policies that are conducive to entrepreneurship.

In *The Spirit of Democratic Capitalism*, Michael Novak argues that a prosperous society involves three distinct systems: economic, political, and moral-cultural. The economic system entails rules, principles, and institutions regulating the production and distribution of goods and services. The political system includes the fundamental norms, laws, and institutions regulating the polity. The moral-cultural system provides the moral values, traditions, habits, and human dispositions that guide and inspire the economy and the polity.[7] To the extent that the moral-cultural system provides the foundation for the effective and efficient functioning of the economy and the polity, prevalent moral values and traditions play a crucial role in fostering or inhibiting development.

Since Christianity is a religion rooted in loving God and loving one's neighbor, churches have an opportunity to teach and nurture the moral development of their parishioners. In her study of development in Guatemala, Amy Sherman showed how personal conversion had resulted in behavioral changes that were conducive to fidelity, trust, and accountability.[8] In 2005, while flying from Chicago to Miami on my way to Honduras, I sat next to an Ecuadorian businessman. When he began to read the Bible, I asked him if he was a Christian and he replied that he was. He then told me how his life had been transformed by his spiritual conversion. He said that for years he had not been a good husband, father, or employer. After becoming a Christian, however, his priorities changed, leading to changes in his values and behavior. These changes, he said, were responsible for improving family life, increasing economic prosperity, and providing greater personal satisfaction. In his view, the improvements in personal and professional life were a direct result of his religious conversion.

Cold War Development

During the Cold War, most of the concern about development focused on the large economic inequalities between the rich countries (the North) and poor countries (the South). Although Western political leaders were concerned with alleviating poverty in the developing nations, much of the public debate among political leaders and international organizations focused on redressing inequalities through financial transfers from the North to the South. An example of this orientation was the work of the Independent Commission on International Development, headed by Willy Brandt, the former head of West Germany, and other influential leaders and academicians. The co-called Brandt Commission report was issued in 1980 under the title *North-South: A Programme for Survival*.[9] The central message of that report was that the developed nations of the North should increase financial transfers to the developing nations in the South.

For their part, the countries in the South, believing that their poverty was due to unjust rules of the global economy, did not focus on economic reforms they could undertake to advance growth. Instead, they sought to transform the rules and institutions of the global economy. Their initiative, known as the New International Economic Order, sought to reform global institutions like the International Monetary Fund and the World Bank and to increase financial transfers from rich countries to poor countries.[10] Not surprisingly, during the 1970s and 1980s most poverty reduction initiatives involved official development aid, government-to-government financial transfers as loans and grants.

In the heyday of the North-South economic conflict, government leaders and economists approached the challenge of poverty reduction from two different perspectives. The first approach called for economic redistribution; the second emphasized indigenous economic growth. The first school, known as *structuralists*, emphasized the need to reduce domestic and international inequalities through government action and were skeptical of trade as an engine of growth. The other school, the *free enterprise liberals*, believed that growth was essential in reducing poverty and that such a task was to be undertaken primarily through private investment. Whereas structuralists were skeptical of foreign trade, liberals believed that international trade could be an engine of economic growth.

By the end of the 1980s, the prevailing consensus was that the liberal perspective provided a more effective way of alleviating poverty. This economic paradigm—known as the *Washington consensus*—was based on the following propositions: economic efficiency was best achieved through free enterprise, trade was an important source of economic growth, growth was essential in poverty reduction, the scope of government needed to be limited, and public policies needed to be conducive to private investment.[11] The economic phenomenon called "globalization" is simply the application of this neoliberal approach to the international economic order.

THE IMPACT OF GLOBALIZATION

Thomas Friedman defines globalization as the integration of markets and states in a way that enables "individuals, corporations, and nation-states to reach around the world farther, faster, deeper, and cheaper than ever before," and enables "the world to reach into individuals, corporations, and nation-states farther, faster, and deeper, and cheaper than ever before."[12] Numerous technological innovations have contributed to the increased integration of the international community.

To begin with, modern telecommunications facilitate the near instantaneous dissemination of information worldwide. The digital revolution has transformed the distribution of information, allowing for rapid, low-cost sharing of data worldwide. The internet, which relies on fiberoptic cables and to a lesser extent on satellites, facilitates global information flows, allowing direct telephone contact as well as visual display on a computer screen. Whereas the traditional telephone system required lines to connect users, the mobile phone has eliminated the costly and ugly need of hundreds of wires hanging among buildings. It is estimated that by 2023 most of the world's people, including those in the poorest countries, had a cell phone. This development has had a profound impact on poor countries since it has permitted connectivity in rural areas where transportation was limited and sporadic. The subsequent development of the smartphone has had an even more dramatic impact on connectivity among people. As of 2023, the world had over eight billion smartphones, or roughly one phone per person.

Another important development that has facilitated global trade is the invention of the storage container. Essentially, a container is a metal box twenty or forty feet long that allows standardize shipping of goods via rail, road, or sea. This invention is important because it increased security and protection of goods while lowering the costs of shipping. A company in central India can fill a container with cotton sheets, transport it by truck or rail to a port, load the container onto a ship (typically carrying from ten thousand to twenty thousand containers), unload the container upon arrival at the destination port, and transport the container by land to its destination. The tracking of this container is facilitated by digital information between producers and buyers.

Globalization has been an engine of economic growth. China's economic growth, which averaged 10 percent per year from 1990 to 2010, is chiefly due to its adoption of market economics and a focus on growth based on exports. I still recall visiting a handicrafts store near our home in the late 1980s and buying some simple handcrafted lacquered baskets from China, soon after the country had begun to export simple products. When I saw the beautiful, intricate lacquered baskets, which came in many shapes, sizes, and designs,

I was so impressed with these handmade products that I bought a dozen of them—for our home and to give away as gifts. Remarkably, the baskets were priced at ninety-nine cents! In the intervening years, China's exports have become more sophisticated, involving industrial products and electronic goods that are in demand worldwide. Now, many of the tools and electronic equipment that we use are made in China. The result of China's extraordinary rise in economic output has led to a dramatic transformation of the standard of living for most Chinese. It is estimated that China's economic growth is responsible for bringing some six hundred million people out of abject poverty. India, the nation with the second largest population, has similarly increased the standard of living for its citizens by adopting market-friendly economic policies.

But human wellbeing involves more than material progress. Even more important are the subjective perceptions of individuals to their social, economic, and political environment. In recent years, social scientists have sought to measure people's overall life satisfaction through subjective surveys. The surveys, which cover such areas as health, social support, freedom, generosity, corruption, and positive and negative affective measures, are used in developing an index of overall life satisfaction. According to the most recent "World Happiness Report," the countries with the highest levels of happiness (satisfaction with life) are: 1) Finland—7.804, 2) Denmark—7.586, 3) Iceland—7.530, and 4) Israel—7.473. The countries with the lowest indices were: 137) Afghanistan—1.859, 136) Lebanon—2.382, 135) Sierra Leone—3.138, and 134) Zimbabwe—3.207.[13]

Despite the significant improvements in living conditions resulting from neoliberal economic policies, globalization has been increasingly challenged in some developed countries, especially the United States. The concern with globalization has various sources, but two of them are especially noteworthy: rising domestic economic inequalities fostered by changes in domestic investment priorities, and mass migration by irregular migrants. Although foreign trade produces absolute gains for nations, not all sectors of society benefit equally. Indeed, globalization has involved significant changes in both developed and developing nations. In developed countries, globalization has shifted economic resources toward the service, technology, and informational sectors and decreased industrial production. In the emerging economies, by contrast, globalization has fostered investment in low-wage assembly plants and small-scale manufacturing. Employment in both countries remains relatively robust, but the shift away from industrial production in some developed nations has resulted in wage declines for the working class. This perceived loss, coupled with the rise of irregular migrants from poor countries, has contributed to a rise of populism and more specifically to increased protectionist economic policies.

Economist Paul Collier argues that the rise in political polarization is not simply the result of economic changes but rather is due to a shift in values. Whereas traditional social democracy was based on a communitarian ethos that nurtured social caring, contemporary political ideologies are rooted in a utilitarian worldview that prioritizes individualism over a shared identity. According to the progressive perspective, the state was now responsible for redistributing resources to "victims" with the greatest needs. The traditional communitarian view of duties based on reciprocity was replaced by an ethic of social paternalism. As a result, the reciprocal obligations of citizens were no longer encouraged.[14] If Collier's analysis is valid, the only way to reduce anxiety, distrust, anger, and polarization is to strengthen communal ties and social cohesion. In effect, if a country is to respond to people suffering from economic dislocations, it must have robust institutions based on social solidarity. In Collier's view, only with a strong shared identity can "far-sighted reciprocity" work.[15]

It is unclear how the concern with the unequal distributional effects of globalization will affect the future of global trade. What is clear, however, is that neoliberal economics have contributed far more to poverty reduction in poor lands than foreign government assistance. Of course, targeted official development assistance can help to reduce poverty but only if it contributes to indigenous economic growth. The major improvements in global welfare since the end of the Cold War have not come from economic transfers from rich countries to poor countries. Rather, the rise in the standard of living throughout the word is the byproduct of economic growth, facilitated by domestic improvements in education, health, infrastructure, and effective domestic institutions.

DEVELOPMENT IN THE NEW MILLENNIUM

When the concept of development first became popular in the aftermath of the Second World War, it was associated almost exclusively with economic growth. The level of development was generally defined in terms of average per capita income. Countries with high average incomes were "developed" and those with low income were "developing." In time, the World Bank found this division simplistic and inaccurate. As a result, it began to categorize countries' development status in terms of four categories: low income, lower middle income, upper middle income, and high income. But since development involves more than income, the United Nations subsequently developed a more inclusive concept, the Human Development Index (HDI), that provided a broader measure of the physical quality of life.

The HDI, a composite index based on life expectancy, education, and per capita income, is an improvement over simpler indices, such as per capita income. Still, the HDI provides only a partial index of overall living conditions, since it does not include data on measures such as human rights, human freedoms, political order, and rule of law. Nevertheless, the HDI is a useful index that provides a quantitative measure over time of the physical quality of life among most of the world's countries. One of the most amazing findings is that, based on the HDI, most of the world's countries have improved their living conditions in the post–Cold War era. For some countries, the changes are truly dramatic. For example, China's HDI coefficient in 1990 was 0.484, but by 2021 it had increased to 0.768. The increase in India's HDI coefficient was only a little less dramatic, rising from 0.434 in 1990 to 0.633 in 2021.[16]

Although per capita income and HDI continue to be used by social scientists and political leaders, in the new millennium social scientists now tend to distinguish economic growth from development. Whereas economic growth refers chiefly to increased economic output that makes possible improved living conditions, development is now viewed as a more wholistic, comprehensive, and multidimensional process. Economist Joseph Stiglitz, for example, says that development is "about transforming societies, improving the lives of the poor, enabling everyone to have a chance at success and access to health care and education."[17]

Although economic growth continues to be viewed as a necessary precondition for holistic development, growth itself does not ensure the availability and equitable distribution of goods and services regarded as necessary for a humane existence. As a result, the United Nations adopted an initiative in 2000 to highlight the need for a more comprehensive approach to development. This initiative, known as the Millennium Development Goals, identified eight society-wide goals that should be pursued by the international community.[18] In 2015, this program was replaced with the adoption of the 2030 Agenda for Sustainable Development, a program designed to foster long-term sustainable development that improves living conditions for people in low-income countries and limits pollution and other harmful byproducts of industrialization.

The fifteen-year program involves seventeen Sustainable Development Goals, covering such issues as zero hunger, quality education, clean energy, clean water, gender equality, and reduced inequalities. The sixteenth goal—peace, justice, and strong institutions—is especially important because of its focus on the development of "effective, accountable, and inclusive institutions at all levels." To a significant degree, the Sustainable Development Goals initiative is rooted in two approaches to society-wide development: community development and sustainable development. The first, which became popular during the Cold War era, involved planned socioeconomic change to improve the quality of life for community members. Whereas earlier development had occurred without plans or guidance, the new development initiatives assumed that planned and coordination actions could bring about superior beneficial outcomes compared to those advanced by private groups. Sustainable development is a more recent initiative begun largely in response to the realization that the world's resources are limited, that industrialization has imposed costs on the environment, and that collective action is necessary in addressing climate change.

Although the shift in focus from economic growth to comprehensive social and economic development is laudable, the focus on sustainable development continues to neglect one important element of community life—namely, political institutions. While many poor countries continue to suffer from inadequate living conditions, the barriers to a better life are not simply social and economic. Political underdevelopment is widespread in low- and middle-income countries, and the weakness of political institutions remains a fundamental impediment to progress. For example, Haiti remains impoverished not simply because of social and economic problems but because its political community is weak and fragile. Its society is deeply fractured, the central government has little authority, and crime and corruption are rampant. Until a strong, beneficent state is established, the people of Haiti will continue to suffer from human rights abuses and poverty.

Regrettably, social scientists have not given sufficient attention to the problem of political decay and political underdevelopment. It has been easier to assume that economic progress would inevitably result in communal solidarity. But political development is not an inevitable byproduct of economic growth. Indeed, modernization has often increased expectations without establishing strong social bonds within society. The world is filled with deeply divided states with weak governments. If human rights are to be protected and sustainable development is to be pursued, a capable state is necessary. Poverty and hunger remain major problems in the world, but if these conditions are to be remedied, a stable, strong state is indispensable.

The problem of an imbalance between economic and political development was examined more than fifty years ago by the noted political scientist Samuel Huntington. In his classic *Political Order in Changing Societies*, he argues that the development of political community is the necessary precondition for a humane society. But a political community is not a natural byproduct of social and economic life; it is a distinct human creation. A primary task in building a political community is to establish order by creating organizations. "Organization is the road to political power," he writes, "but it is also the foundation of political stability and thus the precondition of political liberty."[19] For Huntington, institutions are indispensable in creating communal solidarity since they provide the rules and norms that structure human behavior.

As noted earlier, however, foreign powers and external organizations can contribute little to nation building. While foreign governments can provide financial and administrative assistance, the task of fostering communal solidarity is one that only residents can carry out successfully. Indeed, outsiders can unwittingly undermine fragile relationships and undermine existing order. States considering foreign intervention should heed the Hippocratic oath: "do no harm."

THE CHRISTIAN FAITH AND DEVELOPMENT

What contributions can Christians make to the quest for development? As I noted earlier, during the Cold War era, the focus on development was almost exclusively on growth, since increased economic output was viewed as the essential precondition not only for a prosperous society but also for poverty reduction. By the beginning of the new millennium, most developing countries had improved their living conditions considerably and the new challenge was no longer simply growth but rather how to foster societies that were more sustainable, equitable, and humane.

The Christian faith involves ideas and principles that can contribute to both economic growth and community development. Since growth is a material, technical endeavor, Christian teachings provide moral teachings that can inspire and guide the process of job creation and economic growth. Similarly, the Christian faith can provide important insights and principles to the task of building sustainable communities that foster human flourishing.

Christianity and Economic Growth

Economic growth is not an automatic byproduct of social and political life. Rather, it occurs when people apply their reason, initiative, frugality, disciplined work ethic, and integrity to the process of making and distributing goods and services. Productive enterprise can only occur when justice, political order, and social trust are prevalent in society.

Of the Christian principles described in chapter 2, the notions of *personal responsibility* and *stewardship* are especially appropriate to the notion of economic enterprise. While each person is entitled to dignity and respect, individuals bear responsibility for their own spiritual and material wellbeing. As noted earlier, the Christian faith involves a person's personal response to God's grace in Christ. Faith in Christ is not inherited; rather, it involves a personal acceptance of God's love. But this acceptance of divine resources does not lead to passivity but to an ethic of responsibility and stewardship. Although Protestants believe that God's grace is a gift, they also stress the importance of developing and using human gifts and abilities as a manifestation of godly stewardship. And because work is regarded as a human expression of faith, Protestant societies have emphasized the virtues of diligence, frugality, honesty, promise keeping, and faithful service in economic enterprise. These attitudes and dispositions, which are common in northern Europe, are responsible for the prevalence of capitalist values.

A second principle of Christian social ethics relevant to growth is *participation*. As discussed earlier in chapter 2, participation means that people must be involved in the life of communities in which they live, seeking to advance their own welfare but also the welfare of other community members. In his encyclical *Laborem Exercens* (*On Human Work*), Pope John Paul II argues that work is an essential feature of a person. "Work," he writes, "is one of the characteristics that distinguish man from the rest of creatures." Work is important because it provides humans with the capacity to fulfill the creation mandate, which he defines as follows: "Man is the image of God partly through the mandate received from his Creator to subdue, to dominate the earth. In carrying out this mandate, man, every human being, reflects the very action of the Creator of the universe."[20] The importance of work as an essential part of human flourishing was developed further by a group of lay Catholic leaders three years later. In their study of Catholic social teaching and the US economy titled *Toward the Future*, they argue for the imperative economic participation. They write that, "Creation is not finished," and then declare: "Humans become co-creators through discovery and invention, following the clues left by God."[21]

Participation in the economic and social life of a nation is both a right and a moral responsibility. It is a right because the inherent worth of a person depends in part on work. And it is a responsibility because people need to care for their own material wellbeing as well as the welfare of others. Scripture similarly emphasizes the responsibility to be stewards of the gifts and talents that God has entrusted to each person. Because believers are called to be co-creators with God, they have a responsibility to continue the divine process of creation.

Christian churches have an important role in teaching and modeling moral behavior—or what might be termed "culture care." As noted earlier, Michael Novak argues that moral values, habits, traditions, and human dispositions are the basis for a society's moral-cultural system that sustains a society's institutions.[22] One of the reasons for the early economic success of northern European nations was that Protestant Christianity encouraged personal responsibility and made work an expression of religious faithfulness. To this day, northern European countries have higher levels of social trust and less corruption than southern European nations.[23] The different impact of the Catholic and Protestant faiths has been historically evident in the different values that Spanish conquerors brought to Central and South America and those brought to North America by the Protestant pilgrims. The different moral-cultural traditions have had a profound effect on the subsequent social and economic development of countries in North and South America.

Notwithstanding the different value systems of Catholics and Protestants, both faiths share a common concern with improving living conditions and meeting basic human needs. While both Catholic and Protestant charities have emphasized health care and education, their approaches and strategies to development differ. For example, the approach of Roman Catholics emphasizes a more hierarchical and institutional orientation, while the Protestant approach emphasizes decentralization and individualism. Not surprisingly, the Protestant approach has been more supportive of free enterprise and democratic governance. In addition, as Robert Woodberry and Timothy Shah have shown, Protestantism played a critical role in the rise and expansion of civil society. This development took place because Protestants maintained a decentralized church structure and emphasized dispersed authority that encouraged pluralism. In time, the emphasis on individual responsibility and personal freedom facilitated the development of mediating institutions (e.g., unions, professional associations, nongovernmental organizations) between government and society.[24]

In his pioneering study on the role of Protestant missionaries, Woodberry shows that missionaries played a critical role in disseminating concepts and ideas that are foundational to economic growth. These included equality, human sin, the inherent dignity of persons, personal accountability, and distrust of authority.[25] Such ideas have nurtured individual creativity and responsibility and stimulated individual enterprise. While different circumstances influenced how such ideas were expressed and applied in different societies, it is evident that they affected people's religious views and contributed to a more modern political and social perspectives. It is important to stress, however, that missionary activity was not motivated chiefly by humanitarian needs. Rather, missionaries traveled to distant lands to share the gospel of Christ, and in carrying out their evangelistic work, they concurrently built schools, clinics, and met human needs as a manifestation of faith.

Christians are not unaware of the dangers posed by a relentless pursuit of economic growth. From a moral perspective, economic development is important because it can improve the basic conditions of life. But when greater personal wealth is the sole aim of development, the resulting materialist values can impair human dignity and compromise authentic faith. Development is important, but it is not the most important goal in building humane nation-states. The aim of authentic development is to create the communal preconditions where persons can flourish by developing and using their God-given gifts and abilities. The Church can contribute to this task by teaching and modeling values and behaviors that are consistent with authentic, long-term development.

Christian Principles and Community Development

Of the Christian principles and teachings that I described in chapter 2, the most relevant to sustainable community development are human dignity (personalism), the common good, solidarity, caring for the poor, and participation.

Human dignity: Because of God's love for each human being, it is important that each person be able to flourish and use the gifts and abilities that they are endowed with at birth. Fundamentally, the aim of economic life is to affirm human dignity. From a Christian perspective, the purpose of development is not to increase wealth but to enhance the quality of life. Although every person is born with a soul, the ability of a person to flourish will depend on the material, educational, and spiritual resources available within society. Development is therefore important insofar as it enables people to develop and use their inherent gifts and abilities. Finally, while development is generally focused on the material improvement of society, there can be no collective or societal progress without individual empowerment. The capacity of individuals to initiate, create, and distribute goods and services within communities provides the foundation for society-wide economic growth.

Common good: Since humans are social creatures, their identity is found not as isolated individuals but in association with other community members. The common good of a community requires that each community member's basic and material needs should be met as much as possible through cooperation with others. If the principle of common good is to be advanced, radical disparities in power and income must be reduced and the welfare of the poor must be addressed.

Solidarity: This principle means that members of society must pursue fraternal friendship and civic caring within society. Solidarity demands that individuals must treat community members as neighbors. Communal solidarity is an expression of Christ's love for the world.

Caring for the poor: Scripture declares that caring for those in need is an expression of faith. As noted earlier, because God's love is universal, ensuring that all humans have the material and social resources to live a dignified life is essential to individual flourishing and society's common good. Indeed, the US Catholic Bishops declared in a pastoral letter on economic life that the poor have the single most urgent claim on society.[26]

Finally, *participation* is also relevant to the pursuit of sustainable community development. In the previous section, I highlighted the principle of participation because of its important role in fostering an ethic of responsibility toward work. But participation is also vital in advancing the common good and fostering strong communal bonds.

How are such principles to be applied in fostering community development? First, the church should emphasize moral education not only to parishioners but also to all of society. It is not the task of the church to tell a mayor, legislator, or government official what actions to take. Rather, the task is to highlight moral principles and to illuminate how they can help guide and structure public policies. Second, the church should respond to human needs. Churches, like charitable nongovernmental organizations, can distribute food and resources to people in need, especially in the aftermath of natural disasters. The aim of such relief should be to restore the health of the afflicted community as quickly as possible. Third, the church can model behaviors that strengthen groups, associations, and community life. Since the church is a social organization, it can illuminate values and attributes that foster communal solidarity.

In conclusion, the economic, social, and political development of societies is important in that it increases the physical quality of life and expands the possibilities for human flourishing. For the Christian, ensuring human dignity remains a fundamental value of any political or economic initiative that seeks to improve the standard of living. Christians have historically contributed to the development process by nurturing such values as fidelity, trust, thrift, and individual accountability. In modeling such behaviors, Christians have played an important role in strengthening social capital and fostering community development. The latter task has been especially important in the developing world, where believers have built clinics, schools, and other institutions. Such institutions, including individual churches, are important because they can foster human cooperation and thereby strengthen a community's social solidarity. Since more than a billion people continue to suffer from disease, crime, poverty, and other impediments to a humane life, the task of development remains unfinished. Although fostering economic growth, strengthening communities, and relieving suffering remain important concerns, what the world needs most of all is an ethic of caring, manifested by the Good Samaritan who treated a stranger as a neighbor.

NOTES

1. Paul Collier, *The Bottom Billion: Why the Poorest Countries Are Failing and What Can Be Done About It* (New York: Oxford University Press, 2008), 38–52.
2. "World Happiness Report 2023," https://worldhappiness.report (August 6, 2024). One statistical organization, the Statista Research Department, reported the following: During a survey in 2022, the level of happiness with the topmost population in Cuba in a scale from 0 to 10 (being 0 not happy at all and 10 very happy) was for 20 percent with only 1, followed by the citizens not feeling happy at all with a 0 level with a 13 percent.
3. "The Legatum Prosperity Index 2023," www.prosperity.com (August 6, 2024).

4. See, for example, Daron Acemoglu and James A. Robinson, *Why Nations Fail: The Origins of Power, Prosperity, and Poverty* (New York: Crown Business, 2012).

5. See, for example, David S. Landes, *The Wealth and Poverty of Nations: Why Some Are so Rich and Some so Poor* (New York: W. W. Norton, 1999).

6. See, for example, Jagdish Bhagwati and Arvind Panagariya, *Why Growth Matters: How Economic Growth in India Reduced Poverty and the Lessons for other Developing Countries* (New York: PublicAffairs, 2013).

7. Michael Novak, *The Spirit of Democratic Capitalism* (New York: Simon & Schuster, 1982).

8. Amy Sherman, *The Soul of Development: Biblical Christianity and Economic Transformation in Guatemala* (New York: Oxford University Press, 1997).

9. Independent Commission on International Development, *North-South: A Programme for Survival* (Cambridge: MIT Press, 1981).

10. The South's proposed reforms, which were not supported by the major Western economies, had little impact. The major reason was that the South had become deeply divided among its members in the 1980s. The fracturing of the South was due to rising inequalities among its members, due partly to rapid wealth that accrued to the oil cartel after raising petroleum prices and the growing prosperity of some emerging economies after they had adopted market-friendly policies.

11. For a more expansive exposition of this perspective, see Petersen Institute for International Economics, "What Is 'the Washington Consensus'?" www.piie.com/blogs/realtime-economic-issues-watch/what-washington-consensus (August 6, 2024).

12. Thomas L. Friedman, *The Lexus and the Olive Tree: Understanding Globalization* (New York: Anchor Books, 2000), 9.

13. "World Happiness Report 2023."

14. Paul Collier, *The Future of Capitalism: Facing the New Anxieties* (New York: HarperCollins, 2018).

15. Collier, *The Future of Capitalism*, 213.

16. UN Development Programme, "Human Development Index (HDI)," 2023, https://hdr.undp.org/data-center/human-development-index#/indicies/HDI (August 6, 2024).

17. Joseph E. Stiglitz, *Globalization and Its Discontents* (New York: W. W. Norton, 2002), 252.

18. These goals included the eradication of extreme poverty, reducing child mortality, combating such diseases as HIV/AIDS and malaria, improving maternal health, and fostering gender equality.

19. Samuel P. Huntington, *Political Order in Changing Societies* (New Haven: Yale University Press, 1968), 461.

20. Pope John Paul II, *On Human Work* (The Vatican, 1981), www.vatican.va/content/john-paul-ii/en/encyclicals/documents/hf_jp-ii_enc_14091981_laborem-exercens.html (August 6, 2024).

21. Lay Commission on Catholic Social Teaching and the U.S. Economy, *Toward the Future: Catholic Social Teaching and the U.S. Economy: A Lay Letter* (New York: Lay Commission on Catholic Social Teaching and the U.S. Economy, 1984).

22. Novak, *The Spirit of Democratic Capitalism.*

23. Esteban Ortiz-Ospina and Max Roser, "Trust," OurWorldInData, https://ourworldindata.org/trust (August 6, 2024).

24. Robert D. Woodberry and Timothy S. Shah, "Christianity and Democracy: The Pioneering Protestants," *Journal of Democracy* 13 (April 2004): 50.

25. Robert D. Woodberry, "The Missionary Roots of Liberal Democracy," *American Political Science Review* 106, no. 2 (2012): 244–74.

26. US Conference of Catholic Bishops, *Economic Justice for All: Pastoral Letter on Catholic Social Teaching and the U.S. Economy*, 1986, www.usccb.org/upload/economic_justice_for_all.pdf (August 6, 2024).

Chapter 7

The Christian Faith and Climate Change

The environmental challenge of climate change, like the issues of migration and development, is global in nature. But it differs from them in that any success in addressing climate will demand much greater cooperation and collaboration among states. Since the earth's atmosphere has no specified boundaries, success in addressing climate change will require cooperation among states, especially the rich countries that generate a disproportionate amount of pollution.

Fundamentally, the problem posed by the earth's changing climate is that the earth's atmosphere is a collective good, or what social scientists call a *public good*.[1] Examples of such goods include peace, clean air, financial stability, and political order, and may be national or global in scope. The earth's atmosphere is a global public good because it extends across territorial borders. To a significant extent, the earth can be viewed as a global commons where the soil, atmosphere, and water are shared resources. In caring for these goods, it is important that states work collaboratively to prevent the misuse or overuse of the earth's common resources.

Who provides for public goods? Within nation-states, governments are responsible for protecting such public goods as clean air, airline safety, potable water, and automobile safety. Governments can do so because they have the authority to make and enforce laws. The international community, by contrast, has no central authority to ensure compliance. As a result, states must cooperate to address global concerns. They do so by enacting treaties and conventions to foster collective actions to protect and care for the earth. One of the most significant international initiatives on the environment is the 1992 UN Conference on Environment and Development in Rio de Janeiro, Brazil. Billed as "the last chance to save the planet," the 1992 summit adopted the UN Framework Convention on Climate Change (known as the

Climate Treaty), which serves as the basic international treaty for addressing greenhouse gas emissions and their impact on the earth's climate.

Since the United Nations does not have the authority to enforce multilateral treaties, caring for the earth is largely up to each member-state, working individually and collaboratively. But in seeking to protect the world's environment, the United Nation's decentralized, voluntary structure suffers from weak governance and the free-rider problem. This problem arises because some states may be tempted to let others bear the costs while still benefiting from any improvements arising from collective action. This condition emerges because a public good is available to everyone, regardless of who contributes to it. Thus, since there is no legal accountability in global society for fulfilling treaty commitments, states may be tempted to let others bear the costs of collective action.

This chapter has four parts. First, I examine the nature of the problem posed by global warming. Second, I describe how states, and especially the United States, have sought to address the challenge of climate change. Third, I examine major international initiatives to address climate change, focusing on the role of the United Nations as the primary international organization. Finally, I address the role of the Christian faith with regards to climate change. I describe and assess some major church statements about creation care and the challenge of global warming.

THE NATURE OF THE PROBLEM

The earth's temperature is determined principally by the balance between energy received from the sun and the energy radiated back to space. Water vapors and human-made gases (chiefly carbon dioxide), however, can impair this balance by trapping solar radiation, much like the glass of a flower or vegetable greenhouse. The "greenhouse effect" thus occurs because vapors and gases allow more of the sun's heat to be absorbed by the earth than is released back into space. Although water vapor, methane, and other gases contribute to greenhouse gas emissions, the major source is carbon dioxide, resulting from the burning of fossil fuels (coal, oil, natural gas). According to the Environmental Protection Agency, the principal sources of US greenhouse gas emissions in 2021 were transportation—28 percent, electric power—25 percent, industry—23 percent, commercial and residential—13 percent, and agriculture—10 percent.[2] For the world, the source of global emissions is slightly different: agriculture and land use—24 percent, electricity and heat production—25 percent, industry—21 percent, and transportation 14 percent.[3] In his book *How to Avoid a Climate Disaster*, Bill Gates, the founder of Microsoft, describes the principal sources of greenhouse gas emissions from things people do. He describes the major human activities as: "making things" (such as cement, steel, plastic)—31 percent, "plugging in" (electricity)—27 percent, "growing things" (plants, animals)—19 percent, "getting around" (planes, trucks, cargo ships)—16 percent, and "keeping warm and cool" (heating, cooling, refrigeration)—7 percent.[4]

Since economic development requires energy, and since fossil fuels are the chief energy source, the world has experienced a persistent and inexorable growth in greenhouse emissions in recent decades. This means that if the growth in greenhouse emissions is to be contained or reduced, the burning of fossil fuels will also have to be reduced significantly. If economic growth is not to be compromised, however, alternative energy sources must be developed along with innovations that increase the efficient use of energy.

Over the past centuries, the earth's climate has shown significant natural variability. Nonetheless, the global average temperature in recent years has increased at a rate greater than that which natural variability can explain. Indeed, according to many scientists, the rise in carbon dioxide and other greenhouse gases is responsible for most climate warming in the past fifty years. Since modern economic development involves an increased demand for energy, and since the principal global source of energy has been the burning of fossil fuels, most scientists assume that global warming is chiefly due to human actions.

Climate change became a global concern in the latter part of the twentieth century. In 1988, the United Nations established the UN Intergovernmental Panel on Climate Change (IPCC), a group of hundreds of the world's leading climate scientists who work collectively to issue periodic assessment reports about the climate. The group does not carry out original research; rather, it reviews relevant scientific studies on global weather and then issues a comprehensive assessment on the latest scientific findings. In its first report, issued in 1990, the IPCC expressed concerns about the possible role of human activity on the earth's climate. The second report in 1996 was more significant since it declared that continued reliance on fossil fuels would inevitably increase the earth's temperature. Whereas the world's temperature had risen by about 1.8 degrees Fahrenheit in the twentieth century, the continued rise in carbon dioxide would result in an increase of three to eight degrees Fahrenheit in the twenty-first century. The most recent IPCC report (the sixth, issued in 2023) declared that it was issuing its "the final warning" on global warming before damage to the climate became irreversible. Given the threat posed by continued greenhouse gas emissions, scientists declared that it is essential that global warming be kept at or below an increase of 1.5 degrees Celsius (2.7 degrees Fahrenheit) over pre-industrial (1750) levels.[5]

What are the likely effects of continued global warming? Although warming could bring about some beneficial developments, such as an increase in agricultural land in the Northern Hemisphere, environmental scientists have warned that climate change could also bring about significant, long-term harm. Harmful effects include a rising global surface temperature, storms and floods, drought, and loss of biodiversity. Additionally, a rise in the sea level due to thermal expansion could result in the flooding of coastal lowlands and the destruction of numerous tropical islands. According to the United Nations, "climate change is the biggest health threat facing humanity."[6] Most significantly, climate change poses a disproportionate threat to poor societies who have limited resources to adapt to significant environmental changes. Because climate change poses significant harm to poor countries, this issue is a major ethical concern.

In recent years, the world has experienced significant environmental threats from climate change. These weather-related harms include the loss of sea ice, the melting of glaciers, increased drought, intense heat waves (Europe in 2023), and heat-induced wildfires (especially in Greece and Canada, in 2023). Many observers believe that weather has contributed to such recent environmental disasters.

In sum, the key issue on climate change is not whether there is global warming but what to do about it. Because generating energy is a basic requirement of modern economic life, the challenge is how to do so efficiently while protecting the global environment. Although the shift to renewable energy is desirable, fossil fuels will continue, in the foreseeable future, to play an important role in generating energy.

Responding to the problem of global warming will necessarily involve personal and institutional strategies. At the individual level, persons concerned with climate change will adopt behaviors that reduce their carbon footprint. The reduction in carbon usage can be achieved through such actions as limiting consumption, traveling less, using less plastic, thermostat adjustments at home, relying on energy-efficient products, and increased use of public transportation. In effect, the personal strategy will seek to simplify life by using fewer products and less energy.

The institutional strategies of local organizations, national governments, and intergovernmental organizations are far more difficult and complex than those facing individuals. Since the making of public policies is a probabilistic enterprise, estimating the short-term and long-term results can be elusive. For example, anticipating the costs and benefits of relying on solar or nuclear power is difficult and can be only estimated. Moreover, deciding which actions are most effective and efficient in advancing the goal of green energy is similarly complex and difficult.

Economist Bjorn Lomborg has suggested that if we want to make the world a better place, we should not be fixated on a single problem like climate change. Instead, we should explore alternative problems and determine which policies might use scarce economic resources most effectively. When Lomborg assembled a team of social scientists to identify some of the most effective and efficient ways of improving the human condition, the group concluded that climate change was not a top priority. Instead, the group identified increasing economic growth through freer trade, ensuring universal access to contraception, expanding immunization, and reducing child malnutrition as more compelling initiatives.[7]

The moral trade-offs for a poor, developing nation are likely to be far different than those for a modern industrial state. For example, the challenge in African countries weighing the threat of climate change against health threats from deadly communicable diseases poses difficult moral issues. Why should a low-income state use scarce resources to contain fossil fuel use when it could devote those resources to address the immediate threat of a deadly disease like malaria or limited clean water? Clearly, in addressing climate change, it is important to incorporate competing societal needs and realize that trade-offs among competing goods is necessary in prudent policymaking.

DOMESTIC (CHIEFLY US) RESPONSES TO CLIMATE CHANGE

In view of the growing global concern over climate change, countries, provinces, and cities have undertaken a variety of initiatives to encourage clean energy and reduce reliance on carbon. Such initiatives involve regulations that increase energy efficiency, stimulate technological innovation, and increase reliance on renewable energy sources. Industrial states are also shifting automobile and truck production from combustion engines to electric motors. In my domestic and foreign travels in recent years, I have seen increased evidence of alternative energy production. For example, while driving in the French province of Burgundy, I was surprised by the widespread presence of wind turbines throughout the countryside. And in the United States solar panel farms have become more commonplace, especially in southern states like California, Arizona, and New Mexico.

Technically, sustainable development requires the development of new technologies that reduce pollution, conserve energy, and foster alternative energy sources. Developed nations, especially in Europe and North America, have made significant progress in generating energy more efficiently and in expanding the use of renewables. Still, much more needs to be done.

In seeking to reduce greenhouse emissions, governments have pursued a variety of strategies. Four common initiatives are as follows:

1. *Taxing fossil fuels:* The goal of such a policy is to increase the cost of oil and coal and thereby curb their use. This is the mostly widely used

approach, and it is especially practiced in European countries, who rely heavily on the taxing of carbon.
2. *Cap and trade:* Under such a program, governments allocate or sell pollution permits to companies and other entities to limit emissions to a specific limit. Such permits then allow companies that emit less than their allowance to sell the remaining rights to companies that have exceeded their emissions limit.
3. *Clean energy:* Public policies are established to encourage companies to generate a defined percentage of their electricity from noncarbon sources.
4. *Investment in technology:* Tax incentives are used to encourage business investments in clean energy and foster desirable energy practices, while government funds are allocated to support research in alternative energy sources.

Although there is widespread support for initiatives to protect the environment, public support varies among countries. According to a 2022 Pew Research Center survey, majorities who viewed climate change as "a major threat" in developed countries were: Greece—86 percent, Japan—82 percent, France—81 percent, Netherlands—77 percent, the United Kingdom—75 percent, and the United States—54 percent.[8] The lower level of American concern with climate change is due to the skepticism about the sources of global warming and the economic costs involved in adopting green energy. A 2023 Pew Research Center survey found that the American public regarded climate change as a less important issue than the economy, health care, crime, and immigration.[9] This lukewarm support may explain why developing national policies on curbing greenhouse emissions has been a major domestic political challenge in the United States.

Besides limited public support, the challenge of addressing climate change faces an additional difficulty. Since economic growth requires increasing levels of energy, the challenge for countries is how to generate increasing energy while curbing greenhouse gas emissions. Alternative energy sources (wind, solar, hydro), however, are unlikely to provide the energy required in industrial economies. As a result, fossil fuels will continue to be an important energy source in the future.[10] Nuclear power could of course help meet energy needs, but governments have, with few exceptions, been reluctant to increase reliance on such an energy source given the risks associated with radiation fallout from plant disasters. After the Fukushima disaster in 2011, Germany decided to phase out its existing nuclear plants. Currently, only France gets most of its electricity (around 70 percent) from nuclear power plants. By contrast, nuclear plants in the United States generate roughly 20 percent of the nation's electricity.

INTERNATIONAL RESPONSES TO CLIMATE CHANGE

In 1992, world leaders gathered in Rio de Janeiro, Brazil, to address the challenge of economic development and the protection of the earth's environment. At this global summit, the world's leaders adopted two treaties: one on climate and another on biodiversity. The climate treaty did not call for any specific actions but established a framework to address the impact of pollution on climate. As a result, world leaders gathered in Kyoto, Japan, in December 1997 and adopted an addendum to the treaty. The addendum or protocol called on industrial countries to reduce their greenhouse emissions by about 5 percent below their 1990 level by 2012. The effort to establish binding reductions in greenhouse emissions proved especially difficult, however, since the United States and China, the two largest emitters of carbon dioxide, refused to be a part of the agreement. In the end, the Kyoto initiative contributed little to the world's reduction of greenhouse emissions.

Since the Kyoto agreement was ending in 2012, climate leaders sought to develop a new approach to climate change—one that involved both developed and developing nations. Accordingly, the United Nations sponsored a global conference in Copenhagen in December 2009 to devise a new framework for addressing climate change. Although the conference sought to establish a regulatory system involving binding commitments, the delegates were able to achieve only nonbinding goals, including constraining carbon usage and assisting poor nations with sustainable development.

In 2015, global leaders adopted the Paris Agreement—an accord that called on nations to limit the rise in the world's average temperature in the current century to less than 2 degrees Celsius. Since the earth had already warmed by about 1.2 degrees Celsius, the new accord presents a daunting challenge.[11] A second feature of the Paris Agreement is that it places the responsibility of curbing fossil fuel use on each state. Since the carbon-reducing commitments are made individually and unilaterally by each country, there are no binding obligations to the international community.

Since global warming is a "public goods" problem, the challenge of how to reduce greenhouse emissions among sovereign nation-states remains unchanged—namely, how to develop realistic limits on the use of fossil fuels. The international community has hosted many climate conferences and developed several conventions to highlight the problem of global warming.[12] To date, however, the world has been unable to agree on binding curbs on greenhouse emissions.

Anatol Lieven argues that expecting the international community to bring about necessary changes in energy generation to contain climate change is unrealistic. In his view, the only effective way for states to undertake the costly and difficult reductions in fossil fuel use is through the policies of sovereign states. He writes: "The gulf between declarations of global responsibility and inability to mobilize national action has lain at the heart of the failure adequately to address the danger of climate change." As a result, he argues that the problem needs to be reframed in "nationalist" terms, involving "the defense of nation states, their interests, and their future survival."[13]

Even though European and North American countries have been reducing their gas emissions, total global emissions have continued to rise. Despite efforts to curb gas emissions, the Global Carbon Project estimates that global emissions from fossil fuels will rise in 2023 by 1.1 percent, with much of this increased attributed to the burning of oil and coal by China and India. The good news, however, is that gas emissions annual growth has continued to decline. According to one estimate, the carbon dioxide emissions growth for all countries declined from 2.6 percent in the 2003–2012 decade to 0.5 percent in the past decade, while the rate of growth for developing nations (non–Organisation for Economic Co-operation and Development) declined during the same period from 3.3 percent to 1.5 percent.[14]

In his book *What's Wrong with Climate Politics and How to Fix It*, environmentalist Paul Harris claims that the fundamental impediment to curbing greenhouse emissions is the decentralized global order—or what he terms the "cancer of Westphalia." To overcome the limitations of state sovereignty, he argues that climate politics should become more focused on the welfare and rights of people, especially the victims of climate change. In other words, climate politics should direct attention "away from state-centric responses to the problem toward a globalization of climate justice—from thinking most in terms of nations' rights toward thinking and acting much more in terms of human rights."[15] Although the national interests of states continue to dominate the politics of climate change, a shift away from our existing global order is unlikely.

THE CHRISTIAN FAITH AND CLIMATE CHANGE

How can Christians contribute to the ongoing challenge of global warming? What distinctive insights can the church provide to the public policy debate about sustainable development and especially to the needs of poor societies? Although there is widespread consensus about the rising temperature of the earth, there is less agreement about how individuals and nations should respond to the challenge of reducing gas emissions.

Church Declarations

Given the complexity of how to address the challenges of climate change, it is not surprising that churches have emphasized general principles about human dignity, creation care, and sustainable development but have been reticent to offer specific public policy advice. In 2022, for example, the House of Bishops of The Episcopal Church issued a general statement of concern about the climate, one that is similar in many respects with other denominational statements. The Episcopal Church declaration states: "As people of faith, we are not without hope, but the sustainability of God's creation demands our action. Confronting climate change and environmental degradation has never been more urgent. As members of The Episcopal Church, we are committed in baptism to resist evil, seek God's will, treat all people with dignity, and strive for justice and peace. Living into these promises we must face the climate crisis for the sake of love of God and neighbor."[16]

In 2022, the National Association of Evangelicals, an association of most Evangelical denominations in the United States, issued a report on climate change. Titled "Loving the Least of These," the document provides a biblical perspective on the environment, a description of the harmful effects of climate change, and how weather changes are likely to impact the poor. The report, based on an earlier version issued in 2011, declares that protecting the environment is a biblical mandate. It states: "We worship God by caring for creation. . . . As Christians, we know that God loves his world and the people he created. He placed us in a special role as caretakers of this earth. We are to encourage the fruitfulness of all God's creatures and promote the flourishing of humanity."[17] To confront climate change, the National Association of Evangelicals report calls for a reduction in carbon use. The report states: "We need to severely cut greenhouse gas emissions, such as carbon dioxide and methane, and switch to non-fossil fuel energy sources. We also know that such a clean energy transition needs to be done in a just way." The report does not explain, however, how this should be done or what a "just way" would entail. A 2022 Pew Research Center survey found that, among religious groups, White Evangelicals are the group least likely to regard climate change as a problem.[18]

The Southern Baptist Convention, the largest Protestant denomination in the United States, has taken a cautious approach to climate change. Because the denomination has no central governing authority, responsibility to address issues like the environment are largely determined by local churches. And since Southern Baptists have divergent views on the nature and causes of global warming, church leaders have been reticent to make declarations about global warming. In 2008, a group of more progressive leaders issued "A Southern Baptist Declaration on the Environment and Climate Change," charging that church leaders had been too timid in confronting the harms of greenhouse emissions.[19] But as of 2023, Southern Baptists have continued to downplay the dangers of climate change.

A noteworthy Protestant document on climate change is the report of the Evangelical Lutheran Church of America, issued in April 2023. An initial version of the document was completed and distributed to parishioners in 2022, and after incorporating their suggestions, the final version was distributed to congregations. Titled "The Earth's Climate Crisis," the social message declares that climate change poses "grave dangers to present and future generations." As a result, the report states that the climate crisis presents the church with a *kairos moment*—a critical time "when God is leading us into decisive action."[20] The church's message is that Christians have a duty to be "responsible caretakers of God's creation." While the report cautions that the church should not take part in partisan politics, it encourages individuals to be involved on this issue. The report declares: "Members of our church have a moral obligation to be engaged in setting the direction of our country as we live out our vocation to care for God's creation." The report concludes with specific suggestions, including the need to affirm the scientific evidence that human activity is a source of global warming, encourage stakeholders to develop climate change solutions, foster a shift from fossil fuels to clean energy, assist those "who bear the least responsibility for greenhouse gas emissions but experience disproportionately its costly impacts," and increase incentives for carbon sequestration.

In 2017, the national synod of the United Church of Christ adopted a climate change resolution titled "The Earth Is the Lord's, Not Ours to Wreck: Imperatives for a New Moral Era."[21] The resolution identified three moral imperatives: first, clergy were encouraged to preach on climate change; second, individuals were encouraged to model the changes they desired through personal and communal actions[22]; and third, the church was tasked with speaking "the truth" about climate change. The resolution states: "Let our communities of faith be bold and courageous as we address one of the greatest moral challenges that the world has ever faced."[23]

Other Protestant denominations have also sought to influence the behaviors of their church members. The Anglican Church in England, for example, has encouraged concerns on climate and environmental protection through its "Environment Programme," which disseminates information and suggestions that can contribute to the goal of "net Zero Carbon by 2030." Churches have also tried to influence not only government initiatives but also the behavior of corporations. Some churches have called for divestment from fossil fuel companies. In 2022, for example, the Presbyterian Church (in the United States), decided to divest from five petroleum companies because of a perceived failure to curb carbon emissions. The World Council of Churches—an association of some 350 Christian denominations representing about five hundred million believers—has similarly called for the divestment from fossil fuel companies.

The Catholic Church has also sought to curb greenhouse emissions by calling on its members to seriously consider the destructive impact of fossil fuels. In 2015, Pope Francis issued an encyclical *Laudato Si* (Praise Be to You) to guide the church members' views on climate change and environmental protection. The document, whose subtitle is "On Care for Our Common Home," offers a critique of consumerism, materialism, irresponsible development, and environmental degradation. It also highlights the need to confront climate change. Rather than offering specific guidance on climate change, however, the encyclical critiques modern economic development. According to Pope Francis, economic modernity has brought about harmful results, including pollution, loss of clean water, global warming, and a loss of biodiversity. "Never have we so hurt and mistreated our common home," he writes, "as we have in the last two hundred years."[24]

Although it is important to promote prudent, sustainable economic growth, the pope's broad critique of modern economic development is unlikely to contribute to solving the challenge of climate change. To begin with, modern science and economic growth has resulted in a reduction of poverty, an increase in longevity, and improved living conditions for the vast majority of the earth's people. In critiquing the encyclical, R. R. Reno, the editor of *First Things*, thinks that the document is unnecessarily anti-scientific and anti-progressive. Reno writes: "To be modern is to believe that, for all our flaws, Western societies are more democratic, more egalitarian, and more inclusive than any in history. This is not the Pope's view. The West is rapacious." To be sure, modernity has brought about unintended harmful byproducts. The challenge is to accept the benefits of modern science and technology while reducing or eliminating its destructive consequences. Reno concludes: "Like the prophet Ezekiel, Pope Francis sees perversion and decadence in a global system dominated by those who consume and destroy. The only answer is repentance, 'deep change' and a 'bold cultural revolution.'"[25]

The Christian Century, the leading magazine for Mainline Protestant denominations, has compiled articles relevant to climate change to assist churches and their members in morally addressing the challenges posed by global warming. The 2023 compilation, titled "A Guide for Personal Reflection and Group Discussion,"[26] includes a variety of articles dealing with different theological and social perspectives of the problem. The essays focus chiefly on defining climate challenges posed to individuals and local communities, and avoids the more contentious issues posed by governmental policies. One of the articles provides ideas for congregations and includes such suggestions as installing solar panels, using lightbulbs that are energy-efficient, preaching on creation care, and starting a study group on eco-theology. One of the most critical articles is "Climate Change Is a Symptom" by Ragan Sutterfield, an Episcopalian priest. Sutterfield argues that the problem of climate change is a byproduct of the "systemic pathology of industrial civilization." He writes: "We need reconciliation with the whole, not just a solution for the identified patient. . . . Solar panels on every church rooftop will not be the healing we need." Thus, if Christians are to confront climate change, they need to cultivate a radically different lifestyle that reduces consumption and increases simplicity.

Have Christian churches helped to address the problem of climate change? Based on a review of recent church studies and declarations, church actions have made several contributions to the climate policy debate.

First, church statements and teachings have emphasized the importance of environmental protection. Because Christians view the stewardship of the earth as a moral responsibility, their belief reinforces the importance of addressing global warming as a vital policy concern. Second, church declarations and reports have contributed to the policy debate by highlighting moral principles central to creation care. They have done so by emphasizing the moral dimensions involved in protecting the environment, encouraging sustainable development, and caring for poor people. Third, the environmental concerns expressed by churches have undoubtedly sensitized and influenced parishioners' views about protecting God's earth. By emphasizing long-term sustainable development and short-term curbs on fossil fuel use, churches have challenged parishioners' beliefs and consumption patterns. Finally, churches have contributed to the public policy debates by emphasizing Biblical values and perspectives. While policy advocacy may be desirable, the task of moral education is even more significant since churches' comparative advantage lies in ethics, not public policy. Most importantly, by avoiding partisan stances, the moral authority of churches is not compromised.

Christian Ethics and Climate Change

How should Christians approach the challenge of climate change? What Biblical principles can help structure the moral analysis of this issue?

To begin with, it is important to stress that climate change is an elusive issue. Whereas migration and development involve people directly, the issue of future climate involves people indirectly, affecting where and how they work and live. Moreover, climate change is not easily defined because the problem of global warming is derivative, probabilistic, and future-oriented. It is derivative because future weather patterns are assumed to be based on how humans continue to generate energy. It is probabilistic because the continued rise in the earth's temperature is assumed to be the result of greenhouse emissions from the burning of fossil fuels. And it is future-oriented because the call to reduce fossil fuel use and to shift to alternative energy sources is designed to stabilize the earth's future temperature.

Addressing climate change is also difficult because of the lack of consensus about its causes and remedies. Although there is broad agreement that the earth's temperature has been rising, and that a principal source of this increase is due to greenhouse emissions from the burning of fossil fuels, there is much less international consensus about how to address climate change. Since a clean atmosphere is a public good that can only be pursued through shared, collaborative action, governments differ as to the design and implementation of climate strategies. Finally, climate change is difficult because of the lack of consensus about how to continue to meet the demand for increased energy while simultaneously reducing reliance on fossil fuels.

Acknowledging the ambiguous nature of climate change, we now turn to the challenge of integrating Christian values with the problem of climate change. Of the Christian principles and teachings explored in chapter 2, the norm that is most relevant to climate change is *creation care*. According to the United Methodist Church, this principle means that "all of creation is God's, and that we are responsible for the ways in which we use and abuse it. Our natural world is to be valued and conserved because God has called humanity to be its caretakers" (Genesis 1:26–31).[27] The US Conference of Catholic Bishops defines this principle as follows: "We show our respect for the Creator by our Stewardship of creation. Care for the earth is a requirement of the Catholic faith. We are called to protect people and the planet, living our faith in relationship with all of God's creation."[28]

Since climate is only one element of the earth's environment, caring for God's creation involves other elements. These include land (e.g., deforestation and desertification), oceans (e.g., protection of the seas and fish), biodiversity (e.g., protecting endangered species), and waste disposal (e.g., preventing marine pollution and the safe disposal of hazardous wastes). To the extent that climate change threatens a part of God's earth, Christians should seek to prevent such harm. They can do so through their own individual behaviors as well as through collective public policy advocacy. It is important to stress that any significant political action must be rooted in the individual beliefs and practices of citizens. Advocacy will be far more effective if leaders model behaviors that are consistent with the goals being pursued through public policies. Regrettably, this is not always the case, with the result that hypocrisy compromises the quest for policy effectiveness.

Three additional principles of Catholic social teaching help buttress the norm of creation care: the common good, solidarity, and caring for the poor. Because confronting global warming is a global threat, climate change requires a global perspective—an approach that seeks the world's *common good*. Such a goal can only be pursued effectively through cooperation among nation-states, especially the major industrial powers of the world. Discerning the global common good, however, is a difficult, elusive goal because the world's general welfare involves more than climate and environmental considerations. Indeed, the common good of the world involves different dimensions, including economic, social, political, medical, and moral spheres. Since the global common good is multidimensional, Christians must weigh the merits of curbing fossil fuel use against other essential needs of society. This is especially the case for low-income countries with greater health needs and reduced longevity.

The principle of *solidarity* is also important in confronting climate change. As noted earlier, addressing climate change can only be effective if states cooperate in shifting energy generation from fossil fuels to renewables. But such cooperation is only possible if people value social solidarity with those from diverse nations, cultures, religions, and economic classes. National and global social solidarity is thus a precondition for shared interstate actions to advance climate change and, more generally, to pursue the global common good. Thus, if societies are to carry out the difficult work of curbing the use of fossil fuels, people must be willing to identify with the shared interests of other nations and seek to pursue common interests, even when immediate national wants are qualified.

Finally, creation care must involve *caring for the poor*. Climate specialists generally agree that global warming is likely to be more harmful to low-income, tropical countries than to the more developed nations in the Northern Hemisphere. As a result, providing foreign aid to poor societies is regarded as a necessary component of a comprehensive long-term global climate change strategy. In several annual conferences on climate change, including the ones in Copenhagen in 2009 and in Paris in 2015, developed countries promised financial and other aid to assist poor countries in fostering sustainable development. Such assistance is not only important as a matter of justice but also as an expression of social solidarity.

Based on this analysis, a Christian perspective on climate change should include, at a minimum, the following elements: a) pursue creation care by protecting the global environment through individual and collective actions, b) pursue a simple lifestyle by reducing energy consumption and consumer waste, c) encourage public policies that reduce reliance on fossil fuels and shift to renewables, d) foster multinational initiatives that encourage collaboration among nations to advance sustainable development, e) nurture the environmental common good through multinational initiatives and policies, and f) provide public aid to poor nations that are harmed by climate change.

In conclusion, climate change is an important global issue. Although people remain divided on the severity of the problem and how best to address it, there is widespread agreement that global warming is a problem because of its potential harmful effects. Many scientists agree that a principal cause of climate change is the excessive amount of greenhouse gas emissions in the atmosphere. These emissions are, to a significant degree, the result of the burning of fossil fuels to generate energy. As a result, countries are seeking to reduce reliance on fossil fuels by shifting to alternative energy sources. Since the world's atmosphere is a public good, however, working to reduce total global gas emissions is a major problem because of the decentralized nature of the international community. If greenhouse gas emissions are to be reduced, however, states must curb the use of fossil fuels and adopt policies that encourage alternative energy sources. Since Christians are obligated to care for the earth, they have a special responsibility to model behaviors that protect the environment while fostering sustainable growth that enhances human dignity for all, but especially for those who are poor and vulnerable.

NOTES

1. Economists define a public good as a product or service that is nonexcludable and nonrivalrous. This means that such a good can be consumed freely by any person in society without reducing its availability to others.
2. Environmental Protection Agency, "Sources of Greenhouse Gas Emissions," 2022, www.epa.gov/ghgemissions/sources-greenhouse-gas-emissions (August 2, 2024).
3. Environmental Protection Agency, "Global Emissions by Economic Sector," 2019, www.epa.gov/ghgemissions/global-greenhouse-gas-emissions-data#Sector (August 2, 2024).
4. Bill Gates, *How to Avoid a Climate Disaster* (New York: Alfred A. Knopf, 2021), 55.
5. IPCC, "AR6 Synthesis Report: Climate Change 2023," www.ipcc.ch/report/sixth-assessment-report-cycle/ (August 6, 2024).
6. World Health Organization, "Climate Change and Noncommunicable Diseases: Connections," November 2023, www.who.int/news/item/02-11-2023-climate-change-and-noncommunicable-diseases-connections#:~:text=There%20is%20increasing%20strong%20evidence,serious%20risks%20to%20mental% (August 2, 2024).
7. Bjorn Lomborg, *False Alarm: How Climate Change Panic Costs Us Trillions, Hurts the Poor, and Fails to Fix the Planet* (New York: Basic Books, 2020), 219–21.
8. Pew Research Center, "Climate Change Remains Top Global Threat Across 19-Country Survey," August 2023, www.pewresearch.org/global/2022/08/31/climate-change-remains-top-global-threat-across-19-country-survey/ (August 2, 2024).
9. The survey found that people's top priorities are strengthening the economy—75 percent, reducing health care costs—60 percent, reducing crime—57 percent, and dealing with immigration—53 percent. Confronting climate change, however, was viewed as a top priority by only 37 percent of the people. See Pew Research Center, "Economy Remains the Public's Top Policy Priority; COVID-19 Concerns Decline Again," February 2023, www.pewresearch.org/politics/2023/02/06

/economy-remains-the-publics-top-policy-priority-covid-19-concerns-decline-again/ (August 2, 2024).

10. In the United States, energy sources in 2018 were as follows: petroleum—36 percent, natural gas—31 percent, coal—13 percent, and nuclear—13 percent. Renewables accounted for less than 5 percent.

11. Since then, global leaders have agreed that any rise above 1.5 degrees Celsius will have catastrophic effects on the world's climate.

12. Every year, signatories to the UN Climate Treaty of 1992 gather to update the work and ongoing challenges to the task of reducing greenhouse emissions. These gatherings, known as the Conference of the Parties, have involved over twenty-two different conferences and are important in the ongoing efforts to guide and encourage states in the quest for clean energy. The most important of these were those in Kyoto in 1997, Copenhagen in 2009, and Paris in 2015. The most recent Conference of the Parties was in the United Arab Emirates in 2023.

13. Anatol Lieven, *Climate Change and the Nation State: The Case for Nationalism in a Warming World* (New York: Oxford University Press, 2020), 143.

14. Global Carbon Project, "Briefing on Key Messages Global Carbon Budget 2023," https://drive.google.com/file/d/1gDztPwVlt_pvrH6vffPWqoHhqhM_mAJI/view (August 2, 2024).

15. Paul Harris, *What's Wrong with Climate Politics and How to Fix It* (Malden, MA: Polity Press, 2013), 121.

16. The Episcopal Church, "Expressing the Mind of the House on Climate and Our Vocation in Christ," July 2022, www.episcopalchurch.org/ecojustice/expressing-the-mind-of-the-house-on-climate-and-our-vocation-in-christ/ (August 2, 2024).

17. National Association of Evangelicals, "Loving the Least of These: Addressing a Changing Environment," 2022, pp. 13–14, www.nae.org/wp-content/uploads/2022/08/LovingTheLeastOfThese_0822_FINAL_Pages.pdf (August 2, 2024).

18. Pew Research Center, "Religious Groups' Views on Climate Change," November 2022; www.pewresearch.org/religion/2022/11/17/religious-groups-views-on-climate-change/#:~:text=For%20instance%2C%20about%20a%20third,is%20getting%20warmer%20(32%25) (August 2, 2024).

19. Baptist Press, "Full Text of SBECI Declaration," March 2008, www.baptistpress.com/resource-library/news/full-text-of-sbeci-declaration/ (August 2, 2024).

20. Evangelical Lutheran Church of America, "A Social Message on 'Earth's Climate Crisis,'" April 2023, https://download.elca.org/ELCA%20Resource%20Repository/Earths_Climate_Crisis_Social_Message.pdf?_ga=2.86208536.1231755631.1701644729-1463902495.1701644729 (August 2, 2024).

21. Jim Antal, *Climate Church, Climate World: How People of Faith Must Work for Change*, revised and updated edition (Boulder: Rowman & Littlefield, 2023), 4–5.

22. The resolution declares: "Now is the time for congregations and for every person of faith to set a moral example through our own words and actions."

23. Antal, *Climate Church*, 6.

24. The Vatican, "Encyclical Letter *Laudato Si'* of the Holy Father Francis," www.vatican.va/content/francesco/en/encyclicals/documents/papa-francesco_20150524_enciclica-laudato-si.html (August 2, 2024).

25. R. R. Reno, "The Return of Catholic Anti-Modernism," *First Things* (June 2015), www.firstthings.com/web-exclusives/2015/06/the-return-of-catholic-anti-modernism (August 2, 2024).

26. The compilation is available online at https://www.christiancentury.org/free-guide-climate-change.

27. United Methodist Church, "Creation Care," www.umc.org/en/how-we-serve/social-issues/creation-care (August 2, 2024).

28. US Conference of Catholic Bishops, "Care for Creation," www.usccb.org/beliefs-and-teachings/what-we-believe/catholic-social-teaching/care-for-creation (August 2, 2024).

Chapter 8

The Christian Faith and Global Health

Most problems and concerns in nation-states are domestic in nature. Issues such as education, sanitation, and crime prevention are typically addressed by local authorities. National security concerns, fiscal and monetary policies, border controls, and regulation of trade, by contrast, are typically addressed by national governments. Some issues, however, are transnational in scope and can be addressed effectively only through cooperation with other states. In two of the previous three chapters, we have addressed the issues of migration and development that, while defined largely by national governments, demand cooperation with other states. The challenge of climate change, however, entails much greater cooperation with other states. While national action is essential in reducing fossil fuel use, such action will succeed only through collaboration with other states.

In this chapter, I explore an additional issue that demands transnational collaboration—global health and, more specifically, pandemics. I describe the nature and emergence of global health, an area that emerged in recent decades as the world became more integrated and interdependent. As Randall Packard has observed, "global health emerged as a set of practices, organizations, and ideas in the early 1990s, as the world's health community faced new disease threats."[1]

To illuminate the nature and challenges of global health, I focus on three pandemics—HIV/AIDS, COVID-19, and Ebola. Each of these diseases presented significant challenges in identifying the nature of the illness and how best to curb infection and care for the ill. Since the spread of HIV was through human contact, the disease involved important behavioral moral issues as well as concerns with Christian beliefs. By contrast, since both COVID-19 and Ebola were spread chiefly through contaminated air and fluids, the diseases were addressed primarily at a medical and scientific level.

In the chapter's second section, I explore how a Christian worldview can contribute to the analysis and response to these global health challenges. Since diseases and environmental disasters inflict great suffering on people, they are a direct threat to the dignity and welfare of human beings. And since human dignity is a fundamental value of Christianity, caring for people in need provides an opportunity to express compassion and love to others.

In the final section, I address the role of humanitarian aid in containing the spread of deadly diseases. Since poor countries typically have fragile health systems, they do not have the knowledge or resources to contain the spread of deadly viruses or to care for patients who are ill. As a result, foreign assistance is essential to address pandemics like HIV or COVID-19. The outbreak of diseases or the sudden devastation from a major natural disaster demonstrates the vital role of a capable, beneficent nation-state. But it also demonstrates that, in view of the highly interdependent nature of the international community, transnational collaboration is essential in addressing common health challenges. Although governments are necessarily involved in responding to epidemics and natural disasters, their response often is insufficient—either because the threats are transnational or because the afflicted nation does not have the resources to fully address the threat of diseases. As a result, international cooperation among states is vital, and in the case of poor societies, foreign humanitarian aid is essential.

GLOBAL HEALTH AND PANDEMICS

Randall Packard observes that global health is fundamentally about efforts to improve the health of peoples living in low-income countries.[2] These efforts are not a recent development but rather reflect an increased commitment to the issue because of the growing threat posed by the international spread of diseases facilitated by growing global interdependence. As a result, health care has become a much more prominent concern of governments, multilateral organizations, and nongovernmental organizations.

Governments play a vital role in protecting the health of their people. Depending on the country's level of development, governments provide a variety of health care services, including regulating health care safety, preventing disease, and providing medical care through clinics, hospitals, and public health facilities. According to the Institute for Health Metrics and Evaluation at the University of Washington, total world expenditures on health care in 2019 were 9.2 trillion dollars. Based on the world's total population in that year, the average per capita expenditures were estimated at $1,183—a total that disguises enormous disparities among rich and poor countries. For example, average expenditures for different country groups in

2021 were as follows: high income—$5,938, upper middle income—$575, lower middle income—$117, and low income—thirty-seven dollars.[3] Fortunately, governments from high-income countries, along with private charities, provide significant health aid to poor countries. According to one estimate, development aid for health totaled more than twenty-eight billion dollars in 2019 and increased to more than sixty-seven billion dollars in 2021 because of COVID-19.[4]

Although studies have demonstrated that per capita income is closely correlated with longevity,[5] financial allocations for health care alone do not fully explain the limitations and inadequacies of health care systems in low-income countries. Often the major inadequacies are due to poor training, limited health infrastructure, and inadequate national health care systems. Thus, despite significant foreign assistance to improve basic health services, comprehensive health care in low-income countries remains woefully inadequate. According to Packard, health care foreign assistance has been impaired not simply because it has been driven by intermittent responses to global diseases but also because it has been influenced by questionable values. These include an overemphasis on biomedical technology, inadequate concern with basic health services, and the privileging of Western medical knowledge over knowledge and abilities of local people.[6] In his view, what is most needed in poor countries is the strengthening of comprehensive basic health care systems.

Most premature deaths result from diseases. These deaths are caused either by noncommunicable or communicable agents. The first group—noncommunicable diseases—involves such illnesses as cancers, cardiovascular diseases, chronic respiratory diseases, and diabetes, accounting for nearly three-fourths of all early deaths (forty-one million). The communicable diseases are illnesses caused by bacteria or viruses that are transmitted by air, water, bodily fluids, insect bites, or contaminated surfaces. They include such diseases as HIV/AIDS, tuberculosis, viral hepatitis, malaria, sexually transmitted infections, and tropical diseases. Although communicable diseases account for a much smaller percentage of premature deaths, they inflict great suffering on societies, in part because of the difficulty in containing their growth as well as their unpredictable impact on society. Given the ease with which such diseases can be transmitted internationally, communicable diseases are a major threat to global health. Since communicable diseases are a significant international threat, this chapter focuses on the health threat of pandemics.

A pandemic is an epidemic of an infectious disease that has spread to other regions or countries. Historically, two of the most destructive pandemics were the bubonic plague, known as Black Death, in fourteenth-century Europe and the Spanish influenza of 1918–1919. The plague, which is caused by bacteria and is transmitted by rodents, resulted in the death of roughly fifty million persons, mostly in Central Europe. The Spanish flu, which is caused by a virus transmitted interpersonally through airborne respiratory secretions, impacted most of the world's regions and resulted in fifty million to one hundred million fatalities.

To illustrate the threat posed by pandemics, I examine three recent health threats—HIV/AIDS, COVID-19, and Ebola. While the first two viruses were international health threats, Ebola was chiefly a regional disease, impacting three West African countries: Guinea, Liberia, and Sierra Leone. In all three health crises, however, the threat of global contagion was significant and demanded a response by the international community.

HIV/AIDS

HIV/AIDS was first detected in the United States in the early 1980s, when gay men became ill and died soon thereafter. In 1983, medical scientists discovered the cause of the illness, namely a virus—the human immunodeficiency virus, or HIV—that damages a person's immune system and interferes with the body's capacity to fight infection and disease. The virus is spread through human contact, especially sexual contact or blood transfusions. Since the illness can remain dormant, persons with the virus can unknowingly spread it to others. If HIV is not treated medically, it can result in AIDS (acquired immune deficiency syndrome) and cause death.

In seeking to understand, and to contain, the spread of the disease, the US government played a decisive role in coordinating and funding medical research. The first medical breakthroughs took place in the late 1980s with the discovery of antiretroviral medications. Such medications suppress HIV replication, delay the onset of AIDS, and prolong a patient's survival. Although the first medications were expensive and only partly effective, by the mid-1990s more reliable and less expensive medications had been found. Since the beginning of the new millennium, scientists have discovered additional antiretroviral medications that improve the quality of life for infected persons and reduce the chance of transmitting the disease. Nevertheless, scientists have been unable to find a cure for HIV. Once a person gets the virus, they have it for life. Persons living with HIV, however, can lead a normal life with medications.

When HIV/AIDS began to spread in the 1980s, little medical information was known about the disease. As a result, the virus spread rapidly in developed and developing nations alike. According to the US Centers for Disease Control and Prevention (CDC), by 1995 more than a half million Americans had acquired AIDS, with more than 62 percent of the cases ending in death.[7] The impact of HIV/AIDS, however, was far more destructive to sub-Saharan African nations because of less education, fewer medical resources, and limited access to condoms. Although malaria and other illnesses continued to plague African nations, the devastation brought about by HIV/AIDS was unprecedented. Tens of thousands of adults were dying daily, leaving orphans to care for themselves. According to a UN Children's Fund report, by 2003 Africa had more than twelve million children orphaned by AIDS.[8]

Although significant progress has been made in containing the spread of HIV and in treating those with AIDS, the threat of the disease persists in the present. According to global health officials, thirty-nine million persons were infected with HIV globally in 2022, with close to thirty million receiving antiretroviral treatments. The disease continues to affect most areas of the world, but most HIV infections are in African countries. Of the total global HIV infections, Africa accounted for roughly two-thirds of the total (twenty-five million). As of 2023, the total deaths attributed to HIV/AIDS were 40.4 million, with roughly 630,000 deaths in 2022.[9]

COVID-19

The COVID-19 virus surfaced in Wuhan, China, in mid-December 2019. When the Chinese government realized the danger posed by this new disease, it sealed the city in mid-January 2020. The US government banned air travel from China soon after, but by then, the virus had begun to spread globally. In time, it would result in 775 million confirmed cases of COVID-19 worldwide and the deaths of seven million persons.[10]

When the disease first emerged, health authorities knew little about the nature and lethality of the virus. As a result, there was uncertainty among medical professionals on how best to curb infections and how best to assist those who had succumbed to the illness. But once it became clear that the disease could be spread easily through contaminated droplets in the air and that older people were especially vulnerable, governments began imposing public health restrictions. These measures included limiting social gatherings; requiring facemasks; imposing social distancing in public; the closure of public facilities such as libraries, schools, and colleges; and a variety of restrictions on churches, businesses, restaurants, and public transport.

The COVID-19 disease is caused by the SARS-CoV-2 coronavirus. When health authorities became aware of the spreading virus, no vaccine existed to prevent its harmful effects. Typically, developing a safe and effective vaccine takes four or five years. Fortunately, the US government's Vaccine Research Center at the National Institutes of Health had been studying coronaviruses to find out how best to protect against them. In doing so, it had developed a "prototype" vaccine. Thus, when China published the DNA sequence of the SARS-CoV-2, US scientists used the available "prototype" vaccine as the basis for structuring a modified variant using the data from China. This explains why American scientists were able to develop a vaccine targeted to the SARS-CoV-2 virus in a couple of months, and to carry out clinical trials soon thereafter. In December 2020, US health officials announced that a vaccine was ready for distribution. After scientists had developed a COVID-19 vaccine, the challenge for the government and pharmaceuticals was how to rapidly produce, distribute, and utilize the vaccines to halt the spreading virus.

To contain the spread of the coronavirus, governments imposed a wide variety of restrictions, including lockdowns, school closures, and restricting air and train travel. After a vaccine was discovered, evidence of vaccination was required for public events, such as attending a concert or visiting a museum. Most governments sought to restrict international travel and limit immigrant visas.[11] Given the porosity of the United States' southern border, US immigration authorities imposed a variety of restrictions to curb border crossings. Persons seeking to claim asylum were required to wait in Mexico. Economic and social life in urban centers came to a standstill as retail stores, hotels, and restaurants were barely kept afloat. If people worked, they did so mostly from home. I recall walking on Michigan Avenue on the north side of Chicago in January 2021, and few shops, stores, or restaurants were open. Few people were on the streets. The city appeared to be a ghost town.

COVID-19's impact on community life and leisure was devastating. Many schools closed. Churches stopped having worship services in person and shifted to online services. Schools and colleges and universities similarly shifted to online teaching. While the impact on students' virtual learning is still being assessed, educators now agree that children who were kept away from the classroom for a year or more have suffered significantly. The national economy similarly suffered from dramatic declines in the production of goods and services. The areas that were impacted most severely were travel, dining, and health and social services. Many restaurants were forced to close and retail businesses reduced hours of operation, consolidated operations, or closed stores altogether. According to the Center of Health Policy and Economics at the University of Southern California, the economic cost of COVID-19 in the United States during the 2020–2023 period was estimated at fourteen trillion dollars. Had the United States not had a pandemic, economists estimate that total economic output would have been 14 percent higher at the end of 2023.[12] Although the total cost of the coronavirus to the global economy is still being assessed, the International Monetary Fund estimates that the pandemic resulted in a decline of at least 3 percent in 2020, the first year of the pandemic.[13]

The humanitarian challenge posed by COVID-19 was different from that of HIV/AIDS. Whereas HIV was spread chiefly through sexual relations, the spreading of COVID-19 was largely through close personal contact, especially through contaminated air. Second, given the different ways that the two viruses spread, AIDS affected fewer people in specific communities, whereas COVID-19's dissipation through aerosols affected any gathering of people—in churches, classrooms, offices, hotels, automobiles, ships, etc. Third, whereas containment of HIV was achieved chiefly through personal hygiene and medicines, containment of COVID-19 involved significant restrictions on business and social life. As a result, the social and economic impact of COVID-19 was much greater than that of AIDS. Fourth, whereas medications for AIDS were costly, the vaccines for COVID-19 were relatively inexpensive. Fifth, whereas AIDS inflicted the greatest suffering on the poor countries of Africa, the countries that experienced the greatest harm from COVID-19 were the developed, globalized countries of North America and Europe. According to the World Health Organization, deaths attributed to COVID-19 were distributed as follows: Americas—2.9 million, Europe—2.2 million, South and East Asia—806 thousand, Western Pacific—416 thousand, and Africa—175 thousand.[14] Ironically, the United States, the first country to develop an effective vaccine, suffered more deaths (1.2 million) than any other country. China, the source of the virus and the most populous country in the world, experienced only 175,000 deaths.[15]

Although global health officials have made significant progress in containing the spread of the coronavirus, the spread of the disease continues. As of early 2024, there were roughly sixty-two thousand new weekly infections worldwide, and 1,119 weekly deaths attributed to the disease.[16] Fortunately, there is now much more knowledge and widespread availability of vaccines to contain the spread of infections.

Ebola

The Ebola virus disease, which was first discovered in 1976 in central Africa, is a highly contagious, deadly illness. It has one of the highest mortality rates among infectious diseases and is found chiefly in sub-Saharan Africa. The disease is spread through contact with infected animals (chiefly fruit bats) or contaminated human blood or bodily fluids. After a person becomes infected with the virus, the incubation period can last many days before symptoms develop. But once the fever begins, and the person starts losing bodily fluids from vomiting and diarrhea, the illness can intensify rapidly. Unless the person receives adequate treatment through fluid replacement, death follows quickly.

In March 2014, an outbreak of the Ebola virus occurred in West Africa. According to the World Health Organization, a case of Ebola virus disease was discovered in the forested rural region of southeastern Guinea and quickly spread to Conakry, the country's capital. Given the weak border controls with neighboring countries, the disease soon spread to Liberia and Sierra Leone. Because of the rapidly expanding threat posed by the virus, World Health Organization officials issued a public health emergency advisory, calling for a coordinated international response to the West African pandemic.

When the Ebola virus erupted in West Africa, many of the health institutions had been depleted because of ongoing political strife and civil war in the region. As a result, soon the hospitals, clinics, and health centers were inundated with patients, many with insufficient protective equipment to care for infected patients. Since the virus spreads easily in health centers treating infected patients, it is not surprising that even with some protective gear, a significant percentage of health professionals contracted the disease. According to Paul Farmer, a noted professor and activist for global health who was involved in containing the West African Ebola virus, close to one thousand health professionals from Guinea, Liberia, and Sierra Leone became infected with Ebola, and more than half of them subsequently died.[17] According to the CDC, the total Ebola virus disease cases in the three West African countries affected by the pandemic was 28,616, resulting in the death of 11,308 persons. By the end of 2016, the three countries were considered free of Ebola.[18]

Francis Fukuyama argues that three factors are responsible for effectively containing pandemics: state capacity, social trust, and leadership. He suggests that "strong state action" is essential in curbing pandemics.[19] Indeed, while some pundits had been predicting the demise of the nation-state, the actions undertaken by states to contain the spread of the coronavirus demonstrated the vital role of political leadership in confronting a major health threat. To be sure, multilateral cooperation was also important in addressing the pandemic. But in the author's view, no recent international development has demonstrated both the need for sovereign authority and competent leadership as has the COVID pandemic.

THE CHRISTIAN FAITH AND GLOBAL HEALTH

No inherent conflict exists between medical science and religion. Thus, when infectious diseases threaten societies, it is imperative for medical personnel to use all available scientific knowledge and medical resources to identify and respond to the diseases. The Christian faith does not provide moral guidance on how scientists should do their scientific work, nor does it provide guidance on how the church should respond to public health concerns. Instead, the church should support the medical and scientific communities as they address illnesses and inspire and model compassionate care for those who are ill.

Regrettably, some clergy and religious leaders fail to follow these constraints and go beyond their pastoral responsibilities by issuing declarations and making statements that are beyond their competence. For example, some church leaders seek to account for diseases by through religious interpretations, such as viewing illnesses as divine judgment for human sin. I recall hearing a sermon in the late 1980s by a pastor who claimed that AIDS deaths were directly due to homosexual sex and was God's way of calling people to repentance. Fortunately, as people became more knowledgeable about HIV/AIDS, religious leaders were far more nuanced about the nature, causes, and implications of the epidemic. As Anthony Petro, a professor of religious studies, observes, "Most American Christians, even most [E]vangelicals, downplayed or even rejected the idea that AIDS was God's punishment. Or they layered this interpretation with calls for compassion."[20]

While the Christian worldview does not provide principles about how to carry out science, it does provide insights about how individuals and communities should respond to the personal and social needs of individuals and communities. In addressing health challenges, a Christian perspective can contribute to human dignity by emphasizing the inherent worth of all persons, sick or healthy, and the need for compassion and loving care. Additionally, the tradition of Catholic social teaching calls attention to the importance of participation, human solidarity, and the common good in responding to transnational health concerns.

The Church and HIV/AIDS

In the early phase of the AIDS crisis, most Christian denominations issued simple declarations about the need for compassionate care. But given the uncertainty about the nature and cure for HIV/AIDS, and the tensions arising from compassionate care and sexual fidelity, most Protestant churches and Evangelical denominations failed to explore how the Christian faith could help structure the moral analysis of this health crisis. Religious associations like the National Council of Churches and the National Association of Evangelicals avoided the topic altogether. Some denominations issued short declarations of compassion and concern. For example, leaders of the Presbyterian Church adopted a resolution in 1986, declaring that AIDS was an illness, "not punishment for behavior deemed immoral."[21] And in November 1988, the Lutheran Church issued a statement expressing concern for those suffering from the disease.[22] Nevertheless, since the spread of HIV/AIDS in the early 1980s was associated with homosexual sex, and since such behavior was inconsistent with traditional church teachings about marriage and sexual morality, it is noteworthy that neither the Catholic Church nor Protestant denominations developed teaching documents on how to respond to people living with AIDS.

The most important early effort by a church to investigate the relationship of faith to HIV/AIDS was undertaken by the Catholic Church. In 1987, the

Administrative Board of the US Conference of Catholic Bishops approved a statement titled "The Many Faces of AIDS" that had been drafted by a select group of bishops, headed by Cardinal Bernardin. That statement called on Catholics to care for those suffering from AIDS and to avoid discrimination against them. The statement also urged, following traditional Catholic teaching on sexual morality, abstention as the primary means of prevention. It took note, however, that many persons would disregard this moral injunction. As a result, it addressed the use of condoms as a lesser evil.[23] Because this conclusion was upsetting to numerous clergy, the US Conference of Catholic Bishops called for a comprehensive investigation of Catholic teaching and the disease.

This subsequent study resulted in a report issued in December 1989. Titled "Called to Compassion and Responsibility: A Response to the HIV/AIDS Crisis," the document describes the nature and impact of the disease, affirms traditional Catholic principles on social morality, and sets forth a pastoral response to those suffering from the disease. The bishops argue that a Christian response to the crisis should be characterized by compassion, personal integrity, responsible living, and social justice. According to the report, the disease is not simply a biomedical phenomenon, but "a social reality rooted in human behavior." Since scientific knowledge about how to contain HIV/AIDS was still being developed, the church emphasized the importance of living life with integrity and fidelity. As a result, the report condemned the "safe-sex" approach being encouraged by public health officials and instead called for limiting sexual intercourse to those who are married. "Sexual intercourse," the bishops wrote, "is appropriate and morally good only when, in the context of heterosexual marriage, it is a celebration of faithful love."[24]

Interestingly, Wheaton College, the Evangelical institution where I taught, issued a statement on the disease in April 2007. The statement, titled "HIV/AIDS: A Biblical and Theological Response," declares: "The suffering and death resulting from HIV/AIDS stands in stark contrast to God's intentions for abundant life." Given the threat posed by the disease, the statement sets forth key elements of a biblical approach to the illness. The statement states, "We acknowledge our responsibility to proclaim the Gospel of Jesus Christ and embody his commands for justice, sexual purity, forgiveness, and compassionate action for those who suffer."[25]

The most important contribution that Christians made to the US AIDS epidemic was the prioritization of compassion and nondiscrimination in treating those with the disease. By contrast, churches played a far more important and active role in addressing the global AIDS pandemic. This phase of political action toward low-income countries was facilitated by two developments. First was the realization that the disease was afflicting both men and women and was being spread through means other than homosexual sexual relations.

Secondly, was the discovery of antiretroviral drugs that inhibited AIDS. The focus of political action thus shifted to the world, and more specifically to Africa. The health challenge for low-income countries in the early 1990s was how to contain the spread of the disease and more specifically, how to provide medicines to those infected with HIV.

Christians played a pivotal role in the debate about US foreign aid on HIV/AIDS. Leading Evangelical pastors and heads of charitable organization organized meetings among themselves and with government officials to discuss how best to respond to the crisis. According to Peter Wehner, a White House aide in the George W. Bush administration, much of the inspiration and motivation for addressing the AIDS humanitarian crisis was rooted in the Christian community.[26] Senator Jesse Helms, the chairman of the Senate Foreign Relations Committee, for example, declared that he had changed his mind about the government AIDS initiative and was now strongly in favor of a US government program. In a 2002 conference, he declared: "I was wrong, and I'm going to take the latter days of my time in the Senate to do everything I can to help push this [comprehensive anti-AIDS initiative]."[27] According to Senate Majority Leader Bill Frist, Christians had an important role to play in addressing the pandemic, stating, "The ultimate cure [to the AIDS crisis] cannot be found without the church."[28] In the final cabinet meeting on the proposed AIDS initiative, President Bush turned to his chief speechwriter and advisor, Michael Gerson, and asked for his opinion. Gerson said: "If we can do this and we don't, it will be a source of shame."[29]

The Church and COVID-19

Unlike the difficult moral issues raised by the HIV/AIDS crisis, COVID-19 presented less demanding moral concerns. Given the nature of the disease, which was spread chiefly through the atmosphere, the major challenge for public health authorities was to determine which practices were most necessary in containing the spread of the virus. Accordingly, local, state, and national governmental institutions established a wide variety of rules and prohibitions designed to contain the spread of the virus. Some states, like California, Illinois, and New York, for example, imposed severe restrictions, such as lockdowns, limitations on social gatherings, required facemasks in public, and social distancing in buildings. Public schools in many states were closed and relied on virtual teaching. Some governments, like Florida, established fewer constraints, allowing businesses and schools to reopen after lockdowns. Since hospital care was limited to those suffering from the illness or who needed immediate medical care, ongoing health care concerns were relegated to a later time. My cardiologist told me that several of his patients had died during the pandemic because official medical priorities had limited hospital work to those requiring urgent care.

As with all aspects of social life, church life was significantly impacted. Under the varied health regulations, the major responsibility of churches and religious organizations was to comply with the health ordinances. The prohibition against social gathering led churches to curtail worship services and to shift to online services. The important role that Christian communities play in marriage and death was similarly affected. Although some church groups, citing separation of church and state, refused to comply with local ordinances, most religious organizations followed health restrictions. One of the major criticisms of some church leaders was that restrictions were not enforced impartially. For example, some public officials allowed some businesses and public events to take place in person, while prohibiting church services and restricting religious events.

Given the American tradition of separating church from the state, some Christian churches refused to comply with governmental lockdown rules. For them, they regarded governmental restrictions as being illegitimate and a threat to the spiritual work of churches. In their view, government had overstepped its boundaries and was intruding on the sphere that belonged to the Kingdom of God. Some churches went so far as to question the legitimacy and need of the COVID-19 vaccine, leading many church members to refuse vaccination, even though the vaccines were free and strongly encouraged by health officials. Although the COVID-19 threat has now receded, the conflict between government and churches continues to linger in many fundamentalist congregations, providing an ongoing source of Christian nationalist fervor.

Since churches are social institutions, a major constraint on their religious work was the inability to demonstrate and provide compassionate care. Virtual communication is no substitute for authentic interpersonal relations. The common good and social solidarity are best advanced through interpersonal and communal interaction. While technology can aid in fostering communication, technological instruments are no substitute for authentic interpersonal ties. Since churches and religious institutions are a part of the social and political fabric of nations, they should comply with health policies, unless such policies directly contravene biblical norms.

For example, Christians can express love to neighbors and support social solidarity by following health guidelines, such as wearing facemasks, complying with vaccinations, and practicing social distancing. Such cooperation is an act of charity, and it is consistent with the common good of society.

As with COVID-19, the Ebola pandemic was essentially a public health crisis that demanded swift and effective medical care. Given the suffering imposed by the disease, a Christian perspective calls on the church to care for those who are infected and dying. Given the highly contagious nature of the disease, carrying out this mandate was possible only for medical personnel who had the training and access to the proper protective equipment to care for those with Ebola. Religious leaders and even family members were encouraged to avoid contact altogether with those with the illness.

Given the contagious nature of Ebola and risks involved in caring for those with the disease, are there valid constraints in how Christians should provide medical care? Are believers called to risk their own lives in the service of others? Fundamentally, how should Christians weigh the risks of contracting a contagious disease with the need to relieve human suffering? Such questions raise difficult moral issues that are beyond the scope of this book. While love and compassion are fundamental values of the Christian faith, this does not mean that they should take precedence over considerations of safety, security, and the health of the personnel caring for those in need. Thus, in providing compassionate service, it is also important to be wise and prudent.

HUMANITARIAN AID

As noted earlier, HIV/AIDS was far more destructive to African countries than to Western, developed nations. Because of the tens of thousands of adults who were dying throughout the African continent, leaving millions of children without parents, foreign assistance to combat the deadly disease was essential if the humanitarian disaster was to be alleviated. Thus, soon after assuming the presidency in 2001, George W. Bush supported an UN-inspired initiative on AIDS, tuberculosis, and malaria, by allocating two hundred million dollars to this program. He was aware, however, that such support was woefully inadequate given the magnitude of the threat posed by AIDS. As a result, different agencies of the federal government, along with congressional leaders, began exploring a more comprehensive response to the virus.

In the January 2003 State of the Union speech to Congress, President Bush announced an AIDS initiative, known as the President's Emergency Plan for AIDS Relief (PEPFAR). As initially advanced, PEPFAR was a five-year, fifteen billion dollar program providing both medical and humanitarian assistance. The initiative sought to prevent new HIV infections, increase testing, provide medicines to those with the virus, and help care for orphans who had lost parents to AIDS. It is estimated that when PEPFAR was announced some thirty million African were infected with HIV and nearly three million had died. In subsequent years, the US government allocated more than one hundred billion dollars to this initiative, resulting in saving the lives of at least twenty-five million persons. By some estimates, the anti-AIDS program is the largest and most successful US humanitarian initiative.

Since the United States initiated PEPFAR, it has continued to be the major global donor to HIV/AIDS, providing more than three-fourths of all foreign assistance to low-income and middle-income countries. Other major donors that have contributed significant aid to combat the virus include France, Germany, The Netherlands, and the United Kingdom. In 2022, total annual donor HIV aid was estimated at $8.2 billion.[30] Because of the continuing threat of HIV, additional humanitarian aid is important if the rate of infection is to be reduced. In 2022, there were 1.3 million new infections, down from about two million in 2012, and almost half as many AIDS-related deaths. Additionally, the threat is now not simply focused on Africa but also on other regions, including Eastern Europe, Central Asia, the Middle East, and North Africa.

As noted previously, when the COVID-19 pandemic broke out in 2020, it affected primarily the developed, highly interdependent countries of North America and Europe. But within a short period of time, COVID-19 threatened other regions of the world, especially Latin America and Asia. After developed countries had vaccinated a large portion of their citizens and established domestic practices to contain the spread of the virus, they distributed vaccines to many foreign states. As of February 2024, the US government had donated more than 692 million vaccine doses to 117 countries.[31] As with HIV, the United States has been the major donor to assist low-income and middle-income countries in containing the spread of the coronavirus. As of 2022, the total US foreign assistance to combat the global COVID-19 pandemic was estimated at about ten billion dollars. The countries receiving the most aid included Ethiopia, India, Somalia, South Sudan, Sudan, Syria, and Yemen.[32]

Donor governments also contributed significantly to the West African Ebola pandemic by providing financial assistance and sending medical personnel to train and help prevent and care for those with the illness. For example, the CDC helped train more than 24,500 health care workers on infection prevention and control practices. Western European countries, including Belgium, France, Germany, and Sweden, similarly provided health care professionals as well as mobile laboratories to test patients. The Chinese government responded by carrying out its largest humanitarian health initiative in the country's history. Drawing on its experience in responding to the SARS epidemic in 2003, Chinese health officials helped to contain the spread of the virus and to treat patients while avoiding contaminating themselves. In addition to government aid, nongovernmental organizations also were also involved in training and caring for the sick. As a result of these efforts, the three West African countries that had battled Ebola were virtually free of the virus by late 2016.

In conclusion, pandemics impose great human suffering. Given the high level of global integration, the outbreak of a deadly virus in one country can quickly spread to other countries and regions of the world. While national health authorities play a vital role in establishing health guidelines to curb the spread of the illness and to provide basic care for infected persons, international cooperation is essential in curbing the spread of the pandemic. As a result, collaboration among developed countries is essential in identifying the nature of the infection and in providing medical and financial assistance to care for those suffering from the disease. This is especially the case when pandemics afflict low-income countries. Since human dignity is a foundational value of the Christian faith, the Christian norms of love, compassion, solidarity, and the common good can help guide and inspire humanitarian assistance to meet essential human needs.

NOTES

1. Randall M. Packard, *A History of Global Health: Interventions into the Lives of Other Peoples* (Baltimore: Johns Hopkins University Press, 2016), 273.

2. Packard, *A History of Global Health*, 7.

3. Institute for Health Metrics and Evaluation, University of Washington, "Financing Global Health 2021," 11–12 (August 2, 2024), www.healthdata.org/sites/default/files/files/policy_report/FGH/2023/FGH_2021.pdf (August 2, 2024).

4. Institute for Health Metrics and Evaluation, "Financing Global Health 2021," 48. Of the total development assistance for health in 2021, nearly 70 percent was earmarked for COVID-19.

5. See, for example, McKinsey Global Institute, "Pixels of Progress," December 2022, www.mckinsey.com/mgi/our-research/Pixels-of-progress-introduction (August 2, 2024).

6. Packard, *A History of Global Health*, 8–9.

7. CDC, "First 500,000 AIDS Cases—United States," 1995, www.cdc.gov/mmwr/preview/mmwrhtml/00039622.htm (August 2, 2024).

8. UN Children's Fund, "Africa's Orphaned and Vulnerable Generation: Children Affected by AIDS," 2006, https://digitallibrary.un.org/record/586337?ln=en (August 2, 2024).

9. World Health Organization, World Health Observatory, www.who.int/data/gho/data/themes/hiv-aids (August 2, 2024).

10. KFF, "Global COVID-19 Tracker," March 18, 2024, www.kff.org/coronavirus-covid-19/issue-brief/global-covid-19-tracker/ (August 2, 2024).

11. There is considerable debate about the efficacy of travel bans and lockdowns. For a critique of these practices see, Charles Kenny, *The Plague Cycle: The Unending War Between Humanity and Infectious Disease* (New York: Scribner, 2021), 179–86.

12. University of Southern California Schaeffer Center for Health Policy & Economics, "COVID-19's Total Cost to the U.S. Economy Will Reach $14 Trillion by the End of 2023," https://healthpolicy.usc.edu/article/covid-19s-total-cost-to

-the-economy-in-us-will-reach-14-trillion-by-end-of-2023-new-research/#:~:text=The%20big%20idea,and%20other%20experts%20have%20estimated (August 2, 2024).

13. International Monetary Fund, *World Economic Outlook, April 2020: The Great Lockdown* (Washington, DC: International Monetary Fund), www.imf.org/en/Publications/WEO/Issues/2020/04/14/weo-april-2020 (August 2, 2024).

14. World Health Organization, "WHO Coronavirus (CVD-19) Dashboard: Situation by Region, Country, Territory and Area," 2023, https://covid19.who.int/table (August 2, 2024).

15. Many scholars and epidemiologists question the reliability of statistics on deaths attributed to COVID-19, especially those from China.

16. KFF, "Global COVID-19 Tracker."

17. Paul Farmer, *Fevers, Feuds, and Diamonds: Ebola and the Ravages of History* (New York: Farrar, Straus and Giroux, 2020), xix.

18. CDC, "2014–2016 Ebola Outbreak in West Africa," www.cdc.gov/ebola/outbreaks/index.html (August 2, 2024).

19. Francis Fukuyama, "The Pandemic and Political Order," *Foreign Affairs* (July/August 2020), 26–30.

20. Rich Barlow, "How the AIDS Crisis Became a Moral Debate," The Brink: Boston University, December 2015, www.bu.edu/articles/2015/how-the-aids-crisis-became-a-moral-debate/ (August 2, 2024).

21. Presbyterian Church: "Resolution on Acquired Immune Syndrome Deficiency (AIDS)," www.presbyterianmission.org/wp-content/uploads/resolutionbehaviorcarepcusapolicies198ga1986_.pdf (August 2, 2024).

22. Lutheran Church, "AIDS and the Church's Ministry of Caring," www.elca.org/Faith/Faith-and-Society/Social-Messages/AIDS (August 2, 2024).

23. US Conference of Catholic Bishops, "The Many Faces of AIDS, November 14, 1987," www.usccb.org/resources/statement-many-faces-aids-november-14-1987 (August 2, 2024).

24. US Conference of Catholic Bishops, "Called to Compassion and Responsibility: A Response to the HIV/AIDS Crisis," www.usccb.org/resources/called-compassion-and-responsibility-0 (August 2, 2024).

25. Wheaton College, "HIV/AIDS: A Biblical and Theological Response," April 2007, www.wheaton.edu/about-wheaton/stewardship/hivaids-a-biblical--theological-response/ (August 2, 2024).

26. Speech by Peter Wehner at Wheaton College (Illinois) on September 11, 2023.

27. Quoted in Mark R. Amstutz, *Evangelicals and American Foreign Policy* (New York: Oxford University Press, 2014), 161.

28. Amstutz, *Evangelicals*, 161.

29. George W. Bush, "Michael Gerson's Words Make the Case for PEPFAR," *Washington Post*, September 13, 2023.

30. KFF/Joint United Nations Programme on HIV and AIDS, "Donor Government Funding for HIV in Low- and Middle-Income Countries in 2022," https://files.kff.org/attachment/Report-Donor-Government-Funding-for-HIV-in-Low-and-Middle-Income-Countries-in-2022.pdf (August 2, 2024).

31. US Department of State, "COVID-19 Vaccine Donations," www.state.gov/covid-19-recovery/vaccine-deliveries/ (August 2, 2024).

32. KFF, "U.S. Global Funding for COVID-19 by Country and Region," www.kff.org/global-health-policy/issue-brief/u-s-global-funding-for-covid-19-by-country-and-region-an-analysis-of-usaid-data/ (August 2, 2024).

Chapter 9

The Importance of Public Service

In the previous chapters, I have described major features of the international community and have explored how Christian values and perspectives can contribute to the order, prosperity, and justice of the world. Given the political constraints imposed by the decentralized system of nation-states, the task of strengthening international peace, improving human rights, and raising the living conditions for the poor may seem to be a difficult, even elusive, quest. I have written this book in the belief that a better world is possible through the actions of governments in pursuing the common welfare of nations and the common good of global society. Such work will necessarily be rooted in the creative and persistent service of individuals, working through governmental and nongovernmental institutions.

In the previous chapters, I have not sought to provide public policy solutions to the instability and chaos of global politics. Rather, my aim has been to encourage individuals—whether in public or private life—to advance the common good using Christian perspectives and biblical principles. While government service is essential in advancing the common good of nations and the world, individuals play a critical role in fostering the welfare of their own communities through service in local charities, professional associations, churches, nongovernmental organizations (NGOs), and related institutions.

Scripture tells us that "it is more blessed to give than to receive" (Acts 20:35). I believe that all persons can give something to a cause beyond their immediate personal interest. Responsible citizens, and especially Christians, can express their moral concern for others through public service.

One way of caring for others is through financial giving. In the late 1950s, my father and I visited the small town of Villarrica, Chile, next to the beautiful lake and active volcano with the same name. The town was small, populated by several hundred people, all poor. As we entered the village on a rainy, winter morning, I noticed a large banner strung across a one-lane gravel road. The banner's message was a call to contribute to a relief fund for the people of an Italian village that had recently suffered a devastating earthquake. Amazingly, poor people in Chile were supporting victims of a natural disaster eight thousand miles away! Since the contemporary world is far more interdependent today than it was seven decades ago, giving to a worthy cause through the electronic media is simple and easy. Thus, when Haiti suffered a massive earthquake in 2010, I responded with a modest financial donation to two relief organizations. Since I used the internet and a credit card, the task was easy, quick, and efficient.

One of the most important ways of showing care is through personal service in public institutions, both governmental and nongovernmental. I was first introduced to public service as a college student during my summer break in 1963. The previous summer, I had been successful in book sales and had made enough money to travel to Chile to visit my parents, who were serving as missionaries in Osorno, a lovely small city about nine hundred kilometers south of Santiago, the capital. During my six-week visit, I met two Peace Corps volunteers when they came for dinner in our home. The two young men had graduated from Ivy League universities and had decided to delay graduate studies by serving with the Peace Corps, a new government program established by the Kennedy administration.[1] The two men were truly outstanding, both having graduated with academic honors and one having been selected as a Woodrow Wilson Scholar. The two volunteers, who were serving a two-year commitment, were living simply in a nearby rural community, teaching indigenous people aspects of modern life, including improved health and hygiene and better agricultural techniques. What a wonderful way to serve the common good!

I previously mentioned that my own life had been profoundly influenced while in college by the challenge of a US diplomat to consider a vocation in public affairs. Sixty years later, I remain convinced, both as a citizen and as a Christian, of the importance of public service. Since Christians express their faith by loving God and loving their neighbor, they can do the latter by serving others in different ways, including public service through government organizations and NGOs. In my many years of college teaching, I would regularly remind students to develop their gifts and abilities and then to give them away for a cause other than their immediate self-interest.

In this closing chapter, I explore how individuals can contribute to the common good through service in governmental institutions, work in NGOs, and individual initiatives. Whether undertaken through public or private channels, every person can make the world a little better through voluntary service that helps to relieve suffering and foster a more peaceful and humane world. Although public service is commonly associated chiefly with work in governmental organizations, any service that advances the common good in society is a manifestation of public service. Indeed, some of the most important initiatives in addressing communal concerns—such as improved health care, poverty reduction, strengthening human rights, or environmental protection—are undertaken by NGOs. Since government is the indispensable agent in providing conditions that ensure public order and protect human rights, the first part of this chapter explores the role of public service in governmental institutions. I then turn to the role of NGOs. Finally, I discuss how individuals can contribute to a more prosperous and peaceful world. I do so by describing the public service of five ordinary Americans whose service has contributed significantly to the common good. Their service is a model for others.

SERVING THE PUBLIC INTEREST THROUGH GOVERNMENT

There are many avenues of serving the public interest in government. Service can involve working in a government agency, the civil service, a local police department, or a public school. Public service also involves technical work in specialized governmental agencies like the Border Patrol, the US Centers for Disease Control and Prevention, or the Federal Aviation Administration. Additionally, public service can involve working for multilateral governmental organizations like the World Health Organization, the North Atlantic Treaty Organization, the European Commission, or the International Court of Justice.

In a democracy, elected officials establish national goals and adopt laws. The task of implementing the laws and governmental initiatives is with the bureaucracy—that is, the agencies and departments of government. The bureaucracy is comprised of the unelected officials who work within specific agencies. Max Weber famously argued that if government agencies were to carry out their work with efficiency and effectiveness, they needed to be guided by an administrative system that was based on rules that prioritized impartiality and fairness. For Weber, an effective bureaucracy needed to be based on six principles: a clearly delimited area of responsibility supported by government authority, hierarchical organization, accountability based on record-keeping, specialized areas of service, professional expertise, and rules-based decision-making.[2] Unlike elected government officials, civil servants carry out their work divorced from politics. The public frequently remains unaware of civil servants' contribution to an effective economy, an efficient welfare system, a competent military, or an effective educational system. As a result, public service rarely receives public recognition for its important role in society. To be sure, not all bureaucracies function efficiently and effectively, but when they do, they help to advance a nation's common good.

When civil servants neglect their assigned responsibilities or fail to advance the public good, agency effectiveness is impaired. Indeed, one of the common criticisms of the American bureaucracy is that the administrative state often fails to implement the specific tasks government leaders have assigned to its agencies. A further criticism is that an agency can undertake initiatives that are not consistent with the guidance given by elected leaders. Clearly, if bureaucracy is to function effectively, governments must provide specific policy guidance and allocate the resources for carrying out the assigned mission. Regrettably, this is not always the case. Sometimes, laws fail to set forth realistic and clearly defined goals. In other cases, laws may set forth a specific mission but fail to provide adequate resources or realistic expectations on fulfilling the desired objectives. Moreover, when laws specify goals but fail to provide guidance on how to achieve the goals, civil servants may end up making rules and regulations that have the appearance of laws. This development in the United States has created a significant backlash against the administrative state, the so-called fourth branch of government. But if the gap between laws and bureaucratic implementation is to be moderated, government leaders must establish clear, realistic guidelines. The problem, of course, is that the issues being addressed, such as environmental protection, the regulation of migration, and the curbing of fossil fuel use, are enormously complex. Passing laws that can address public concerns often results in laws that are long, complex, and often difficult to apply. Indeed, some laws are more than one thousand pages long!

The tensions between the legislature and administrative state are not caused chiefly by civil servants. Indeed, civil servants, whether at the local or national level, serve with competence, humility, and devotion to the public good. This is why honoring those who serve the public interest is important. I have many former students who have worked in local, state, and national governmental agencies and have found their work fulfilling and rewarding. Since I was a professor of international relations, many of my students have pursued government careers in international affairs, serving in a wide variety of roles.

Service in international organizations is also another way of serving the common good. Such organizations include the many specialized agencies affiliated with the United Nations, such as the World Health Organization, the Food and Agriculture Organization, the UN High Commissioner for Refugees, and the UN Development Programme. Although the chief purpose of the United Nations is to deter war and foster peacekeeping, some of its most successful programs involve social, health, and economic services, not political conflict resolution. For example, international organizations like the World Trade Organization, the International Monetary Fund, and the World

Bank have played a pivotal role in providing principles and rules that have facilitated global economic expansion. Similarly, international organizations have similarly played an important global role in addressing such issues as environmental protection, climate change, and health care.

An important function of the United Nations is peacekeeping. The logic of peacekeeping is not to make peace between enemies but to prevent an outbreak of fighting by keeping the warring parties apart. Peacekeeping missions are undertaken only after the opposing parties agree to a cease-fire. The UN peacekeeping forces, which include soldiers and police from a variety of nations, function under UN authority. UN Peacekeepers are lightly armed and are authorized to use force only in self-defense. Since UN Peacekeeping was established in 1948, seventy-one peacekeeping missions have been authorized. In 2023, there were twelve missions involving some ninety thousand UN personnel.

SERVING THE PUBLIC INTEREST THROUGH NONGOVERNMENTAL ORGANIZATIONS

NGOs are independent, mission-driven societal organizations whose primary aim is to promote shared goals at the national or international level. Such organizations, which are typically private, not-for-profit institutions, play an important role in advancing common interests and support the work of governmental institutions.

NGOs are typically classified as either advocacy organizations or direct service organizations. The former aim to influence local, national, and international governmental organizations. While their goal is ultimately to achieve desirable policy goals and programs, advocacy organizations also seek to influence public opinion. For example, tens of thousands of climate change NGOs are seeking to encourage green energy, limit pollution, and reduced fossil fuel use by influencing people's beliefs and values and thereby fostering public policy changes. Their aim is to reduce greenhouse emissions through clean energy.

The second type of NGO provides direct services in a wide variety of social, medical, and economic areas. Such humanitarian organizations provide a much-needed way of supplementing governmental humanitarian, medical, and social programs. Examples of such NGOs include *Médecins sans Frontières* (Doctors Without Borders), which provides emergency medical care; International Rescue Committee, which provides humanitarian aid to refugees; Save the Children, which provides care and support to children in need; and World Vision, which provides humanitarian aid to people suffering from poverty and environmental disasters.

Currently, hundreds of thousands of NGOs exist at the local, national, and international levels, and they cover every conceivable problem or public concern. Typically, the largest and most numerous NGOs are in the developed democracies. Indeed, since NGOs operate independently of the government, authoritarian regimes frequently seek to regulate or prohibit their operations, especially if the organization is viewed as a threat to government authority.

Since NGOs arise in response to a perceived need or concern, their role and number has increased dramatically as societies have become more modern and complex. Their growth is also associated with the expanding role of mediating institutions that help to connect people with governmental institutions.[3] The increase in NGOs was especially significant following World War II and especially at the end of the Cold War. The growth was a direct byproduct of the strengthening of civil society worldwide as countries became more democratic and more economically developed. According to Freedom House, a think tank concerned with democratic expansion, the number of democratic states in 1977 was forty-four of 148 countries, but by 2023 the number had increased to eighty-four of 195 countries.[4] It is estimated that the world in 2023 had around ten million NGOs involved in local, national, and international issues. The Department of State estimates that 1.5 million NGOs are in the United States.

In advancing specific interests, NGOs have several advantages over government. First, since NGOs are more flexible and adaptable than government, they can modify their initiatives as conditions change far easier than governmental agencies. Second, since NGOs emerge from perceived needs, they enjoy a high degree of public support. As a result, NGOs enjoy a high degree of legitimacy and maintain close ties with the people they serve. Third, because they are private institutions, their functioning depends upon the voluntary support from concerned citizens. Such voluntarism contributes to high morale within the organization and to communication effectiveness at all levels. Finally, since NGOs are independent, they have great flexibility in hiring staff and face fewer constraints in setting policy than government agencies.

As noted earlier, NGOs play an important role in caring for human needs and reducing poverty. Although they have fewer resources than governmental aid programs, they often are more efficient in meeting human needs. Some of the reasons for humanitarian NGOs' effectiveness include deep knowledge of the local environment in which they serve, greater flexibility to adapt programs to local needs, enhanced financial accountability, greater local involvement in the allocation and distribution of resources, and close collaboration between donors and recipients, contributing to shared ownership.

In the heyday of the Cold War, development assistance was channeled through governments. Basically, the bulk of humanitarian assistance involved loans, grants, and goods from one government to another. This is no longer the case. Because of the advantages of nongovernmental agencies, most US humanitarian assistance is now allocated through private charities, local organizations, and humanitarian NGOs, while official development aid is undertaken through contracts with private organizations. In 2004, the United States established the Millennium Challenge Corporation, a government agency that administers grants to countries. The grants are allocated only when countries meet basic preconditions, including democratic governance, investment in people, and economic freedom. The grants are conditional and structured on evidence-based accountability.

THE VITAL ROLE OF INDIVIDUALS

Individuals can advance the common good by giving time, money, ideas, and professional skills. While governments and organizations are essential in promoting peace and prosperity, institutions depend upon individuals who initiate and guide their work. Personal service in organizations is important in providing direct humanitarian services as well as political advocacy. But individuals also contribute to the common good in surprising ways. Indeed, what is amazing about individuals' contribution to human wellbeing is the love and compassion that they express when facing challenges or adversity. In the examples described subsequently, neither wealth, education, nor social class seem to have influenced human actions. Rather, what mattered was the moral character of persons—their capacity to act on behalf of the interests of others.

Where does courageous and virtuous behavior come from? Pakistani Malala Yousafzai, for example, developed the conviction as a young girl that education was a right for all girls. Since this belief was contrary to the radical Muslim view that only boys should be educated, her activism was inconsistent with prevalent values in her community. As a result, a Taliban gunman attempted to kill her as she returned home from school when she was fourteen years old. Given the gravity of her injury, she was flown to Birmingham, England, for medical care. After recovering, she expanded her campaign for the right to education, and in 2014, when she was seventeen years old, she became the youngest Nobel laureate, in recognition of her advocacy of girls' schooling.

Courage often plays a critical role in advancing human dignity. After Rosa Parks, a Black resident of Montgomery, Alabama, became involved in the civil rights movement, she was on one of the city's segregated buses on December 1, 1955, when the bus driver asked her to give up her seat to a White man. She refused. She was arrested and found guilty of disobeying a lawful order, consistent with the city's segregation rules. Her defiance led to a city-wide boycott of the city's buses—a boycott that lasted over a year. The boycott ended when the Supreme Court ruled that the segregation laws were unconstitutional.

Corrie ten Boom, a Dutch woman, also provides a further illustration of the role of courage in fighting oppression. Corrie and her family, who were devout Christians, sought to protect Dutch Jews from deportation after Germany occupied Holland in World War II. The ten Booms owned a watch/clock business and used their home and business as a means of aiding persecuted Jews. They distributed food ration cards and built a small secret room above their shop, where they could hide as many as six persons. After the Nazis discovered the ten Boom's involvement in the underground resistance in 1944, Corrie, her sister Betsie, and their father Casper were jailed. Casper died soon after going to prison, and the two sisters were eventually sent to the woman's concentration camp in Ravensbrück, Germany, where Betsie died in December 1944. Shortly before the end of the war, Corrie was released from prison through a clerical error. As a result of her heroic service during the war, Corrie was knighted by the Queen of The Netherlands, and in 1967 her name was added to the "Righteous Among the Nations" list at the Yad Vashem Memorial in Israel.

Another example of personal courage in defending human dignity is the covert work of Professor Jan W. Schulte Nordholt during the Nazi occupation of The Netherlands.[5] Professor Nordholt believed that he had a moral responsibility to aid persecuted Jews. He was deeply involved in the underground movement, with much of his secret work focused on identifying and alerting Dutch Jews scheduled for deportation. After Nazi authorities learned of his involvement in the resistance, he was forced into hiding for many months. When I directed Wheaton College's International Studies Program in the 1980s, Professor Nordholt would often give a lecture on US-Dutch relations during our residential program in The Netherlands. A highlight of his talk was his discussion of life during the Nazi occupation.

Whereas Corrie ten Boom continued to speak about her heroic service during the war, Professor Nordholt rarely discussed the difficult years of the Nazi occupation and tended to view his service as an inevitable response to oppression and discrimination, values that were inconsistent with the Christian faith. For both Ms. ten Boom and Professor Nordholt, pursuing the common good did not emerge from apprehending an ideal, but rather was a response to a perceived evil. They were confronted with a moral challenge: they could disregard the injustice and evil, or they could confront it directly, even at great personal peril.

Not all individual action arises from courageous and virtuous living. Occasionally, important initiatives emerge from the depths of despair and personal failure. Charles Colson, who was a senior advisor in the administration of

President Richard Nixon, for example, was sent to prison for his involvement in the Watergate scandal. The scandal stemmed from efforts to cover up the involvement of White House personnel in the illegal break-in of the Democratic National Committee headquarters in Washington, DC, in 1972.

Shortly before going to prison, Mr. Colson became a Christian, a development that radically transformed his life and subsequent work. Soon after he was released from the Maxwell Correctional Facility in Alabama, Colson visited Wheaton College, where I was a professor. After meeting him following a chapel service, I invited him to speak to my senior seminar class. He graciously agreed to do so. He began his talk by describing what it was like to go from the White House to prison. He said that the lowest point of his life occurred when he entered prison. "Soon after arriving at the prison," he declared, "officials asked me to take off my clothes and to put on the prison-issued uniforms." He continued, "Do you know what it's like to lose everything you are wearing and be given prison clothing?"

What is remarkable about the life of Chuck Colson is that he used the life-shattering experience of imprisonment to establish Prison Fellowship—an NGO committed to serving prisoners, ex-prisoners, and their families. After its establishment, the organization grew rapidly and soon became the largest and most influential organization of its kind, responsible for important prison reform initiatives and providing direct support to prisoners. In 1979, Prison Fellowship extended its work to foreign countries, and by the start of the new millennium the organization was serving in more than one hundred countries. In 2008, President George W. Bush presented Colson with the Presidential Citizens Medal for his outstanding service to the common good.

Christians are called to love their neighbors and to care for the poor. Mother Teresa, an Albanian nun who served the poor in Calcutta (now Kolkata) for more than four decades, provides a powerful example of such love and service. After leaving her Albanian homeland in 1928, Mother Teresa traveled to Ireland to join the Sisters of Loreto as a nun. She then went to India as a missionary, where she taught at the Loreto Convent school in the outskirts of Calcutta. In 1948, she left the school to serve the poor in the slums of the city. And in 1950, she received permission to start her own congregation or ministry, which would become the Order of the Missionaries of Charity. When the congregation began its work, the organization had thirteen sisters. By the beginning of the twenty-first century the religious order had more than forty-five hundred nuns serving in clinics, dispensaries, orphanages, shelters for the sick, and homes for the dying throughout the world.

Although these centers provide food, education, and care, their most important gift is love. According to Mother Teresa, what the poor, the disabled, and the dying want above all else is the recognition that they matter. She states: "we want to make them feel that they are wanted, we want them to know that there are people who really love them . . . to know human and divine love. That they too may know that they are the children of God."[6]

Mother Teresa's desire to care for "the least of these" was based upon her deep faith in Christ. Although Mother Teresa established a Christian ministry to care for the unwanted and uncared persons in society, her influence stems from personally modeling love toward sick, disabled, dying, and neglected children. In an interview she stated her life's purpose as follows: "I wanted to serve the poor purely for the love of God. I wanted to give the poor what the rich get with money."[7] In the mid-1980s, the late Senator Mark Hatfield (Oregon) told me that after he had visited with Mother Teresa in his Washington, DC, office, the nun made a personal request. She asked, "Please pray for me that in serving the poor I would not lose sight of the face of Jesus."[8]

Mother Teresa has received widespread recognition for her humanitarian service. In 1979, for example, she was awarded the Nobel Peace Prize. And six years later, she was introduced to the UN General Assembly by the Javier Perez de Cuellar, the UN Secretary General, who referred to her as "the most powerful woman in the world."[9] Finally in 2016, the Vatican recognized her extraordinary service to the poor and dying by canonizing her as Saint Teresa of Calcutta. Writer Eric Metaxas captures the extraordinary impact of this woman: "Mother Teresa was considered a saint because she was seen to personify an ideal: to love God, and to love one's neighbor. And yet, what she did was so simple that each one of us can do it—in fact, must do it, if we are to obey the command of Christ: to feed the hungry, care for the sick, invite the stranger in, clothe the naked, visit those in prison, and quench the thirst of those who simply need a cup of water."[10]

FIVE CASE STUDIES

The examples of courageous wartime service and loving service to the oppressed, sick, and dying present extraordinary personal accounts few can emulate. Such accounts can inspire but are unlikely to offer examples that ordinary people can emulate given the everyday challenges that most people face in modern societies. I therefore want to describe the service of five ordinary individuals who through their work and life have been able to contribute to the common good. Unlike Corrie or Mother Teresa, these five individuals have been able to use their various skills and abilities for a cause other than their immediate personal gain or professional advancement. The five individuals include a physician, an NGO executive, a researcher, a military officer, and a lawyer.

Samuel Amstutz: My brother, Dr. Samuel Amstutz, an ophthalmologist, periodically travels to low-income countries to provide medical care to people with deficient eyesight. His trips, which are organized through small religious NGOs that make the preparations for travel and clinical work, select communities that have limited medical services. In carrying out humanitarian work in foreign lands, the NGO selects a community in need of the medical services being offered and ensures that visiting medical personnel have the support of the national government, the local authorities, and local medical personnel. Since poor people frequently have access to only basic optical services, his humanitarian work is primarily surgical. Additionally, his work often involves teaching and staff support for overburdened clinics. Over the course of many years Dr. Amstutz has made more than seventeen trips, including to Ecuador, the Dominican Republic, Honduras, Nicaragua, Peru, northern Iraq, Uganda, Azerbaijan, Uzbekistan, and Fiji. These trips typically involve ten or more working days. These short-term medical overseas experiences bring much joy to my brother as he uses his medical expertise to enhance human dignity by improving people's eyesight.

Larry Reed: A former student, Larry Reed has contributed to the global common good through his innovative work in promoting and facilitating micro finance for poor people. Such finance involves small, short-term loans, savings accounts in local, specialized banks, and similar financial services. After completing studies at Harvard's Kennedy Institute, he began working for Opportunity International (OI), a Christian humanitarian organization concerned with poverty reduction. After working in Zimbabwe in the 1980s, he returned home and served as an executive of the organization. As a leader, he used his knowledge and skills to develop and expand a micro-lending and micro-savings programs geared to poor women. His gift to the world was his ideas how to make available loans to poor people and how to encourage them to protect their earnings. Since prospective borrowers had few assets, no collateral was possible. As a result, trust was essential to the success of the program, especially if it was to be sustainable. To assist in accountability, borrowers met periodically to make loan repayments as well as to discuss shared social and business concerns.

Three features have contributed to the success of OI's micro-lending program: first, the vast majority (around 94 percent) of all borrowers are women; second, the program works chiefly through local churches to encourage trust and accountability; and third, the loan-repayment rate is unusually high, close to 98 percent. Since the loans are small (less than two hundred dollars) and typically short term, the impact of any loan itself is modest. But because of the broad scope of the program, the societal impact is significant, providing loans to more than seven million persons and contributing to the improvement in living conditions for millions of family members and others impacted by the loans.

OI eventually realized that loans alone were not sufficient to ensure increased prosperity. As a result, the organization decided to expand its financial services to include savings accounts. The addition of a savings program was important because it helped clients protect their hard-earned money, help meet family needs, provide education for children, and help make plans for the future. The expansion into banking and savings accounts led to a dramatic increase in clients, reaching nearly fifteen million savings accounts in 2022. Currently, OI provides financial services to more than eighteen million clients.[11] Given its success in providing financial services to the poor, OI has served as a model for numerous other charitable organizations concerned with poverty reduction.

Since leaving his position at OI, Mr. Reed has continued to work in micro finance, serving at the Boulder Institute, Micro-finance Transparency, and the Micro-credit Summit Campaign. Reed summarizes his service as follows: "I've worked for more than thirty years in the field of financial services, but not in the usual way. I've worked at the bottom end of the market, extending credit, savings, and insurance to some of the poorest people in the world. I've watched as people living in poverty have used these services as tools of liberation, investing in small business activities that enabled them to create a different future for themselves and their children."[12]

Bob Gersony: In *The Good American: The Epic Life of Bob Gersony, the U.S. Government's Greatest Humanitarian*, Robert Kaplan tells the improbable story of an ordinary American whose service had a profound impact on US government institutions as well as on the lives of tens of thousands of people suffering from abject poverty and violence.[13] Gersony, who never graduated from high school, developed an interest in learning about complex social and political situations by interviewing the common folk of society. He believed that the "truth" about a political conflict or human disaster could emerge from the data he collected from ordinary people. Gersony would travel to difficult areas and carry out extended interviews with refugees, farmers, and manual laborers, recording his observations by hand in a notebook. Only after carrying out extended interviews would he seek to analyze and synthesize his findings. His conclusions emerged not from abstract theorizing but from the data that he had collected. Because of his unique capacity to uncover knowledge about difficult conflicts or problems, US government officials found his work especially helpful in decision-making. In his forty years of public service, he carried out fifty-four projects in some of the most difficult and dangerous regions of the world, including Bosnia, Chad, Colombia, El Salvador, Ethiopia, Gaza, Mozambique, Nepal, North Korea, Somalia, Sudan, and Uganda.

Why were Gersony's reports so influential? Because his findings were authoritative, guided by credible fieldwork. In 1991, for example, he was asked to investigate how food aid was being used by North Korea. After interviewing North Korean refugees along the country's border, he found that most aid was being used to prop the dictatorial regime rather than to alleviate hunger. As a result, the US government reduced food aid and established practices that helped reduce the diversion of food to the government. Similarly, when he investigated the violence between the Mozambique government (Frelimo) and the anti-government guerrillas (Renamo), he found that the guerrillas were committing gross human rights abuses. After presenting his findings to Secretary of State George Shultz, the Reagan administration cut its military support to the rebels, even though the US government remained opposed to the Frelimo regime.

Gersony's work is important to humanitarianism. He demonstrates how one individual, guided by courage and the quest for truth, can influence public policy. Kaplan concludes: "To call Gersony great is to diminish him, since greatness usually involves an unusual degree of ambition concealed or unconcealed. Gersony achieved his ambition, over and over again, by recording people's stories in his notebooks while under a tree or inside a tent somewhere with the dulling heat, buzzing flies and wafting dust intensifying the silence. That was his glory."[14]

Arthur Dewey: Arthur (Gene) Dewey's long public service cuts across several practitioner disciplines: military, diplomatic, United Nations, and NGOs. After graduating from the US Military Academy at West Point, Dewey served in the military for twenty-five years in a wide variety of posts. His military service included two tours in Vietnam, a White House Fellowship (working at the Department of State and the US Agency for International Development), commanding officer of a combat helicopter battalion, and chief of the Army's Political-Military Division in the Pentagon. His final three years of military service were in the Pentagon as executive officer to the assistant secretary of defense, international security affairs.

As a result of his outstanding service in facilitating coordination among different organizations and nations on refugee affairs, Dewey was appointed deputy assistant secretary of state in the Bureau of Refugee Programs when he retired from the military in 1981. In his work at the Department of State he played a critical role in fostering cooperation between the US government and the United Nations in addressing war, famine, and refugee issues in Africa. In 1986, he was appointed assistant secretary general at the UN Deputy High Commissioner for Refugees in Geneva, Switzerland—a position he held for four years. Beginning in 1993, he was director for the Congressional Hunger Center, an advocacy NGO that provided relief to refugees in Africa. His public service culminated with his appointment in 2002 as assistant secretary of state for population, refugees, and migration. By the time he retired in 2005, Dewey had helped shape refugee policies and programs that had affected millions of persons. In his last position as assistant secretary of state, he helped shape the return of over four million refugees to Afghanistan after the Taliban government had been replaced.

Dewey credits his success in developing successful refugee programs to his mindset and commitment to solving problems. Although his military background undoubtedly contributed to his organizational effectiveness, he found that addressing complex humanitarian crises required the integration of diplomacy, security, and political concerns with the humanitarian programs of international organizations and donor states. In undertaking such multilateral initiatives, leadership was essential. His work in the 1980s in addressing humanitarian challenges, such as the Indochina refugee crisis of 1979–1981 and the Eritrean/Ethiopian famine of the mid-1980s, demonstrated the crucial role of courageous leadership, effective coordination, and rapid response.[15]

In recognition of more than four decades of public service, Dewey has received numerous awards. These include the West Point Distinguished Graduate Award and the John W. Gardner Legacy of Leadership Award, which is given annually to a former White House Fellow for selfless service to the nation and to mankind. Since 2018, USA for UNHCR, an American refugee NGO, has honored Mr. Dewey through its Gene Dewey Refugee Award, given annually to a person who has demonstrated "visionary leadership and extraordinary dedication to help people forcibly displaced from their homes."

Gary Haugen: Haugen's interest in human rights was kindled through overseas work—first on political reconciliation in South Africa as an undergraduate and then on criminal justice in Rwanda after completing his law degree. His service in Rwanda involved directing a UN team to investigate the 1994 genocide that led to the massacre of more than eight hundred thousand persons. His team's investigative work resulted in findings that were subsequently used in prosecuting leading perpetrators of the genocide. The Rwanda experience challenged Haugen to explore how poor countries might develop more effective criminal legal systems to deter violence and human rights abuses.

Given his work on civil rights and criminal justice, Haugen decided to establish an organization that would help developing nations reduce human trafficking and forced labor through more effective criminal justice systems. Accordingly, in 1997 he started the International Justice Mission (IJM) with a small budget and four staff members. The organization's first work focused on sex trafficking in Southeast Asia. In time, IJM expanded the nature and scope of its work by establishing field offices in the Philippines, India, Thailand, and Cambodia. As of 2023, IJM had twenty-four field offices in fourteen countries with more than twelve hundred employees. Although the US government and private foundations have provided numerous large grants, most financial support comes from individuals.

In pursuing its goal of liberating persons from forced labor, domestic violence, and human trafficking, IJM relies on local teams of lawyers, criminal investigators, social workers, and community staff. The aim of the teams is not simply to rescue victims and bring criminals to justice, but also to provide survivors with restorative assistance. Since IJM seeks systemic change, team members undertake collaborative initiatives and training with local justice systems and community leaders. They do so to prosecute offenders and deter human rights abuses. Peter Wehner notes that the IJM's basic goals are "to serve survivors, deter criminals and dramatically decrease violence."[16] According to the IJM 2022 annual report, the organization was providing protection to thousands of victims, helping to convict hundreds of perpetrators of violence and training thousands of staff of justice systems in many countries.[17]

In sum, Christians are called to love and serve their neighbor. They can do so through individual acts of caring, such as assisting a refugee family, supporting a homeless shelter, or providing food for a poor family. But they can also do so through governmental organizations and NGOs. I have stressed public service in this chapter because of the pivotal role that it can play in fostering the common good of nations and the world. Because public institutions establish and implement society-wide policies to address national and global concerns, public service vocations provide an important means of demonstrating concern for the wellbeing of others. The case studies covered in this chapter illustrate how people with different skills and backgrounds can contribute to human dignity. While all persons have distinct interests, capabilities, and resources, everyone can contribute something to the welfare of others. The gift could be time, money, knowledge, skills, or the intangibles of love and care. The recipients could be family members, neighbors, church members, citizens, or foreign individuals. Although this chapter has highlighted public service through institutions, the common good is advanced in everyday life—at home and at work as individuals serve and care for one another and bring hope to people facing intractable problems. Our world will become more peaceful, harmonious, and prosperous if we make service to others a more important part of our own lives. And it will also be a source of profound joy as we share with others what God has entrusted to us.

NOTES

1. President John F. Kennedy initiated the program in 1961 to encourage volunteers to provide development assistance. The program trains and deploys volunteers, who serve a two-year commitment, in areas where they can provide development and humanitarian aid.

2. Max Weber, *Rationalism and Modern Society*, volume 3, edited and translated by Tony Walters and Dagmar Walters (New York: Palgrave Macmillan, 2015).

3. Sociologist Peter Berger defines mediating institutions as "those institutions standing between the individual in his private life and the large institutions of public life." Examples of mediating institutions include labor unions, professional associations, churches, clubs, lobbies, and educational organizations.

4. Freedom House, "Freedom in the World 2023," https://freedomhouse.org/report/freedom-world/2023/marking-50-years (August 2, 2024).

5. Professor Nordholt was a leading Dutch scholar of American history and culture. For most of his professional life, he was a distinguished professor of American Studies at Leiden University in The Netherlands.

6. Malcolm Muggeridge, *Something Beautiful for God* (New York: Harper & Row, 1971), 91–92.

7. Quoted in Muggeridge, *Something Beautiful*, 90.

8. Personal visit with Senator Mark Hatfield, US Senate, Washington, DC, in the mid-1980s.

9. *The New York Times*, October 27, 1985.

10. Eric Metaxas, *Seven Women and the Secret of Their Greatness* (Nashville: Nelson Books, 2015), 190.

11. OI, "Microenterprise," https://opportunity.org/what-we-do/micro-banking (August 2, 2024).

12. Larry Reed, "Does Finance Have a Soul?" Soul of Finance, www.souloffinance.com/about/ (August 2, 2024).

13. Robert D. Kaplan, *The Good American: The Epic Life of Bob Gersony, the U.S. Government's Greatest Humanitarian* (New York: Random House, 2021).

14. Kaplan, *The Good American*, 467.

15. Interview with Arthur (Gene) Dewey on January 5, 2024.

16. Peter Wehner, "The Faith of Gary Haugen," *The Atlantic*, May 12, 2023, www.theatlantic.com/ideas/archive/2023/05/gary-haugen-south-africa-apartheid-religion-civil-rights/674012/ (August 2, 2024).

17. In 2022, IJM and its global partners accomplished the following: relieved 9,295 victims from violence and oppression, restored 434 survivors to safety, restrained 4,097 suspected criminals, convicted 1,178 perpetrators in local courts, and trained 20,746 justice system officials in addressing cases of violence. International Justice Mission, "A Future Defined by Freedom: 2022 Annual Report," www.ijm.org/2022-year-in-review#:~:text=This%20year%2C%20our%20updated%20numbers,to%20protect%20500%20million%20people (August 2, 2024).

Bibliography

Acemoglu, Daron, and James A. Robinson. *Why Nations Fail: The Origins of Power, Prosperity, and Poverty*. New York: Crown Business, 2012.
Amstutz, Mark R. *Evangelicals and American Foreign Policy*. New York: Oxford University Press, 2014.
———. *Just Immigration: American Policy in Christian Perspective*. Grand Rapids: Eerdmans, 2017.
———. "Two Theories of Immigration." *First Things*, December 2015.
Antal, Jim. *Climate Church, Climate World: How People of Faith Must Work for Change*. Revised and updated edition. Boulder: Rowman & Littlefield, 2023.
Bennett, John C. *Foreign Policy in Christian Perspective*. New York: Charles Scribner's Sons, 1956.
Berger, Peter. "Moral Judgment and Political Action." *Vital Speeches of the Day* 56 (December 1, 1987).
Betts, Alexander, and Paul Collier. *Refuge: Rethinking Refugee Policy in a Changing World*. New York: Oxford University Press, 2017.
Bhagwati, Jagdish, and Arvind Panagariya. *Why Growth Matters: How Economic Growth in India Reduced Poverty and the Lessons for other Developing Countries*. New York: PublicAffairs, 2013.
Bigger, Nigel. *Between Kin and Cosmopolis: An Ethic of the Nation*. Eugene, OR: Cascade Books, 2014.
Bonhoeffer, Dietrich. *The Cost of Discipleship*. New York: Macmillan, 1961.
Brunner, Emil. *Justice and the Social Order*. New York: Harper and Brothers, 1945.
Bush, George W. "Michael Gerson's Words Make the Case for PEPFAR." *Washington Post*, September 13, 2023.
Campbell, John L., and John A. Hall, *The World of States*. London: Bloomsbury Academic, 2015.
Carroll, M. Daniel R. *Christians at the Border: Immigration, the Church and the Bible*. Grand Rapids: Baker Academic, 2008.

———. *The Bible and Borders: Hearing God's Word on Immigration.* Grand Rapids: Brazos Press, 2020.

Catholic Bishops of Mexico and the United States. "Strangers No Longer: Together on the Journey of Hope." 2003. www.usccb.org/issues-and-action/human-life-and-dignity/immigration/strangers-no-longer-together-on-the-journey-of-hope (August 6, 2024).

Cavanaugh, William T. *Migrations of the Holy: God, State, and the Political Meaning of the Church.* Grand Rapids: Eerdmans, 2011.

Chartier, Gary. *Christianity and the Nation-State: A Study in Political Theology.* Cambridge: Cambridge University Press, 2023.

Claude, Inis L. Jr. *Swords into Plowshares: The Problems and Progress of International Organization.* Fourth edition. New York: Random House, 1971.

Collier, Paul. *The Bottom Billion: Why the Poorest Countries Are Failing and What Can Be Done About It.* New York: Oxford University Press, 2008.

———. *The Future of Capitalism: Facing the New Anxieties.* New York: HarperCollins, 2018.

Courtois, Stéphane, et al. *The Black Book of Communism: Crimes, Terror, Repression.* Cambridge: Harvard University Press, 1999.

Deutsch, Karl. *Nationalism and Its Alternatives.* New York: Alfred A. Knopf, 1969.

The Editors. "A Christian Declaration of American Foreign Policy." *Providence*, September 21, 2016. https://providencemag.com/2016/09/christian-declaration-american-foreign-policy/ (August 2, 2024).

Evangelical Lutheran Church of America. "AIDS and the Church's Ministry of Caring." www.elca.org/Faith/Faith-and-Society/Social-Messages/AIDS (August 2, 2024).

———. "A Social Message on 'Earth's Climate Crisis.'" April 2023. https://download.elca.org/ELCA%20Resource%20Repository/Earths_Climate_Crisis_Social_Message.pdf?_ga=2.86208536.1231755631.1701644729-1463902495.1701644729 (August 2, 2024).

Falk, Richard. "World Order." *The Princeton Encyclopedia of Self-Determination.* https://pesd.princeton.edu/node/696 (July 29, 2024).

Farmer, Paul. *Fevers, Feuds, and Diamonds: Ebola and the Ravages of History.* New York: Farrar, Straus and Giroux, 2020.

French, David. "One Reason the Trump Fever Won't Break." *The New York Times*, October 1, 2023.

Friedman, Thomas L. *The Lexus and the Olive Tree: Understanding Globalization.* New York: Anchor Books, 2000.

Francis, Pope. "Encyclical Letter *Laudato Si'* of the Holy Father Francis." www.vatican.va/content/francesco/en/encyclicals/documents/papa-francesco_20150524_enciclica-laudato-si.html (August 2, 2024).

Freedom House. "Freedom in the World 2023." https://freedomhouse.org/report/freedom-world/2023/marking-50-years (August 2, 2024).

Fukuyama, Francis. *State Building: Governance and World Order in the 21st Century.* Ithaca: Cornell University Press, 2004.

———. "The Pandemic and Political Order." *Foreign Affairs* (July/August 2020).

Gates, Bill. *How to Avoid a Climate Disaster.* New York: Alfred A. Knopf, 2021.
Goodhart, David. *The Road to Somewhere: The Populist Revolt and the Future of Politics.* London: Hurst & Company, 2017.
Haas, Hein de. *How Migration Really Works: The Facts About the Most Divisive Issue in Politics.* New York: Basic Books, 2023.
Haass, Richard. *A World in Disarray: American Foreign Policy and the Crisis of the Old Order.* New York: Penguin Press, 2017.
Harris, Paul. *What's Wrong with Climate Politics and How to Fix It.* Malden, MA: Polity Press, 2013.
Hastings, Adrian. *The Construction of Nationhood: Ethnicity, Religion and Nationalism.* Cambridge: Cambridge University Press, 1997.
Henry, Paul B. *Politics for Evangelicals.* Valley Forge, PA: Judson Press, 1974.
Holsti, Kalevi J. *The State, War, and the State of War.* Cambridge: Cambridge University Press, 1996.
Huntington, Samuel P. *Political Order in Changing Societies.* New Haven: Yale University Press, 1968.
Ignatieff, Michael. *Blood and Belonging: Journeys into the New Nationalism.* New York: Farrar, Straus and Giroux, 1993.
———. *The Ordinary Virtues: Moral Order in a Divided World.* Cambridge: Harvard University Press, 2019.
———. "The Return of Sovereignty." *The New Republic*, February 16, 2012.
Ikenberry, John. *After Victory: Institutions, Strategic Restraint, and the Rebuilding of Order after Major Wars.* Princeton: Princeton University Press, 2001.
Independent Commission on International Development. *North-South: A Programme for Survival.* Cambridge: MIT Press, 1981.
Inglehart, Robert. *Modernization and Postmodernization: Cultural, Economic and Political Change in 43 Societies.* Princeton: Princeton University Press, 1997.
Intergovernmental Panel on Climate Change. "AR6 Synthesis Report: Climate Change 2023." www.ipcc.ch/report/sixth-assessment-report-cycle/ (August 6, 2024).
International Justice Mission. "A Future Defined by Freedom: 2022 Annual Report." www.ijm.org/2022-year-in-review#:~:text=This%20year%2C%20our%20updated%20numbers,to%20protect%20500%20million%20people (August 6, 2024).
International Monetary Fund. *World Economic Outlook, April 2020: The Great Lockdown.* Washington, DC: International Monetary Fund. www.imf.org/en/Publications/WEO/Issues/2020/04/14/weo-april-2020 (August 2, 2024).
Isaacson, Walter. *Henry Kissinger: A Biography.* New York: Simon & Schuster, 1992.
John Paul II, Pope. *On Human Work (Laborem Exercens).* The Vatican, 1981. www.vatican.va/content/john-paul-ii/en/encyclicals/documents/hf_jp-ii_enc_14091981_laborem-exercens.html (August 1, 2024).
Jones, Dorothy. *Code of Peace: Ethics and Security in the World of Warlord States.* Chicago: University of Chicago Press, 1992.
Judis, John B. *The Nationalist Revival: Trade, Immigration, and the Revolt Against Globalization.* New York: Columbia Global Reports, 2018.

Judt, Tony. *Postwar: A History of Europe since 1945*. New York: Penguin Press, 2005.

Kagan, Donald. *On the Origins of War: And the Preservation of Peace*. New York: Anchor Books, 1996.

Kagan, Robert. *The Jungle Grows Back*. New York: Alfred A. Knopf, 2018.

———. *The Return of History and the End of Dreams*. New York: Alfred A. Knopf, 2008.

Kaplan, Robert D. *The Good American: The Epic Life of Bob Gersony, the U.S. Government's Greatest Humanitarian*. New York: Random House, 2021.

———. *The Tragic Mind: Fear, Fate, and the Burden of Power*. New Haven: Yale University Press, 2023.

Keck, Margaret E., and Kathryn Sikkink. *Activists Beyond Borders: Advocacy Networks in International Politics*. Ithaca: Cornell University Press, 1998.

Kenny, Charles. *The Plague Cycle: The Unending War Between Humanity and Infectious Disease*. New York: Scribner, 2021.

Kirby, Jeffrey. "'Personalism' in the Social Teaching of John Paul II." https://frkirby.com/wp-content/uploads/2014/01/Personalism.pdf (July 31, 2024).

Kissinger, Henry. *World Order*. New York: Penguin Press, 2014.

Landes, David S. *The Wealth and Poverty of Nations: Why Some Are so Rich and Some so Poor*. New York: W. W. Norton, 1999.

Lay Commission on Catholic Social Teaching and the U.S. Economy. *Toward the Future: Catholic Social Teaching and the U.S. Economy: A Lay Letter*. New York: Lay Commission on Catholic Social Teaching and the U.S. Economy, 1984.

Lieven, Anatol. *Climate Change and the Nation State: The Case for Nationalism in a Warming World*. New York: Oxford University Press, 2020.

Lind, Michael. "The Case for Cultural Nationalism." *National Review*, September 11, 2017.

Lomberg, Bjorn. *False Alarm: How Climate Change Panic Costs Us Trillions, Hurts the Poor, and Fails to Fix the Planet*. New York: Basic Books, 2020.

Lowry, Rich, and Ramesh Ponnuru. "For Love of Country." *National Review*, February 6, 2017.

Lutheran Church—Missouri Synod. "Immigrants Among Us: A Lutheran Framework for Addressing Immigration Issues." November 2012. www.cui.edu/Portals/0/uploadedfiles/AboutCUI/Immigrants_Among_Us-FINAL_(English)%20(1).pdf?ver=mawv7apNkeNyf2rao3tj1w%3d%3d (August 6, 2024).

Mandelbaum, Michael. *Mission Failure: America and the World in the Post-Cold War Era*. New York: Oxford University Press, 2017.

Metaxas, Eric. *Seven Women and the Secret of Their Greatness*. Nashville: Nelson Books, 2015.

Micklethwait, John, and Adrian Wooldridge. *The Fourth Revolution: The Global Race to Reinvent the State*. New York: Penguin Press, 2014.

Miller, David. *On Nationality*. New York: Oxford University Press, 1997.

Miller, Paul D. *The Religion of American Greatness: What's Wrong with Christian Nationalism*. Downers Grove, IL: IVP Academic, 2022.

Morgenthau, Hans. *Politics Among Nations: The Struggle for Power and Peace.* Seventh edition. Boston: McGraw-Hill, 2006.

Mouw, Richard. *Abraham Kuyper: A Short and Personal Introduction.* Grand Rapids: Eerdmans, 2011.

Muggeridge, Malcolm. *Something Beautiful for God.* New York: Harper & Row, 1971.

National Association of Evangelicals. "Loving the Least of These: Addressing a Changing Environment," 2022. www.nae.org/wp-content/uploads/2022/08/LovingTheLeastOfThese_0822_FINAL_Pages.pdf (August 2, 2024).

———. "Resolution on Immigration." 2009. www.nae.org/immigration-2009/ (July 31, 2024).

Neuhaus, Richard John. "Christianity and Democracy: Statement of the Institute on Religion and Democracy." Washington, DC: Institute on Religion and Democracy, 1981.

Niebuhr, H. Richard. *Christ and Culture.* New York: Harper & Row Torchbooks, 1975.

Niebuhr, Reinhold. *The Children of Light and the Children of Darkness: A Vindication of Democracy and a Critique of Its Traditional Defense.* New York: Charles Scribner's Sons, 1964.

———. *The Nature and Destiny of Man.* Volume 1: "On Human Nature." New York: Charles Scribner's Sons, 1964.

———. "Why the Christian Church Is Not Pacifist." In *The Essential Niebuhr: Selected Essays and Addresses*, edited by Robert McAffee Brown. New Haven: Yale University Press, 1986.

Novak, Michael. *The Spirit of Democratic Capitalism.* New York: Simon & Schuster, 1982.

Nussbaum, Martha C. "Patriotism and Cosmopolitanism." In *For Love of Country: Debating the Limits of Patriotism*, edited by Joshua Cohen. Boston: Beacon, 1996.

Opportunity International. "Microenterprise." https://opportunity.org/what-we-do/micro-banking (August 2, 2024).

Packard, Randall. *A History of Global Health: Interventions in the Lives of Other Peoples.* Baltimore: Johns Hopkins University Press, 2016.

Philpott, Daniel. "There Is a Wideness in God's Justice." *Nova et Vetera*, English edition 18, no. 4 (2020).

Presbyterian Church USA. "Resolution on Acquired Immune Syndrome Deficiency (AIDS)." www.presbyterianmission.org/wp-content/uploads/resolutionbehaviorcarepcusapolicies198ga1986_.pdf (August 2, 2024).

Purcell, James N., Jr. *We're In Danger! Who Will Help Us? Refugees and Migrants: A Test of Civilization.* Bloomington, IN: Archway Publishing, 2019.

Putnam, Robert. *Bowling Alone.* New York: Simon & Schuster, 2000.

Rawls, John. *The Law of Peoples.* Cambridge: Harvard University Press, 1999.

Reno, R. R. "The Return of Catholic Anti-Modernism." *First Things* (June 2015). www.firstthings.com/web-exclusives/2015/06/the-return-of-catholic-anti-modernism (August 2, 2024).

Saiya, Nilay. "Christian Nationalism's Threat to Global Democracy." *The Review of Faith and International Affairs* 22, no. 1 (2024).

Scolnic, Benjamin. "The Prophets and Social Justice." www.ibjewish.org/wp-content/uploads/2014/10/Scolnic-Prophets-and-Social-Justice.pdf (July 31, 2024).

Scott, James C. *Seeing Like a State: How Certain Schemes to Improve the Human Condition Have Failed*. New Haven: Yale University Press, 1998.

Shah, Timothy Samuel. "Some Evangelical Views of the State." In *Church, State, and Citizen: Christian Approaches to Political Engagement*, edited by Sandra Joireman. New York: Oxford University Press, 2009.

Sherman, Amy. *The Soul of Development: Biblical Christianity and Economic Transformation in Guatemala*. New York: Oxford University Press, 1997.

Singer, Peter. *One World: The Ethics of Globalization*. Second edition. New Haven: Yale University Press, 2002.

Slaughter, Anne-Marie. "How to Succeed in the Networked World: A Grand Strategy for the Digital Age." *Foreign Affairs* (November/December 2016).

Smith, Stephen B. *Reclaiming Patriotism in an Age of Extremes*. New Haven: Yale University Press, 2022.

Snyder, Jack. "The Broken Bargain: How Nationalism Came Back." *Foreign Affairs* (March/April 2019).

Soerens, Matthew, and Jenny Yang. *Welcoming the Stranger: Justice, Compassion and Truth in the Immigration Debate*. Downers Grove, IL: IVP Books, 2009.

Stephens, Bret. *America in Retreat: The New Isolationism and the Coming Global Disorder*. New York: Sentinel, 2014.

Stiglitz, Joseph. *Globalization and Its Discontents*. New York: W. W. Norton, 2002.

Strand, Daniel. "A Better Christian Nationalism." *Providence* (January 14, 2021). https://providencemag.com/2021/01/better-christian-nationalism/ (August 1, 2024).

Summers, Lawrence. "How to Embrace Nationalism Responsibly." *The Washington Post*, July 10, 2016.

Tamir, Yael. *Liberal Nationalism*. Princeton: Princeton University Press, 1993.

Tinder, Glen. "Can We Be Good Without God?" *The Atlantic Monthly* (December 1989).

Tooley, Mark. "Are National Borders Ungodly?" *Juicy Ecumenism* (October 23, 1918). https://juicyecumenism.com/2018/10/23/are-national-borders-ungodly/ (August 1, 2024).

United Methodist Church. "Creation Care." www.umc.org/en/how-we-serve/social-issues/creation-care (August 2, 2024).

US Conference of Catholic Bishops. "Called to Compassion and Responsibility: A Response to the HIV/AIDS Crisis." www.usccb.org/resources/called-compassion-and-responsibility-0 (August 2, 2024).

———. "Care for Creation." www.usccb.org/beliefs-and-teachings/what-we-believe/catholic-social-teaching/care-for-creation (August 2, 2024).

———. "Economic Justice for All: Pastoral Letter on Catholic Social Teaching and the U.S. Economy, 1986." www.usccb.org/upload/economic_justice_for_all.pdf (August 1, 2024).

———. "Forming Consciences for Faithful Citizenship: A Call to Political Responsibility from the Catholic Bishops of the United States." www.usccb.org/issues-and

-action/faithful-citizenship/upload/forming-consciences-for-faithful-citizenship.pdf (July 31, 2024).

———. "The Many Faces of AIDS." November 14, 1987. www.usccb.org/resources/statement-many-faces-aids-november-14-1987 (August 2, 2024).

Walzer, Michael. *Spheres of Justice: A Defense of Pluralism and Equality.* New York: Basic Books, 1983.

———. *Thick and Thin: Moral Argument at Home and Abroad.* Notre Dame, IN: University of Notre Dame Press, 2019.

———. "Justice and Injustice in the Gulf War." In *But Was It Just? Reflections on the Morality of the Persian Gulf War*, edited by David E. DeCosse. New York: Doubleday, 1992.

Weber, Max. *Rationalism and Modern Society.* Volume 3, edited and translated by Tony Walters and Dagmar Walters. New York: Palgrave Macmillan, 2015.

Wehner, Peter. "The Faith of Gary Haugen." *The Atlantic*, May 12, 2023. www.theatlantic.com/ideas/archive/2023/05/gary-haugen-south-africa-apartheid-religion-civil-rights/674012/ (August 2, 2024).

———. "The Polite Zealotry of Mike Johnson." *The Atlantic*, October 31, 2023. www.theatlantic.com/ideas/archive/2023/10/polite-zealotry-mike-johnson/675845/ (July 31, 2024).

Weiner, Myron. "Ethics, National Sovereignty and the Control of Immigration." *International Migration Review* 30 (Spring 1996).

Whitehead, Andrew L., and Samuel L. Perry. *Taking America Back for God: Christian Nationalism in the United States.* New York: Oxford University Press, 2020.

Williams, Rowen. "The Ethics of Global Relationships." In *Who Is My Neighbour? The Global and Personal Challenge*, edited by Richard Carter and Samuel Wells. London: Society for Promoting Christian Knowledge, 2018.

Wimmer, Andreas. *Nation Building: Why Some Countries Come Together and Others Fall Apart.* Princeton: Princeton University Press, 2018.

———. "Nation Building: Why Some Countries Come Together While Others Fall Apart." *Survival* 60, no. 4 (2018).

———. "Why Nationalism Works: And Why It Isn't Going Away." *Foreign Affairs* (March/April 2019).

Wolf, Stephen. *The Case for Christian Nationalism.* Moscow, ID: Cannon Press, 2022.

Wolterstorff, Nicholas. *Until Justice and Peace Embrace.* Grand Rapids: Eerdmans, 1983.

———. "Theological Foundations for an Evangelical Political Philosophy." In *Toward an Evangelical Public Policy*, edited by Ronald J. Sider and Diane Knippers. Grand Rapids: Baker Books, 2005.

Woodberry, Robert D. "The Missionary Roots of Liberal Democracy." *American Political Science Review* 106, no. 2 (2012).

———, and Timothy S. Shah. "Christianity and Democracy: The Pioneering Protestants." *Journal of Democracy* 13 (April 2004).

World Health Organization. "WHO Coronavirus (CVD-19) Dashboard: Situation by Region, Country, Territory and Area." 2023. https://covid19.who.int/table (August 2, 2024).

Index

accountability, 110, 166
Acton, Lord, 29
administrative state, 164
Afghanistan, 14, 85, 86, 106, 113
Africa, xvi, 14, 94, 147, 149
aggression, 16, 36, 65
AIDS, 146, 147, 151, 153, 155; see also HIV/AIDS
"America First," 52, 73
Amish believers, 34
Amstutz, Samuel, 170–171
amnesty, 94
Anabaptist believers, 34
anarchy, 6
Anglican Church, 28, 134
Annan, Kofi, 16
Arab Spring, 17
Argentina, 16
Asia, xvi, 156
asylum, 13, 19, 86, 91, 92, 95. 148
asylum-seekers, 85, 91, 93
Augustine, Saint, 28
Australia, 95
autarky, 3, 6, 8
authoritarian regime, xiv, 12
authority, 44, 45, 47, 54, 57
autocratic regimes, xvi, 12, 17, 46, 76

balance of power, 9,
Bennett, John C., 23
Berger, Peter, 39
Betts, Alexander, 91
Bible, 23, 24, 25, 27, 29, 35, 36, 110; see also Scripture
biblical ethics, xii, 136
biblical principles, 24–27, 136
biblical worldview, 26, 39, 136, 161
Biden, Joe, xiii. 86, 87, 92
Bigger, Nigel, 53
Bodin, Jean, 5
Bonhoeffer, Dietrich, 29, 35
borders, 53–54, 69, 86, 89, 90, 93, 94, 98, 99
Brandt, Willy, 111
Brazil, 9
Bretton Woods System, 11
Britain, 11, 86, 91, 94; see also United Kingdom
Brunner, Emile, 27
bubonic plague, 145
bureaucracy, 163
Bush, George W., xi, 153, 155

Caesar, 28, 35
Canada, 11, 95

Index

caring for the poor, 24, 26, 31, 34, 99, 120, 136, 137, 138
Carroll, M. Daniel, 98
Castro, Fidel, 12
Catholic Church, 24, 31, 72, 97, 151–52; *see also* Roman Catholic Church
Catholic Social Thought (CST), 31, 33, 96, 118, 137
Catholicism, 24, 31, 96
Cavanaugh, William, 53, 84
Chartier, Gary, 54
Chile, 12, 109, 161–62
China, xvi, 9, 11, 17, 46, 72, 112–13, 115, 131, 132, 147, 149, 156
Christian anthropology, 54
Christian churches, xii, 36, 96, 118, 119
Christian community, 96
Christian ethics, 100, 118, 136
Christian faith, xix, 23, 27, 33, 34, 44, 53, 80, 100, 105–106, 117, 138, 157; and climate change, 132–39; and development, 117–21; and global health, 150–55; and the international community, 71–74; and migration, 95–98; and the nation-state, 53–55; and politics, 33–39
Christian morality, xii, 72, 100
Christian Nationalism, 55–57; *see also* nationalism
Christian perspectives, xvii, 6, 27, 53, 72, 120, 138
Christian religion, xii, xix
Christian traditions, 24
Christian values, xvii, 80, 98, 137
Christian worldview, xii, 38, 95, 133
Christians, xii, xvii, xix, 24, 25, 34, 55, 60, 96, 117, 119, 121, 137; and global problems, 74–76
Churchill, Winston, 54
citizens, xii xv, 52
citizenship, xvi, xxn4, 43, 68
City of Man, 28
City of God, 28
civil rights, xiv, 5
civil servants, 163, 164

civil society, 60, 119. 166; *see also* mediating institutions
civil wars, xvi, 2, 18
Claude, Inis, Jr., 60
clean energy, 155, 129, 133
climate change, 18, 38, 125, 129, 136; and the Christian faith, 132–36; public opinion on, 130
Climate Treaty Conferences, 140m2
climate justice, 132
Clinton, Bill, 16
code of peace, 7
Cold War, xvi, 6, 14, 95, 105, 110, 114, 115, 117, 166
collective security, 9, 67
Collier, Paul, 43, 46, 48, 91, 107, 114
Colson, Chuck, 168–69
common good, xvi, xvii, 18, 31, 32, 34, 52, 82, 99, 120, 137, 138, 151, 161, 162, 163, 167, 175
common grace, xii
communal solidarity, 48, 60, 100, 114, 116
community development, 115, 117, 120
communism, 12, 45, 48, 61n10, 73, 108
communitarianism, 68–69, 74, 89, 96
compassion, xii, 80, 98, 100, 130, 150, 151, 152, 153, 154, 155
compliance, 44, 45
conflict resolution, 33, 38, 67
Congress of Vienna, 9, 65
constitutional state, 10
corruption, 58
cosmopolitanism, 69–70, 74, 90, 96
covenant, 26, 55, 67
COVID-19, xvi, 11, 15, 143, 147–49; deaths attributed to, 149; economic impact of, 148
creation care, 29, 32, 137, 138
creation of wealth, 106, 107, 108
culture, 109–10
culture care, 105, 118
Cuba, 12, 45, 108, 109
Cynics, 69

Darien Gap, 94
democracy, xiv, 31, 46, 51, 52, 54, 72, 76, 77, 163; satisfaction with, 77
Denmark, 107
deportation, 93
development, 105, 115, 119, 120; and the Christian faith, 117–21; in the Cold War, 110–11; types of, 115–16
development aid, 145
Deutsch, Karl, 50
Dewey, Arthur (Gene), 91, 92, 173–74
dictatorship, 46, 47
diseases, 14, 144, 145–46; types of, 145
disorder, 12–15, 81
distributive justice, 71, 86, 108
divestment, 134
Donne, John, 8
Dreamers, 94–95
dual citizenship, 28–29, 34, 97, 100
dual kingdoms, 28, 98

earthquakes, 15, 162
Ebola, 143, 149–50, 156
economic development, xiii, 115, 116, 127; see also development
economic enterprise, 118
economic growth, 2, 106–107, 109, 112, 114, 115, 121, 127, 129; and the Christian faith, 117–19
economic migrants, 13
emigration, 85, 87, 88
entrepreneurship, 110
Environmental Protection Agency, 126
Episcopal Church, 133
equality, 7, 34, 49, 54, 56, 63, 67, 80, 99, 100
equity, 7, 108
Ethiopia famine, 174
European Union, 10, 91

failed state, 2, 13, 18, 47, 77, 87
Falkland Islands, 16
Farmer, Paul, 150
fidelity, 110, 121

foreign policy, 52
foreign aid, xv, 38, 138, 144, 153, 156
forgiveness, 25, 79, 80, 152
Founding Fathers, 29, 55
France, 11, 91, 94, 130, 156
Francis, Pope, 135
free enterprise, 46, 108, 111
free-rider problem, 126
freedom, xiv, 6, 7, 12, 29, 29, 44, 67, 78, 80; see also liberty
Freedom House, xiv, 166
French, David, 56
Frist, Bill, 153
Fukushima, 38, 130, 150
Fukuyama, Francis, 45, 47, 49, 60

Gaddafi, Muammar, 17
Gates, Bill, 126
Gaza, xiv
General Agreement on Tariffs and Trade (GATT), 11
genocide, 13, 16
Germany, 11, 71, 91, 94, 130
Gerson, Michael, 153
Gersony, Bob, 172
global common good, 18, 52, 82, 138
global commons, 125
global ethics, 25
global health, 143, 144–46, 150; and the Christian faith, 150–55
global integration: obstacles to, 76–77
global order, xvii, xviii, 2, 18, 29, 52, 67, 68, 80; see also world order
global society, 3, 8, 9, 19, 43, 48, 49, 52, 65, 66, 68, 69, 79, 80, 82, 90
global solidarity, 79, 80, 88
global warming, 38, 126, 127, 131, 136, 137
globalization, 49, 79, 111, 112–14
God's love, 25; see also love
God's sovereignty, 24
Goethe, Johann Wolfgang von, 6
Goodhart, David, 49
governance, 126

government, 3, 6, 18, 28, 29, 30, 34, 44, 47, 53, 58, 60, 100, 108, 111, 125, 144
government service, 161, 162, 164, 166; *see also* public service
governmental authority, 44
governmental legitimacy, 45; *see also* legitimacy
green energy, 128
greenhouse gas emissions, 126, 127, 129, 130, 134, 137
Group of Seven, 11
Group of Twenty, 11
Guinea, 149

Haas, Hein de, 87
Haass, Richard, 8
Haiti, xiii, 10, 13, 20n25, 58, 59, 75, 87, 98, 116, 162
Hamas, xiv, 2, 14, 77
Harris, Paul, 132
Hastings, Adrian, 53
Haugen, Gary, 174–75
health care, 144–45; *see also* global health
Helms, Jesse, 153
Henry, Paul, 7
Hezbollah, 2, 14, 77
HIV-AIDS, 2, 14, 143, 146–47; the role of the church in, 151–55
Hobbes, Thomas, 59
Holsti, Kalevi, 14, 45
Houthi, xiv, 14, 77
Human Development Index (HDI), 114–15
human dignity, xii, 17, 24, 25, 29, 31, 32, 34, 54, 67, 72, 89, 99, 100, 120, 144, 151, 175
human flourishing, 18
human needs, 87, 121
human rights, xviii, 14, 18, 44, 46, 47, 54, 67, 86, 87, 116
humanitarian aid, 155–57, 165, 167
humanitarian relief, 75, 144, 155–57, 167

humility, 39
hunger, xiv, 69, 115, 116
Huntington, Samuel, xix, 5, 116
Hussein Saddam, xi

Ignatieff, Michael, 79, 80
immigration, 88, 89
immigration courts, 93
immigration policies, 93–95
"Immigrants Among Us," 97
impartiality, 27
India, 115, 132, 156
individual responsibility, 11, 67, 121
individualism, 78
Indonesia, 15
inequality, xiii, 18, 69, 87, 108, 111
Inglehart, Robert, 49, 78
injustice, 6, 12–15, 27; responses to, 15–17
institutions, xvii, 44, 51, 55, 57, 58, 68, 109, 110, 116
intergovernmental organizations (IGOs), 10, 101, 164, 165
international community, xi, xvii, xviii, 2, 7, 8, 47, 65, 125, 131, 161; and the Christian faith, 71–74; and justice, 70–71
International Justice Mission, 174–75
international law, 17
international organization, 65, 66, 67, 70; emergence of, 66–67
international politics, xii, xvii, xix, 37, 47
international relations, xii, xvii, xviii, xix, 8, 18
International Monetary Fund, 11, 111, 148, 164
Iran, 9, 14
Iraq, xi, 10, 14, 36, 77–78
irregular migration, 18, 87, 93, 98, 113
irregular migrants, 87, 90, 93–95, 98, 100
Iskar, Andrew, 55
Israel, xiv
Italy, 11, 91, 94

Japan, 9, 11
job creation, 87; *see also* creation of wealth
John Paul II, Pope, 118
Johnson, Mike, 35
Jones, Dorothy, 7
Judis, John, 52
Judt, Tony, 6
jus sanguinis, xx
jus solis, xx
just global order, 69, 74
just war theory, 24, 33
justice, 6, 7, 26, 27, 31, 34, 38, 47, 55, 66, 70, 96, 97, 98, 100, 108, 117, 152; and the international community, 70–71; as a process, 7, 71, 99; as a substantive end, 7, 71, 100; as right relationships, 27

Kagan, Donald, 18
Kagan, Robert, 9, 77, 81
Kaplan, Robert, 6, 172–73
Keck, Margaret, 79
Kenya, xiii
Kidd, Thomas, 56
Kingdom of God, xvii, 28, 30, 31, 34, 57, 72, 96, 100
Kingdom of Man, xvii, 28, 34, 96, 100
Kirby, Jeffrey, 32
Kissinger, Henry, xviii, 6, 10, 102n23
Korea, 14
Kosovo, 14
Kuyper, Abraham, xix, 24
Kuwait, xi, 36, 107
Kyoto, 131

law, 27, 30, 47, 164; rule of, 47
League of Nations, 65, 66
Lebanon, 2
Legatum Prosperity Index, 109
legitimacy, 44, 45, 47, 57; types of, 45
liberal economic system, 11, 73
liberal global order, 9, 71, 73
Liberia, 146, 150

liberty, 25, 67, 72, 116; *see also* freedom
Libya, 2, 10, 17, 45, 48, 58, 59
Lieven, Anatol, 51, 131
limited government, 54, 55
Lincoln, Abraham, 37
Lind, Michael, 50
Lomborg, Bjorn, 128
love, xii, 24, 25, 57, 70, 73, 96, 99, 105, 120, 133, 152, 154, 155; *see also* self-love
"Loving the Least of These," 133
Lowry, Rich, 50
Luther, Martin, 23, 28
Lutheran Church, 34, 35, 97, 98, 134, 151

Macron, Emmanuel, 49
Maduro, Nicolás, xiii, 87
Mandelbaum, Michael, 50
market economy, 109
Metaxas, Eric, 170
Mead, Walter Russell, 81
mediating institutions, 166
mercy, 100
Mexico, 86, 97, 148
Micklethwait, John, 49
micro enterprise, 171, 172
migration, 86, 87, 88, 90, 98; alternative conceptions of, 89–94; and the Christian faith, 95–101; opinions on, 88; sources of, 86–87
migrants, 2, 86, 87, 88, 92, 95
Millennium Challenge Corporation, 167
Millennium Development Goals, 115
Miller, David, 4
Miller, Paul, 51, 56
Minerath, Roland, 4
modernization, 116
moral analysis, 101
moral compass, 39
moral-cultural system, 110
moral development, 75, 110
moral education, 120, 136
moral ideals, xviii, 73, 74

moral transformation, 31
moral values, 136; impact of, 119
morality, 80
Mozambique, 173

nation, 3, 4, 48, 55; fusion with state, 5
nation building, 59–60, 116
nation-state, xix, 3, 5, 10, 19. 43, 44, 45, 46, 60, 132, 144; loss of faith in, 48–50; shortcomings of, 47–48; strengthening of, 57–60
National Association of Evangelicals, 23, 97, 133, 135, 151
National Council of Churches, xi, 36, 154
national health, 145
national identity, 44
national interest, 18, 52, 81
national security, 8, 14, 18, 143
national solidarity, 59, 60
nationality, xvi
nationalism, xix, 3, 4, 50–53, 56; *see also* Christian Nationalism
NATO, 9, 17, 78, 163
natural law, 31
Nazi, 34
Netherlands, The, 107, 156
networks: types of, 99
Neuhaus, Richard, 31
New International Economic Order, 111
New York City, 93
Niebuhr, H. Richard, xvii, 39
Niebuhr, Reinhold, xix, 25, 26, 55, 73
nongovernmental organizations (NGOs), xix, 60, 70, 78–79, 101, 161, 162, 165; advantages of, 166
nonintervention, 7, 17
non-refoulement principle, 111
Nordholt, Jan W. Schulte, 168
North Korea, 45, 58
North Sea, 107
North-South conflict, 111
Novak, Michael, xix, 110, 118
nuclear power, 38, 128, 130
Nussbaum, Martha, 69

Old Testament Prophets, 26
Opportunity International, 76, 171–72
Orban, Viktor, 51, 58
order, xviii, 3, 6, 7, 9, 29, 38, 44, 46, 59, 81, 117
order of removal, 93
"ordinary virtues," 79
Organization of American States, 10

Packard, Randall, 143, 145
pandemics, 18, 143, 144, 148
Paris Agreement, xiv, 131
Parks, Rosa, 167
participation, 7, 32–33, 45, 151
paternalism, 114
patriotism, 50, 51
peace, xv, xvii, xviii, 3, 6, 9, 18, 34, 52, 81
Peace Corps, 162
Peace of Westphalia, xviii, 5; *see also* Treaty of Westphalia
peacekeeping, 9
peacemaking, 38
Perry, Samuel, 56
persecution, 18, 89, 90
personal responsibility, 117
personalism, 31, 32
Peru, 1
Petro, Anthony, 151
Philpott, Daniel, 27
polders, 107
political community, 68, 70, 116
political culture, 68
political decay, 116
political development, 116
political engagement: principle of, 37–39
political morality, 79, 80
Ponnuru, Ramesh, 50
popular sovereignty, 46
populism, 113
postmaterialist values, 49
poverty, xiv, 2, 106, 108; *See also* privation
power, 5, 9, 30, 44, 45, 47, 67, 100; configurations of, 20n14

President's Emergency Plan for AIDS Relief (PEPFAR), 155
preferential option for the poor, 33; *see also* caring for the poor
preferential option for nonviolence, 33
Presbyterian Church, 28, 37, 134, 151
Prison Fellowship, 169
privation, 106–107
procedural justice, 7, 99, 100; *see also* justice
promise keeping, 75, 76
property rights, 110
prosperity, xii, xv, xviii, 3, 6, 8, 17, 19, 52
Protestant missionaries, 26, 119
Protestant principles, 24, 27–31, 53; impact of, 119
Protestantism, 24, 26, 27, 28, 117, 118, 119, 133–34
public good, 60, 125, 126, 131, 137, 139n1
public interest, 163
public policies, 35, 36, 97, 98, 138; priorities of states, 139n9
public service, 161, 162, 163
Purcell, James, 91
Putin, Vladimir, 16, 51
Putnam, Robert, 4

Rawls, John, 46, 69
reason, 26, 31
realism, xviii
reconciliation, 74, 79
redistribution, 106, 111
Reed, Larry, 171–72
Reformation, 27, 28
Reformed theology, xviii, 24
refugee, xiv, 85, 89, 90–93, 95
renewable energy, 128, 129
Reno, R. R., 135
responsibility: principle of, 117
Responsibility to Protect Principle (R2P), 8, 17
"ride-free" problem, 19
Roman Catholic Church, 29, 31, 96

rule of law, 110
rules-based international order, xvi, 2, 81–82; *see also* liberal global order
Russia, xvi, 9, 16, 17, 46, 77
Rwanda, 13, 16

Saiya, Nilay, 56
Salvation Army, 26
Samaritan's Purse, 74, 75
sanctions, 36, 38
sanctuary city, 93
Saudi Arabia, 14
Save the Children, 165
Scolnic, Benjamin, 27
Scott, James, 48
Scripture, xii, 23, 28, 31, 35, 36, 38, 53, 55, 72, 96, 118, 161; *see also* Bible
self determination, 7
self-love, 25, 28
Shah, Timothy, 30, 119
shalom, 27, 70
Sherman, Amy, 110
Shultz, George. 173
Sierra Leone, 113, 146, 150
Sikkink, Kathryn, 79
sin, 25, 30, 34, 53, 55; confession of, 29
Singer, Peter, 70
Slaughter, Anne-Marie, 79
smartphone, 112
Smith, Steven, 51
Snyder, Jack, 3
social capital, 4, 105; types of, 4; *see also* trust
social democracy, 46
social justice, 152
social media, 77
social solidarity, 100, 121, 138; *see also* communal solidarity
solar power, 129, 135–36
solidarity, 5, 31, 32, 46, 48, 60, 77, 96, 99, 108, 120, 137, 138, 151; obstacles to, 76–78
Somalia, 77
South, 110, 111; failed reforms of, 122n10

sovereignty, 4, 5, 72
Spanish influenza, 145
spiritual conversion, 110
spiritual life, 30
state, xiii, 3, 5, 7, 9, 30, 44, 45, 46, 47, 52, 68, 69, 85, 89, 98, 116; collapse of, 90; strength of, 44, 45; failure of, 47
state building, 57–59
statecraft, 6
stewardship, 29–30, 117, 136
Stiglitz, Joseph, 115
Stoics, 69
storage container, 112
Strange, Daniel, 57
"Strangers No Longer," 97
Strategic Defense Initiative, 39
subsidiarity, 31, 32, 72
substantive justice, 7, 71, 100; *see also* distributive justice
Sudan, xiii
Sudetenland, 71
Summers, Lawrence, 52
supply chain, 11
sustainable development, xiv, 78, 115, 129, 136
Sutterfield, Ragan, 135
Syria, 2, 8, 14, 15, 45, 48, 77, 86, 91, 156

Taliban, xiii, 167
Tamir, Yael, 50
Temporary Protected Status (TPS), 92
Teresa, Mother, 169–70
"The Earth's Climate Crisis," 134
Thirty Years' War, 5
Tinder, Glen, 25, 26
Tooley, Mark, 53
Torba, Andrew, 55–56
tradition, 26, 31
Transparency International, 58
Treaty of Westphalia, 72
Trump, Donald, 51, 55
trust, 4, 5, 58, 68, 75, 79, 110, 117, 118, 121, 150; *see also* social capital
Turkey, 13, 15

Ukraine, 16, 38, 52, 85, 86
United Kingdom, 94; *see also* Britain
United Nations, xviii, 10, 16, 17, 65, 67, 69, 92, 115, 126, 128, 131, 164, 173
UN Charter, 6, 7, 10, 13, 16, 67
UN Conference on Environment and Development, 125
UN Framework Convention on Climate Change, 125
UN Intergovernmental Panel on Climate Change (IPCC), 127
UN High Commissioner for Refugees UNHCR), 86, 90, 164, 173
UN Peacekeeping, 10, 13, 16, 165
UN Security Council, xi, 17, 36, 67
Universal Declaration of Human Rights, xvi, 68, 88
United Church of Christ, 134
United States, x, xi, 1, 3, 4, 9, 11, 81, 86, 88, 91, 92, 95, 97, 113, 130, 131, 144; and its economy, 118; policies on immigration, 97; public opinion on immigration, 88
US Center for Disease Control and Prevention (CDC), 146
US citizen, xii, 94
US Conference of Catholic Bishops, 32, 120, 137, 152
US Constitution, 30
US economy, 118
US government, 38, 39, 86, 155, 156
US immigration, 94, 97

Venezuela, xiii, 38, 87
Vietnam, 109
Villarrica, 161
visa, 87, 99
voluntary compliance, 44

Walzer, Michael, xix, 36, 68, 80, 89
war, 14, 18, 69, 90; *see also* civil war
Washington Consensus, 111
wealth, 107, 119; *see also* creation of wealth
Weber, Max, 163

Wehner, Peter, 175
Weiner, Myron, 89
Westphalian order, xiii, xix
Wheaton College, 153
Whitehead, Andrew, 56
Williams, Rowan, 25
Wimmer, Andreas, 4, 51, 60
Wolf, Stephen, 56
Wooldridge, Adrian, 49
Woodberry, Robert, 119
work, 30, 117
World Bank, 11, 58, 111, 114
World Council of Churches, 134
world government, 54, 70
World Happiness Report, 109, 113, 121n2
world health, 2; *see also* global health
World Health Organization, 15, 78, 149, 150, 163, 164
world order, xviii, xxn6, 10, 73, 74, 81; problem of, 81–82; *see also* global order
World Trade Organization (WTO), 11, 13, 15
World Vision, 74, 75, 165
World War I, 5, 9, 12, 14, 66
World War II, 5, 12, 14, 71, 92
Wolterstorff, Nicholas, 27, 29

Yemen, xiv, 14, 45, 48, 58, 98, 156
Yousafzai, Malala, 167

Zakaria, Fareed, 81
Zelensky, Voledymyr, 16
Zuiderzee, 107

About the Author

Mark R. Amstutz initiated and developed the political science department in Wheaton College (Illinois), serving as its first chair for two decades. He also directed six overseas programs in Europe and Latin America. As a scholar, he contributed to the development of the field of international ethics with his scholarship on the role of ethics in international relations. He is the author of numerous publications, including *International Conflict and Cooperation: An Introduction to World Politics*, second edition; *The Healing of Nations: The Role and Promise of Political Forgiveness*; *The Rules of the Game: A Primer on International Relations; International Ethics: Concepts, Theories, and Cases in Global Politics*, fifth edition; *Evangelicals and American Foreign Policy*; and *Just Immigration: U.S. Policy in Christian Perspective*.

www.ingramcontent.com/pod-product-compliance
Lightning Source LLC
Chambersburg PA
CBHW020410230426
43664CB00009B/1250